COMMUNITY DEVELOPMENT

A critical approach

Second edition

Margaret Ledwith

THE BRITISH ASSOCIATION OF SOCIAL WORKERS

First published in 2005
Second edition published in Great Britain in 2011 by

The Policy Press
University of Bristol
Fourth Floor, Beacon House
Queen's Road
Bristol BS8 1QU
UK
Tel +44 (0)117 331 4054
Fax +44 (0)117 331 4093
e-mail tpp-info@bristol.ac.uk
www.policypress.co.uk

North American office:
The Policy Press
c/o The University of Chicago Press
1427 East 60th Street
Chicago, IL 60637, USA
t: +1 773 702 7700
f: +1 773-702-9756
e:sales@press.uchicago.edu
www.press.uchicago.edu

© The Policy Press 2011

Reprinted 2012

British Library Cataloguing in Publication Data
A catalogue record for this book is available from the British Library.

Library of Congress Cataloging-in-Publication Data
A catalog record for this book has been requested.

ISBN 978 1 84742 646 8 paperback
ISBN 978 1 84742 647 5 hardcover

Cover design by Qube Design Associates, Bristol
Front cover: image kindly supplied by Eye Wire Images
Printed and bound in Great Britain by Hobbs, Southampton
The Policy Press uses environmentally responsible print partners

Dedicated to Constance Mary Elizabeth, my beloved grandmother, and Grace Constance, my adored mother; but most of all in celebration of the life of Grace, my inspirational granddaughter, who has woven together the fractured threads of my life.

Other books by Margaret Ledwith

Ledwith, M. and Springett, J. (2010) *Participatory practice: Community-based action for transformative change*, Bristol: The Policy Press.

Ledwith, M. (1997) *Participating in transformation: Towards a working model of community empowerment*, Birmingham: Venture Press.

Contents

List of figures and tables

Figures

Table

Foreword to the second edition

Margaret Ledwith's first edition of this book merited a 'bestselling title of all time' award from The Policy Press. Its popularity is due to the way that she effortlessly brings theory alive in practice, making democracy work from the bottom up, community by community, at a juncture in time when we are witnessing globalised shifts in power, with corporate interests and the pursuance of profit taking priority over the common good of people and planet. This has accelerated world crises of social justice and environmental sustainability and calls for urgent grassroots action for change that prioritises democratic rights and a sustainable future.

In her chapters, Margaret models the approach she recommends, wonderfully merging conceptual and practical matters in regard to community development. Few books of scholarly merit move so seamlessly between theoretical and practical matters as does this one. Her thoughtful chapters offer a searching review of the literature while also pulsing with the author's own experience in community activism. In these ways, the pages connect scholarship, practice and experience to provide a unity of approach to address the challenges of our troubled times.

With exemplary focus, my colleague Margaret Ledwith rethinks community development as critical pedagogy for our times, within the context of globalisation and British political changes on the one hand, while reflecting on the legacies of two philosophical landmarks of the last century, Paulo Freire and Antonio Gramsci. In this revised edition, she develops her feminist and anti-racist analyses, reworking ideas around white privilege and bringing theory alive through stories from grassroots practice in diverse international contexts, from Rio to Barrow, from Calcutta to Cumbria. She also critiques the rapidly changing political context in relation to social justice and environmental justice, and emphasises the challenges to any community-based practice with a social justice intention. The great strength of the book is that it provides such comfortable travelling between theory and practice, philosophy and history, and practical social justice activism, the outcome of Margaret's own productive years as an activist and scholar.

As this book makes clear, we live in complex times which require complex thinking from the bottom up to deal with the global policies being imposed from the top down. Hard-won rights of working families are eroding as quickly as the environment itself. What is sometimes called the 'social contract' is being rewritten unilaterally now by multinational conglomerates who have wielded enormous power since the end of the Cold War and the emergence of a borderless one-world market. A religion of the marketplace has emerged whereby market forces are considered too sacred to be touched by local and social concerns; human needs that contradict market needs are fast becoming expendable; indeed, it appears that the market religion is superseding regional planning, community desires and elected governments at all levels. As power gets sucked upwards into the hands of a few world businesses, how can communities, citizens and families educate and organise themselves to protect their political rights, their livelihoods, homes, neighbourhoods, children, health and environment? The wealthy, who benefit greatly from this new world order, live protected from the consequences of their own policies, while the working majorities of the world suffer the worst consequences.

Unlike the privileged, the great bulk of the world live in communities undermined by policies favouring the wealthy and the corporations. This book is written for them. All those who work for democracy and social justice, who oppose racism and sexism and favour solidarity across difference need to learn from each other about our successes and failures in educating and organising for transformation. A great deal is at stake and this book helps us know how to do our work better. It must be read by scholars, students and community activists, indeed, by all civic-minded individuals.

What a pleasure it is to read Margaret's continuing contributions now, nearly a decade and a half after I first met her in Omaha, Nebraska, at the third annual Pedagogy of the Oppressed Conference in April 1997, just weeks before Paulo Freire died. Before and after that gathering, an international debate has been under way about the very questions she takes up in this volume, which makes a major and hopeful statement about a way forward.

Professor Ira Shor
City University of New York Graduate Center
March 2011

Acknowledgements

I wish to acknowledge the ways in which my analysis has become more incisive due to the lived experience of:

Wendy Derbyshire, White community activist and organic intellectual, who continues to stimulate my thinking on the intersection of class and gender.

Paula Asgill, Black activist and critical educator, who shared her profound critical insights into the complexity of 'race' and gender over the years, and retrospective reflections on our alliance continue to deepen my understanding beyond her sudden and premature death in May 2005.

I also wish to thank **Jean McEwan-Short** for her helpful feedback, particularly on Chapter Four.

Storytellers

My sincere thanks go to the many people who have told their stories for this book (and those who play a role in their stories), from their diverse countries, cultures and perspectives, bringing alive theory in action:

Asoke Bhattacharya
Avila Kilmurray
Carolina Leonardini Aris
Chris Cavanagh
Colin Kirkwood
Diane Warner
Diane Watt
Eurig Scandrett
Flavio Wittlin
Gary Craig
Geraldine Ling
Gerri Kirkwood
Gonzalo Aroaz
Helen Lowry
Hilda Regaspi
Mae Shaw
Naomi van der Velden
Phil Teece
Porfirio Garcia Canaviri
Stan Reeves
Steve Robson

When we interrupt the stories we tell by questioning their meanings, we unlock the key to seeing ourselves and the world in a different light.

Glossary

Action/reflection: the foundation of community development praxis, where our knowledge base is developed through reflection on action, and our subsequent action is informed by this analysis.

The 'Big Society': the banner of the UK Conservative Party led by David Cameron, strong on the rhetoric of empowerment, but weak on an analysis of equality.

Civil society: in Gramscian theory, civil society is the site in which the dominant ideas of the ruling class invade our minds persuading us that their way of seeing the world is *common sense*. The institutions of civil society which engage us in life – the family, media, schools, religious organisations, community groups, and so forth – play a role in getting us to consent to ideas that favour the already privileged in society. It is also the site for grassroots action for change.

Codifications: in Freirean pedagogy, these are representations of familiar local situations that stimulate critical debate leading to consciousness of the structural sources of oppression in society. They can take the form of photographs, video, drawings, drama and so on.

Communitarianism: a view of community as a homogeneous unity in which values of mutuality and reciprocity are seen as natural and lead to self-help and social cohesion, founded on the ideas of Etzioni, in particular. This is not only a denial of conflict and competing interests in community, but it dilutes the radical concepts of community development into a model of self-help rather than liberation.

Conscientisation: translated from the Portuguese *conscientização*, Freire used this concept for the process of becoming critically aware of the structural forces of power which shape people's lives as a precondition for critical action for change.

Critical alliance: these are strategic alliances across difference, which are built on the collective strength of diversity in mutual collective action for social justice.

Critical analysis: refers to the theories and conceptual tools with which to analyse practice so that subsequent action is targeted at the source, not the symptoms, of oppression and therefore has the potential to bring about change for social justice.

Critical consciousness: involves the 'dynamic between critical thought and critical action' (Shor, 1993, p 32). This is the stage of consciousness needed for the empowerment to collectively act in relation to the wider contexts of power from local to global.

Critical pedagogy: refers to that type of learning that is based on a mutual search rooted in a 'profound love for the world and for people' (Freire, 1996, p 70). It is a democratic process of education that encourages critical consciousness as the basis of transformative collective action.

Cultural invasion: is a Freirean concept which captures the way that the values, beliefs, ideology, cultural norms and practices of a dominant culture are superimposed on the culture of those it oppresses. It links to Gramsci's concept of *hegemony*.

Dialogue: in Freirean pedagogy, is a mutual, respectful communication between people which engages the heart and mind, the intellect and emotions, which Freire saw as the basis of praxis.

Dichotomous thought: refers to a binary, either/or way of seeing the world that defines one thing in relation to its opposite, with a subject/object power implicit in the relationship, for example, working class/middle class, male/female, White/Black.

Difference: is shorthand for the wide range of social differences that create our identities, and which are related to the process of discrimination, for example, 'race', class, gender, faith, ethnicity, age, sexuality, 'dis'ability and so forth.

Discrimination: refers to the process by which people are disadvantaged by their social identity and therefore given unequal access to rights, resources, opportunities and power. Its consequence is oppression, and 'it is a major obstacle to dignity, equality and social justice' (Thompson, 2003, p 78).

Empowerment: people have their dignity and self-respect restored through empowerment, which is the consequence of critical consciousness: the understanding that life chances are prescribed by structural discrimination, an insight which brings with it the freedom to take action to bring about change for social justice.

Enlightenment: this is the philosophy that developed in western Europe in the 17th and 18th centuries, which rejected previous supernatural ways of making sense of the world in favour of an objective, rational, unemotional, scientific knowledge embedded in masculinity.

Environmental justice: calls for action to redress exploitation of the environment by capitalism which is destroying biodiversity and causing climate change, endangered species, pollution and degradation of land and water resources. The impact is experienced disproportionately by already disadvantaged communities and poorer nations, and so is inextricably linked to social justice.

False consciousness: refers to the unquestioning view of the world in which subordinate groups accept their reality in passive and fatalistic ways, leaving the power and privilege of dominant groups unchallenged.

Feminism: feminist theory in community development places patriarchy as an oppressive force alongside that of class and 'race', seeking to create a diverse world where peace, cooperation, participation and sustainability offer a force to change the essentially exploitative system created by capitalism.

Globalisation: refers to the acceleration of capitalism's global reach by the most powerful systems in the West, exploiting the most vulnerable people and environments in the world for economic gain, and invading other cultures with a western worldview which reproduces discrimination on a complex global level.

Hegemony: concepetualises the ways in which one class maintains dominance over the rest of society by a subtle system of coercion and consent. Coercion is maintained through the law, police and armed forces, and ideological persuasion. Gramsci's important contribution gives insight into the way that our minds are colonised by dominant ideas through the institutions of civil society – the family, religious organisations, schools and so on.

Magical consciousness: is Freire's concept for a fatalistic, disempowered and passive way of seeing the world.

Metanarratives: are theories which attempt to explain universal, collective experience, but in doing so reduce diversity to a naively simplistic unity, subsuming difference shaped by gender, 'race', ethnicity, age, sexuality, 'dis'ability and so forth.

Naive consciousness: is Freire's concept for partial empowerment that relates to the symptoms of oppression, engaging with single issues rather than the underlying roots of injustice.

Narratives: people's personal stories contribute to collective narratives, which express the hopes and fears, needs and strengths that are the basis of community development theory and practice.

Neoliberalism: refers to a free market non-interventionist state that emphasises the individual, and justifies the deregulation of trade and finance.

Neoloberal capitalism: refers to the accelerating system of modern capitalism that operates from a profit-over-people-and-planet imperative and has taken on global proportions.

New Labour: maintaining the neoliberal principles of a free market, the Third Way politics of the Blair government, influenced by communitarianism, located community/civil society as the interface between people and the state, building its modernisation agenda on community partnerships.

New Right: an ideology which supported a free market economy rooted in a politics of individualism, associated with Thatcherism in the UK.

Oppression: is the outcome of discrimination. While categories of discrimination can be seen as class, 'race', gender, ethnicity, and so forth, the forms of oppression which result are classicism, racism, sexism, xenophobia and so forth, which are mostly expressed at a cultural level (Thompson, 2003).

Participation: true participation is achieved in community development through the empowerment of people to engage in collective action for justice and democracy from a critical perspective.

Pluralist community work: believes that there is a multiplicity of competing power bases in society, mediated by the state, and that community work is only capable of ameliorative small-scale neighbourhood change and piecemeal reforms.

Positivism: is the basis of sociology's claim to a scientific paradigm which measures human behaviour, often in a decontextualised way and with little concern for the more intangible intuitive, emotional or feeling aspects of being human. People are perceived as objects in either/or categories based on dichotomous thought. This is a consequence of the Enlightenment's emphasis on rational thought and a consensus view of society (Dominelli, 1997).

Praxis: a unity of theory and practice, which, in community development, involves theory generated in action, the link between knowledge and power through critical consciousness which leads to critical action.

Prejudice: can be seen as the expression of discrimination at a personal level in overt or covert ways, and involves judgemental attitudes which are based on stereotyping and resist reason or evidence (Thompson, 2003).

Problematising: the essence of Freirean pedagogy; people are encouraged to ask thought-provoking questions and 'to question answers rather than merely to answer questions' (Shor, 1993, p 26). This calls for strong democratic values as the basis of a mutual, transformative learning context where educators expect to be co-learners.

Radical community development: is committed to the role of community development in achieving transformative change for social and environmental justice, and develops analysis and practice which move beyond local symptoms to the structural causes of oppression.

Social justice: for radical community development social justice aims to create equal worth, equal rights, opportunities for all and the elimination of inequalities reinforced by poverty (Commission for Social Justice, 1994).

Notes on the author

Margaret Ledwith lives in Lancaster where she is Emeritus Professor of Community Development and Social Justice at the University of Cumbria. She has worked for many years in community settings in Scotland and North West England. Her work with Vietnamese refugees in Montrose, North East Scotland, challenged her thinking and changed her direction. David Alexander, passionate traditional intellectual, was pivotal in developing her analysis of power and privilege in the world. Ralph Ruddock, renowned adult educator, was pivotal in developing her confidence to speak truth to power. Time spent in Nicaragua, in inner-city Manchester and in Hattersley, among the harsh realities of the lives of local people, did more than anything else to sharpen her understanding of power and oppression in society today. This was the context in which her search for praxis finally aspired to a unity: where theory came alive in everyday experience, and made sense. Now, the benefits of these insights give ongoing authenticity to the development of her ideas in relation to social justice and environmental justice. Her theoretical analysis is embedded in that of Paulo Freire and Antonio Gramsci, from which it develops a Freirean-feminist-anti-racist pedagogy as a basis for reclaiming the radical agenda for community development.

Opening thoughts: Unprecedented political times

Never has there been a time of greater challenge and opportunity for community development. Since the first edition of this book, in 2005, the escalating world crises of social justice and environmental sustainability, within which I framed our political times, continue unabated, but now we find ourselves entering an unprecedented period of change, a juncture in world history. The banking crisis of 2007, created by excessive corporate greed and inappropriate risk taking, exposed the fragility of capitalism, plunging us into a world recession. Any illusions of stability evaporate as we continue to see national governments bail out banks, and entire nations teeter on the brink of bankruptcy. Economists suggest that this will prove to be the worst financial crisis since the Great Depression of the 1930s. Paula Allman offers a useful analysis of its roots and consequences in global capitalism, emphasising the need for critical education and a global democratic movement if we are to have any influence in steering towards a better world (Allman, 2010).

In the context of ongoing uncertainty in the world economy, we now witness how the poorest of the world are called on to pay for the excesses of the rich. In the UK, the Conservative–Liberal Democrat coalition government, a result of the indeterminate response of the electorate to return the Labour Party (1997–2010) with a majority vote, has introduced immediate punitive policy changes that are hitting the poorest hardest in order to recover economic equilibrium. The 'Big Society', described by David Cameron, Prime Minister, as his passion, remains a rather contradictory idea. He talks about the 'Big Society' as a huge culture change, as something different and bold which encompasses liberalism, empowerment, freedom and responsibility in a dramatic redistribution of power from central government to civil society, a move which will help people to help themselves and their communities. In the wake of this revolutionary thinking, which could almost suggest a new form of participatory democracy, we are paradoxically faced with benefit cuts justified as necessary welfare-to-work incentives, and public sector cuts that undermine democracy's commitment to health, happiness and well-being. The small state, it seems, is one which privatises public sector provision, at the same time as transferring responsibility for human well-being to communities, without any understanding that the poorest communities with least resources will be faced with the biggest responsibilities. These shifting boundaries between the state, civil society and the market (Craig et al, 2011) threaten to add to the already widening gaps between poverty and prosperity. It is important to understand that these patterns are not exclusive to the UK: globalisation escalated while we were distracted, projecting an ideology of the market and its profit-over-people-and-planet imperative across the globe. The result has been increasing global divisions between poverty and prosperity, both within and between countries, as structures of oppression implicit in this ideology are now reproduced on a global level.

According to this strange human profit and loss account, we become differently positioned according to our relevance as consumers and producers. As Giroux (2006) so powerfully puts it, we have created a 'politics of disposability': those who are not central to the processes of production or consumption are dispensable. It is a world in which the poor, the Black, the female, the young, the old, the sick and the disabled are not key players in the game. In these ways, we find that we are entering into a global juncture in history in which the interlinking roots of poverty reinforce discriminatory divisions, laying out a table from which some profit and some lose to exceptional levels, threatening the future for us all. Ironically, this is happening at a time when:

> Further improvements in the quality of life no longer depend on further economic growth: the issue is now community and how we relate to each other … Large inequalities produce all the problems associated with social difference and the divisive class prejudices which go with them, … it also weakens community life, reduces trust and increases violence. (Wilkinson and Pickett, 2009, p 45)

And so we find ourselves at a paradoxical moment in time. We have constructed a western worldview that is unhealthily preoccupied with profit, at the same time as that profit imperative is both undermining human well-being and destroying the planet that is key to our very survival. We also see eruptions of grassroots action for social change spreading around the world.

Never has there been a more important opportunity for community development to redefine its radical agenda and to engage with injustice in the process of progressive social change. 'All activists need to be critical educators, and as such, they need to start demanding the theory they need to effectively challenge capitalism' (Allman, 2010, p 240).

The ideas that are woven through this book are based on five vital dimensions, which I would like you to bear in mind:

- Radical community development is committed to collective action for social justice and environmental justice.
- This begins in a process of empowerment through critical consciousness, and grows through participation in local issues.
- A critical approach calls for an analysis of power and discrimination in society.
- The analysis needs to be understood in relation to dominant ideas and the wider political context.
- Collective action, based on this analysis, focuses on the root causes of discrimination rather than the symptoms.

Community development begins in the everyday lives of local people. This is the initial context for sustainable change. It is founded on a process of empowerment and participation. Empowerment involves a form of critical education that encourages people to question their reality: this is the basis of collective action and is built on principles of participatory democracy. In a process of action and reflection, community development grows through a diversity of local projects that address issues faced by people in community. Through campaigns, networks, alliances and movements for change, this action develops a local/global reach that aims to transform the structures of oppression that diminish local lives. A critical approach calls for a unity of theory and practice (praxis). Informed by anti-discriminatory analyses, and in a symbiotic process of action and reflection, critical analysis deepens in relation to practical experience. In this way, theory is generated in action, and action, in turn, becomes more critical through analysis. Inspired by a vision of a more just, equitable and sustainable world, this aspiration is not only a possibility, but a necessity.

There is an urgency for community development to reclaim its radical agenda. 'We cannot go on the way we have been doing based on the way we have been thinking … the resultant human tragedies will fuel misery and violence, as well as further ecological damage' (Reason, 2002, pp 3 and 15). In these ways, the practice of a more just society starts in the personal everyday experiences that shape people's lives. It builds on grassroots community activism, developing projects that are based on sustainable living, local economies and human values, but reaches out in alliance to change the root causes that give rise to structural discrimination.

The process of community development is based on confidence, critical consciousness and collectivity, consciousness being the linchpin between the two. Confidence grows as people begin to question their reality, and act together for change. Collective action grows in strength as individuals form groups, groups identify issues and develop projects, and projects form alliances that have the potential to become social movements. This process is cemented together by the connections between people that are based on values of respect, trust, mutuality, reciprocity and dignity, and which result in conviviality, compassion and cooperation. A critical engagement with community resonates outwards in common humanity for people facing injustice everywhere. People perceive that they are part of a greater unity, a more coherent whole, rather than alienated fragments without the power to change the issues that are affecting their lives. In this sense, the entire process is about interconnectedness and balance. The hopelessness that gives rise to anger or apathy transforms into a more dignified and determined hopefulness. A world held in common is one in which we are able to reach across all aspects of difference to act together on issues that are wrong. In these ways, an altered way of 'knowing' the world (epistemology) results in changed ways of 'being' in the world (ontology).

Community development occupies a contested space between top down and bottom up, which attracts many competing agendas. Assimilated, as it has been, into policy development, it has become diluted and distracted, and has lost its way (Pitchford with Henderson, 2008). This is due, in large part, to the divide between theory and practice that results in 'actionless thought' and 'thoughtless action' (Johnston, cited in Shaw, 2004, p 26).This tendency to emphasise 'doing' at the expense of 'thinking' renders us vulnerable to the manipulations of the state. Gary Craig captures some of the consequences:

> Community work is too often drawn into the latest fashions of government policy agendas because that is where the funding is, rather than developing and maintaining a clear analysis to inform action. Increasingly, the emphasis on training seems to be on skills to the exclusion of thinking about the theory and politics of community work (at both micro and macro levels): there remains a paucity of good literature to help students think through the implications of their work. Government, on the other hand, has implicitly recognised the lessons of the CDPs [Community Development Projects] in that it now provides an employment base which is fragmented, short-term and insecure. I think that practice is dominated by the policy and political context rather than creating it. (Craig, quoted in Shaw, 2004, p 42)

By failing to be vigilant, analytic and focused on our principles and purpose, we lay ourselves open to manipulation and dilution.This book sets community development in its political times and develops a critical analysis for a radical approach to practice with social justice and participatory democracy at its heart. It leaves the reader in no doubt about what it is, how to analyse it, and how to 'do' it! I emphasise that the key to this approach lies in praxis: a unity of theory and practice, action and reflection, thinking and doing. In order to achieve this, every stage of the process is rooted in the strong ideological base that informs community development. Democratic values of respect, dignity, reciprocity and mutuality together form a practical framework for checking the validity of everything we do in the name of community development, from personal encounters to global action. I will refer to this as an *ideology of equality*. Through this ideological lens, our skills are shaped and our theories evolve. It provides consonance between our purpose and our practice, ensuring that we remain true to our purpose throughout every aspect of our work.This is the critical pedagogy of Paulo Freire, re-visioned for our current times.

The use of personal narratives to reveal the political nature of our lives is fundamental to Freirean pedagogy (Freire, 1972). In reflection on experience, we engage in what Freire saw as a process of 'denunciation and annunciation': the 'act of analyzing a dehumanizing reality, [and to] denounce it while announcing its transformation' (Freire, 1985, p 57).This narrative approach also engages with feminist pedagogy, locating the *personal as political* by linking voice to narrative through the myriad of 'little stories' of everyday life that make the vital connection between the deeply personal and the profoundly political. For these reasons, I use stories from practice to bring alive the more abstract theoretical ideas.

From classroom to community: in search of praxis

I will begin with a personal story that illustrates the way in which ideas and experience influence the way we act in the world, first told in the Introduction to *Participatory practice* (Ledwith and Springett, 2010).

I began this life as the daughter of Grace Constance: I now find myself the grandmother of Grace. It feels like the wheels have turned full circle. Reflecting back on those austere but optimistic post-Second World War years, life welcomed me into the bosom of a loving extended family headed by adoring grandparents and surrounded by a stable community. So much of my sense of self was formed in that Birmingham suburb, nestling at the bottom of the steep hill that led to Erdington Parish Church, a church that witnessed all our family births, marriages and deaths. I can still name our neighbours and local shopkeepers, can still picture Mr Shute, the chemist, in the High Street, who would make up a 'cough bottle' when I was 'chesty'. Opposite was Dr Treadwell's home and surgery, Coton Cottage, tucked behind a little picket fence. He was the doctor who nursed me through suspected polio when my mother was too scared to hear the word, let alone let me go to hospital. The village green at the other end of the High Street, where I stood to attention in my new guide uniform on Sunday mornings for church parade, had the Victorian public library and baths to one side, and Wrenson's, the local grocers, to the other, the delivery boy's bicycle parked up against the wall outside. All these remain symbols of my early stability. Yet, despite my relative comfort, I had an innate questioning of the injustices I began to notice around me that began very early in childhood, but coming from a family that justified privilege, I was silenced.

Let's jump to 1972, with me in the frame, a newly qualified classroom teacher, nervously facing a class of 36 eight- to ten-year-olds, a sea of expectant faces eagerly weighing me up. The school was Victorian, with classrooms leading off a central hall. Inside, the classrooms had fixed desks and windows were set too high for anyone under six feet tall to see a world outside. As the days went on, I was perturbed by what I saw acted out before my eyes. Three years of teacher training had reinforced over and over again that schools are neutral and classrooms are apolitical spaces. This is an untruth: schools are sites of some of the most profound political experiences that we have. What I witnessed, of course, was the classroom as hegemonic: power acted out in this microcosm of wider society, and relations of 'race', class and gender reinforced. Behind the scenes, in the staff room, I listened to pronouncements that diminished the chances of young children, "Well that's got that lot sorted out: these will make it, and those don't stand a chance".

From the primary classroom, my search for insight and understanding led me in a number of directions, from adult literacy to educational psychology, seeking to put right the damage done by schooling. In the early 1980s, in Montrose, Scotland, quite by chance I found an opportunity to work with Vietnamese refugees, those known as the 'boat people', who had risked their lives on the South China Sea to escape tyranny in their own country, only to find a different kind of tyranny in the West. As I listened to their stories of separation from children, of giving birth on the high seas on rusty old landing craft that offered no dignity and no protection, of facing death as boat after boat from the West abandoned them to their fate, of starvation and dehydration, we held each other for comfort, we became friends in our common humanity, as they taught me more than I could ever teach them. I began to realise that my quest for critical insight was out there in the real world, in community, where everyday lives are shaped. That was the point at which I chose to study for a Master's degree in Community Education and Development at the University of Edinburgh, and it proved to be the context in which my search for a critical analysis of power was realised. David Alexander, with great passion, introduced me to the ideas of Antonio Gramsci, the Italian Marxist who was imprisoned and died under Mussolini in the rise of fascism simply for teaching people to think, and Paulo Freire, the Brazilian adult educator, who was imprisoned and exiled for teaching people to read and to question. Such is the power of ideas! As I read about Gramsci's concept of hegemony, and began to understand his analysis of the way that power is threaded through our everyday lives from our time of birth, it became so obvious, it was hard to believe that I had not spotted it myself. But the way we are taught to see the world is so powerful that it permeates the essence of our being and influences the way we act in the world. Gramsci felt that false consciousness is so pervasive that it takes external intervention from 'traditional intellectuals', as he called them, to act as a catalyst in the process of demystifying power. My experience was certainly testament to that.

The political context of the time saw the New Right in ascendance. Thatcherism took hold, poverty escalated and my life became one of activism. The Miners' Strike of 1984–85 brought support from alliances all over the world as hegemony was acted out before our eyes. As the full impact of social divisions under Thatcher crept up on us and took us by surprise, Stuart Hall, one of the rare political commentators to keep apace, said of Thatcher, "She's probably never heard of *hegemony*, but she sure knows how to do it!". While the power of persuasion was asserted through control of the media, convincing the country at large that the miners were undermining the very moral fabric of society, freedom of movement from mining communities was blocked by the police who were, cleverly, drafted in from other parts of the country to avoid mixed loyalties. The women of the mining communities took immediate action, to the shock of Margaret Thatcher who had expected that she could appeal to them to force the miners back to work. Women Against Pit Closures became their organised action as they rose up in support of their families and communities, threatened in their survival by starvation tactics. Initially they set up soup kitchens to feed families whose benefits had been cut. Many of these women had never been outside their mining communities, built round the pithead to serve the interests of the industry; their role was one of unpaid labour. Their outrage at the burgeoning threat of the government's desire to dismantle the last large union of organised workers gave them the confidence to give public talks all over the country and abroad, seeking support. Alliances across difference emerged, and at many demonstrations coachloads of supporters would swell the numbers. This was the heyday of new social movements and women, gay and lesbian groups, greens and others stood together against injustice. This was the stamping ground of my political activism.

Participatory democracy in Nicaragua captured the hearts of those everywhere who campaigned for a just and peaceful world. The Nicaragua Solidarity Campaign was central to my life. In Nicaragua, in 1985, staying with the people of Puerto Cabezas in particular helped me to experience participatory democracy in action under the Sandinistas, advised by Paulo Freire. Literacy and health campaigns swept the country led by young people, filling this tiny country with hope. As part of a twinning campaign between Manchester and Puerto Cabezas, we organised for John McDonald, the well-respected adult educator, to go to Puerto Cabezas to develop a health centre. He wrote saying, 'How could you do this to me?'. Even for someone like John, with many years' experience in Africa, Puerto Cabezas was at the edge of the world – all those who could get out had left, and the town was under constant threat. Frequent attacks were made by sea from Honduras and overland routes were landmined by the Contra. This little country, striving to achieve true participation, was perceived as such a threat to the USA that sonic booms were heard every day over Managua, creating fear in the minds of everyone. On a bus trip to Bluefields, we were almost swept up into a Contra raid – attacks like this were commonplace. It was terrifying! We worked to support workshops for those disabled as a result of the war, to twin schools with those in Manchester, to set up women's sewing projects as local economies with the support of women's groups in the UK, and to support a community artist to use wall murals with local people as a way of telling their stories. Nicaragua inspired hope in so many people around the world that a harmonious and just way of life, founded on participatory democracy, was possible. In relation to becoming critical through border crossing (Giroux and McLaren, 1994), this was a transformative experience for me. I saw life from an altered perspective. I quickly learnt the meaning of changed thinking leading to changed doing. One particularly critical encounter was when we were invited to meet the head of the army battalion in the northern region, a dangerous area bordering onto Honduras. He willingly agreed to talk to our little group about the struggles they faced on a daily basis, but then took my breath away: "We send money to support your Miners' Strike. Tell me how you have used this struggle as a way to true democracy." In the face of the courage shown by the Nicaraguans, how could I explain that the false consciousness fostered by dominant hegemony had persuaded popular opinion against the miners, who were seen as undermining, rather than acting for, democracy.

Back home, I was very involved in the women's movement. We were active in our local groups reflecting on our lived experience, building practical theory from grassroots action. It was visible and powerful. We organised Greenham support groups to maintain the women's peace action. Campaigning and activism were part of everyday life: we marched the streets carrying banners to say who we represented – Quakers, gay groups, civil rights activists – all joining together as one, demanding, 'Free Nelson Mandela!'. We joined with the anti-deportation campaigns of the civil rights workers. We loaded lorries full of supplies for War on Want, supported Médecins Sans Frontières, the list went on. It was a time of inspiration and hope.

In this period, I first worked in Old Trafford, bordering Moss Side in Manchester, with multicultural inner-city communities, then with the people of Hattersley, a Manchester 'overspill' or 'peripheral' estate invented to house people from 'slum clearance' areas of inner-city Manchester, built on damp land that was no good for farming, on the foothills of the Pennines in North West England. My new-found praxis, a unity of reflection and transformative action, gave me a critical lens through which to see power acted out in everyday lives, in tangible ways, before my very eyes. This not only helped me to understand life on the margins, but it gave me insight into who was destined to occupy this space outside the mainstream. I began to understand the way that poverty is a tool that reinforces discrimination, and that the process is not indiscriminate, but targets very specific social groups. From experience, I began to understand that knowledge is power, and that ideas sold as 'common sense' make no sense whatsoever, but are internalised and obscure the blatant contradictions that we live by in the West. Theories of power gave me conceptual tools to see and understand the world in more critical ways. The theories on their own in the academy would have remained academic, but they came alive in action, in my practice in the community, building knowledge in action from lived experience, a living praxis as my life became intertwined with those of the many Hattersley people who educated me into the real meaning of life on the margins, Wendy Derbyshire in particular. These experiences revealed the ways in which pathologising people in poverty is a distraction that obscures the interests of power in structuring unequal chances through the fabric of society.

I hit a point of dissonance in the theory/practice divide when I decided that my practice would evolve more critically if I integrated it within a PhD framework working with the internationally respected adult educator, Ralph Ruddock. I struggled to make sense of research methodologies that attempted to decontextualise the lives of the people with whom I worked until my colleague, Paul Jones, handed me a copy of Reason and Rowan's *Human inquiry* (1981). This was another critical moment in my politicisation. I read: 'this book is about human inquiry ... about people exploring and making sense of human action and experience ... ways of going about research which [offer] *alternatives* to orthodox approaches, alternatives which ... do justice to the humanness of all those involved in the research endeavour' (1981, p xi), and my eyes lit up. This revolutionary book, the product of new paradigm researchers' action for change, was transformative in my thinking. It gave me insight into participatory action research as a liberating practice, and profoundly influenced my approach to knowledge creation in everyday life. The approaches to research I discovered here were consonant with the value base of community development practice, and offered an integrated praxis, a way of building knowledge in action and acting on that knowledge. A basic model that has stayed with me ever since this time is Rowan's cycle model, which offers a structure for integrating theory and practice as an ongoing dialectical cycle of action and knowledge generation (Rowan, 1981, p 98).

In 1992, I made a move from grassroots community development practice into the academy. I faltered on the interview day, questioning the relevance of locating myself in such a cloistered context after being at the heart of community life for so many years. In my mind's eye, I could see myself sitting in Mottram Churchyard, having a picnic lunch with Paul, a critical space to reflect on our practice. Our partnership was so dynamic for so long, and we thrived on the challenges of Hattersley life; "Could there ever be life after Hattersley?", we asked ourselves. But life moves on, and my challenge was to locate myself where I could make most difference to the process of change, to keep community development critical. In my new role as a community work educator, my life was woven together with Paula Asgill, a woman of Jamaican heritage, who became my close friend and colleague. Through shared experience, we became aware of differences in our lived realities as two women, divided by racism. We worked together on research into alliances between Black and White women in order to gain deeper insight into the process of sustaining alliances for change, and I began to touch at the edges of White power as it manifests itself in daily encounters. She died at the age of 47, 14 years later.

During this period, a young student came bursting into my office, waving a call for papers for the 'Pedagogy of the Oppressed' Conference in Omaha in 1995. He was passionate about the work of Freire, and was urging me to submit a paper. I did, and I found myself beginning a long connection with what is now known as the Pedagogy and Theatre of the Oppressed organisation. In 1996, Doug Paterson, from the University of Nebraska at Omaha, invited Paulo Freire and Augusto Boal to the conference, where it was my great pleasure to meet them just a few months before Freire's death. This was the context for my engagement with such radical educators as Ira Shor, Peter McLaren, Antonia Darder, Peter Mayo, Michelle Fine, Maxine Green, Chris Cavanagh and many others significant in the critical pedagogy movement.

(Adapted from Ledwith and Springett, 2010)

A critical approach

Community development begins in the everyday reality of people's lives by 'extraordinarily re-experiencing the ordinary' (Shor, 1992, p 122). It is a praxis that locates the silenced stories of those who are marginalised and excluded at the heart of any theory of change for social justice. These stories are the basis of community development theory and practice. In a process of action and reflection, theory builds from experience. Praxis is the synthesis of theory and practice to a point where they become a unity, where theory develops in action. The key to this process is problem-posing or *problematising* (Freire, 1972). People are encouraged to ask thought-provoking questions and 'to question answers rather than merely

—

to answer questions' (Shor, quoted in McLaren and Leonard, 1993, p 26). This critical approach to community development exposes structures of power and the way these impact on personal lives. It fundamentally challenges pathologising theories that lay blame and responsibility at the feet of the victims of injustice. However, critical consciousness is not liberating until it becomes a collective process for change. Freire did not believe in self-liberation as an end in itself:

> Liberating education is a social process of illumination.... Even when you individually feel yourself most free, if this feeling is not a social feeling, if you are not able to use your recent freedom to help others to be free by transforming the totality of society, then you are exercising only an individualist attitude towards empowerment or freedom. (Freire, quoted in Shor and Freire, 1987, p 109)

The body of knowledge that informs community development praxis grows in dynamic relation with changing communities, changing contexts and changing knowledge. The way that we understand our world shapes the way we live in our world. It is by challenging the way we see the world that we open ourselves to new worldviews, new possibilities for creating a world that is just, sustainable, and non-violent, and this new understanding, in turn, changes the way we live our lives.

These opening thoughts give you a glimpse of some of the critical aspects of my story and of our times. The relevance of this narrative approach is that it gives you insight into the personal experiences that are woven through my ideas, illuminating the points I make, and grounding them in lived experience. Human inquiry is a lived experience, and is an integral component of community development. I see action and reflection as a process of search, of research, of curiosity and a desire to understand, driven by a commitment to change things for the better. It begins in lived experience, in context, and it reflects the whole tangled complexity of life. It explores different ways of knowing; it also challenges the authority of the knower and relocates authenticity in the reality of people's lives, giving silenced voices the right to be heard. It focuses on understanding power and the way that it is assumed and acted out.

All this may sound chaotic in its complexity, but there are theories, conceptual tools and models that help make sense of the process. In contributing to a body of knowledge that is based on countering discrimination, exploitation and injustice, we push beyond the constraints of our limited understanding to explore new possibilities. Breaking free from a controlled and controlling view of the world, one that we are taught to see as inevitable, we make the choice to step into uncharted territory. This is not only liberating and challenging, but at times frightening and unpredictable. The important point to remember is that it carries the hope that a more socially and environmentally just future based on participatory democracy is a possibility.

A critical approach to community development begins in people's lives in community, but reaches beyond the symptoms of injustice to the root causes by making critical connections between personal experiences and the oppressive political structures that perpetuate discrimination. Collective action is the process by which people join together to bring about change. If we fail to take our practice beyond the good work that goes into local issues and local projects, we fail to realise this potential, and our work is good but not transformative; it is making local lives easier, tolerable, more pleasant, but is not addressing the root source of the problems that give rise to injustice.

Let me illustrate my point. If, in my practice in community, I notice that there are an increasing number of people sleeping rough or in temporary accommodation, and I work with the local community to set up a night shelter and a soup kitchen, this is good practice, but not transformative. It cannot be transformative because it is dealing with the symptoms but failing to reach the causes of the problem. My analysis is not going deep enough to identify the reasons that give rise to this escalating social problem, and the temptation is to stop at the project stage where it remains a local issue. Consequently, the forces generating the problem will continue unabated. To address structural oppression, collective action, through networks and alliances, harnesses collective power beyond local issues to movements for change at national and global levels.

There is much good practice evidenced in community development, but its weaknesses lie in it (i) remaining local, and (ii) having a propensity to divide theory from practice. Do I hear some of you say that this is impossible given the constraints that keep us working with short-term funding, within the parameters of government policies, using indicators that are imposed from outside and limit and fragment our practice? I remind you that, as an occupation, we have always been 'in and against the state', targeted to change things for the better but not to rock the boat; it is the nature of the ambivalent relationship between community work and state (Shaw, 2004). And staying local and untheorised limits our practice to tokenism, failing our professed aim to work for social justice. Without an understanding of the theory and politics of community development, we leave ourselves open to distraction and manipulation.

Community development needs to redefine its critical potential within the current political context if it is to realise its social justice intention. The body of knowledge that informs community development needs to grow in dynamic equilibrium with these rapidly changing times, and we need to engage with and contribute to that body of knowledge if we are to achieve a political analysis worthy of action for a just and sustainable future. This book contributes to a radical, anti-discriminatory practice that is capable of transformative change.

A critical approach to practice calls for reflection on action, and the use of critical questions keeps us focused:

- How is your practice influenced by an anti-discriminatory analysis?
- In what way are national and global changes impacting on the diverse lives of local people?

- What evidence is there that your practice contributes to change for social justice and environmental justice?
- How can you extend collective action beyond the boundaries of community to build national, international and global alliances?

In order to develop a critical approach to practice, I attempt to weave a greater synthesis of theory and practice through this book. Throughout, I choose to emphasise the diverse political nature of the categories 'White' and 'Black' by using capital letters. In the same way, I emphasise the socially constructed nature of 'dis'ability and 'race'. I hope the ideas I share engage you and inspire you to go into the world with new determination.

ONE

Why empower?

'The absence of a coherent political project, it is claimed, inhibits the development of a more radical paradigm in community work', so said Cooke and Shaw in 1996 (1996, p 9). Since then, we have been through a long politics of partnership that has located everyone on the same side, a delusional tactic that has resulted in negating dialectical thought, colonising critical spaces and temporarily halting radical practice in a haze of managerialism, professionalism and the elevation of doing over thinking. Our focus has been blurred on the real issues at stake and left us as uncritical deliverers of policy, not really understanding why we are doing what we do anyway. We have lost our way (Pitchford with Henderson, 2008). At the same time, on a global level, escalating forces of neoliberal globalisation are steering us along a dangerous trajectory, with a free market principle based on a profit imperative systematically fragmenting people and planet. We are left with a world in crisis, a world of increasing social divisions and alarming environmental degradation. This is the radical challenge of our times, and my invitation is for you to join me in exploring just how straightforward it is to reclaim our radical agenda and to locate it in a more global political project for participatory democracy.

> If empowerment is at the heart of critical community practice, then "power" and its utilization are at the core of empowerment. It is only through engaging with structures and processes of social, political and economic power that communities can effectively work to confront the disadvantage, exclusion and oppression that they experience. (Butcher et al, 2007, p 21)

Empowerment is a transformative concept but without a critical analysis it is all too often applied naively to confidence and self-esteem at a personal level, within a paradigm of social pathology, a purpose that is usually associated with personal responsibility for lifting oneself out of poverty, overlooking structural analyses of inequality. The subtle nuances of the concept of empowerment are fundamental to community development analysis, determining whether our practice is informed by pathologising or liberating theories. I am going to use this focus, of power and empowerment, to explore the changing political contexts that have informed the theory and practice of community development. By these means, my intention is to illustrate the ways in which dominant thought influences policy and practice, which, without a critical dimension, skews us towards amelioration rather than transformation. As Emejulu and Shaw (2010) remind us: 'What community development means at any particular time is defined by all those interests which have sought to name, frame and regulate it' (2010, p 5). For those of us who take social justice seriously, those competing interests in these turbulent political times demand vigilance: the creation of 'democratic spaces' in which to engage in critical dissent dialogue are vital to the re-alignment of our principles and our practice.

A brief history of radical community development

Let us begin this exploration by considering the roots of radical practice. Radical practice has a transformative agenda, an intention to bring about social change that is based on a fair, just and sustainable world. In this respect, it locates the roots of inequality in the structures and processes of society, not in personal or community pathology. This has implications for practice. Collective action for change has to follow through from local to structural levels in order to make a sustainable difference. Anything less is ameliorative, making life just a little bit better around the edges, but not stemming the flow of discriminatory experiences that create some lives as more privileged than others. Once we begin to question that everyday taken-for-grantedness, our blinkers are removed and we see life from a more critical perspective.

Community development is never static: its practice is always re-forming in dynamic with current thought, political contexts and lived experience. So, my proposal at this point is that community development is a practice that needs to be constantly re-examined in relation to participatory democracy in order to maintain its integrity and relevance to its commitment to a fair, just and equal world. It is a 'thinking' and 'doing' practice, constantly developing theory in action. Without this necessary vigilance, we leave ourselves open to manipulation from external agendas that may not be operating from the social justice perspective that is central to our purpose.

In the previous edition I traced the foundations of community work to Victorian benevolence, the university settlement movement, particularly Toynbee Hall, and the early examples of feminist action and class action. Here, I want to focus more specifically on the roots of community development as a distinct occupation, and the emergence of radical community development with its commitment to social change for the simple reason that I believe this to be more relevant to the challenges that we face today.

Let us begin by posing the notion that community development is a contested occupation that sits at the interface of reactionary practice and revolutionary practice. By this, I mean that our work is vulnerable to distortion from other agendas if we do not remain vigilant, critiquing the changing times that provide the context for community life.

In the UK, community work began to emerge as a distinct occupation with a strong educational component in the 1960s, following the Younghusband report (1959), which identified community organisation as a key component of social work, based on the North American model. Community organisation was seen as an approach that supported people to define their own needs and identify ways in which these may be met. Based on Younghusband's definition, Kuenstler (1961) presented the first collection of community work material directly relevant to the British context, in relation to social need and current practice at the time. This was the beginning of British community work as we know it today.

The term 'community development' gradually became applied to community work that was based in local neighbourhoods. In 1968, the Gulbenkian report, informed by research into the role of community work in the UK, located community work at the interface between people and social change (Calouste Gulbenkian Foundation, 1968). It defined community work as a full-time professional practice based in neighbourhoods, helping local people to decide, plan and take action to meet their needs with the help of outside resources. Within that, key components were improving the delivery of local services, developing interagency coordination and influencing policy and planning (Calouste Gulbenkian Foundation, 1968). In its broadest sense, the report recommended that community work be a recognised part of professional practice for teachers, social workers, the clergy, health workers, architects, planners, administrators and other community-based services. There was a fundamental split in the recommendations between educationalists, who saw community work as essentially adult/ community education, and others who placed more emphasis on planning and service delivery. In contrast, Scotland, particularly after the publication of the Alexander Report in 1975, chose to place much greater emphasis on community development as community learning (Scottish Education Department, 1975). In the final outcome, despite concerns expressed by community workers, the Gulbenkian report chose to gloss over the contradictory and political aspects of the work (Craig et al, 1982; Popple, 1995).

A number of other influential reports were published around this time, including that of the Seebohm Committee (Seebohm Report, 1968), which recommended the expansion of community work, particularly as a dimension of social services provision, and the Skeffington Report (1969), which recommended increased public participation in urban planning.

The emergence of radical community development

Community work continued to be driven by social work thinking, until another important juncture. Thomas (1983) suggests the desire of the Wilson government to transform British society led to community development becoming a strategy to bridge the gap between the state and the working class, while maintaining capitalist social relations – a reformist rather than revolutionary idea. This was accelerated by increasing social unrest that heightened in 1968. It was a time of transition and change: 1968 is widely acknowledged as a critical juncture in world history, described by Popple (1995, p 15) as a year of 'revolt, rebellion and reaction throughout the world'. It was a year when civil disobedience erupted in the form of 'race' riots, student demonstrations, civil rights marches and anti-Vietnam protests, and which witnessed the assassinations of Martin Luther King and Robert Kennedy. At the same time, there were significant developments in community work practice: the Urban Programme was set up in 1968, and the national Community Development Project (CDP), the largest government-funded action research project, emerged from it in 1969. The Urban Programme was a Labour government response to social unrest generated by unemployment, immigration and 'race' relations, inflamed by Enoch Powell's 'rivers of blood' speech; and the CDP targeted 12 communities in poverty for interventions based on the pathology-based assumptions of Keith Joseph's (Secretary of State for Health, 1972–74) 'cycle of deprivation' theory (Rutter and Madge, 1976, p 3). Action research is a powerful component of community development praxis. The CDP workers, based on theory in action, developed an insightful analysis of the impact of poverty in people's lives and rejected the pathological analysis of the 'cycle of deprivation' theory in favour of structural analyses of power.

Gary Craig, Professor of Community Development and Social Justice at the University of Durham, who worked in Newcastle for the Benwell CDP, comments on how this experience was instrumental in defining community development's radical agenda:

The Community Development Project, 1968–78

"One of the early struggles for the identity of community development followed the emergence of the very substantial volume of writing of the workers on the national CDP. An influential caucus of CDP workers developed what came to be known as the 'structural analysis' of the decline of inner-city areas (where most of the 12 projects were based), pointing to industrial disinvestment and the rundown of public services as the major reason for poverty and deprivation in these areas, rather than, as the governmental literature would have had people believe, the fecklessness of inner-city residents. Virtually every one of the total of 100+ workers on the local CDP projects was engaged in some form of neighbourhood work: their point was that without an understanding of the structural causes of decline, neighbourhood work could be misdirected and ineffective. The analysis, taken forward by others later on, argued instead for the need for alliances, across neighbourhoods, between community activists and trades unions, between women's groups and what had historically been male-dominated organisations, and across ethnic divides, in order to use the analysis for effective political action at local level."

At the same time, the translation of Gramsci's *Prison notebooks* (1971) and Freire's *Pedagogy of the oppressed* (1972) into English had an immense impact on community development praxis, as did Alinsky's *Reveille for radicals* (1969), well-thumbed copies of which poked out of the pockets of any community activist. In these ways, the theory and practice of radical community development came together.

Community work rose against what it saw as 'the social control functions of both the welfare state and the state-sponsored caring professions. Community work presented itself as a radical alternative to social work, which it caricatured as "soft policing". Similarly, youth work was dismissed as a means of simply keeping working-class kids off the streets. The welfare state, it was suggested, was designed to contain rather than cure poverty' (Jacobs, 1994, p 156). It is this commitment to get beyond the symptoms to the root causes of oppression that defines radical community development. At this point, I want to emphasise that this radical perspective on community development was a direct result of a number of dimensions converging at a moment in time. First, I see the influence of action research, in its capacity to engage theory and practice as a living theory that finds its evidence and relevance in the lives of people fully contextualised in community and in society, vital to any form of practice with a social justice intention. Second, the influence of new ideas on practice – Freire, Gramsci, feminism, anti-racism – coincided with the confluence of an historic juncture. Third, the1960s generated a context of hope and optimism, a feeling that a better world was possible for all. All of these factors, in turn, triggered tremendous change through the grassroots activism that evolved as new social movements. We witnessed theory in action rising from lived experience to change policy in alliances that transcended boundaries and, in doing so, began to embrace a more common humanity.

From the epoch of 1968, the distinct approach of community development began to be recognised and expansion took place in both the voluntary and statutory sectors, but as the 1970s progressed there was more emphasis on state sponsorship, with the inevitable consequence that community workers were increasingly located in a contradictory position, 'in and against the state' – working with local people to demand better public services at the same time as being employed by the local state which provided those services. Since that time, there has been a split between the radical agenda, which believes that community development is a locus of change within the struggle for transformation of the structures of society that are the root cause of oppression; and the pluralist agenda, which believes that there is a multiplicity of competing power bases in society, mediated by the state, and that community development is only capable of ameliorative small-scale neighbourhood change and piecemeal reforms. The radical tradition, including class, feminist and anti-racist models of practice (see, for example, Mayo, 1977; Craig et al, 1982; Ohri et al, 1982; Dominelli, 1990), built its knowledge base on critical consciousness and the bigger picture issues of social justice and sustainability. The pluralist agenda rejected a wider political analysis to focus on skills and process issues such as interagency work and service delivery (Henderson and Thomas, 1980; Thomas, 1983; Twelvetrees, 1991).

Working in and against the state, revolution or reform, has presented an ongoing tension for community development. After the election of the Thatcher government in 1979, the anti-state approach of radical community workers became an increasingly ineffective mechanism with which to challenge the declining social democratic consensus and the reactionary ideology of the New Right (Lees and Mayo, 1984). Waddington (1994, p 6) referred to the Conservative government's moralising ideology in which '"enterprise" replaced "greed" in the political lexicon, and the cultivation of "national unity" … disguised the active reinforcement of social divisions'.

Prior to this, Cockburn's (1977) challenge was that community work's function as state-sponsored activity was to defuse escalating conflict by diverting energy into forms of participation that gave an *illusion of democracy*. Waddington (1979) responded by arguing that community work's quest for a just socialist society was inextricably bound up with the state, and that analyses of that relationship must be central to our practice. Blagg and Derricourt (1982) entered this debate, advocating that we move beyond a crude anti-state approach to identify a conflict model that operates within the state to counter the consensus models of community work practice promoted by the Gulbenkian, Seebohm and Skeffington Reports, and perpetuated in the more pluralist approaches of the Henderson and Thomas tradition (Barr, 1991).

Barr (1991, p 129) quotes Peter Marris's analysis, which slices through these positions to state:

> So long as government policy and community action justify themselves by the same ideals, community action has scope for influence on government's own terms, even if its ideology is in other ways radically opposed to the assumptions of government.... Movements for change are empowered by the convergence of social ideals expressed in principles of action ... [and we need] to incorporate into those struggles a demand for effective, open, collective planning, as a crucial part of carrying out any practical ideal of social justice.

Within this model, as Barr (1991, p 129) notes, 'the state, particularly given its planning powers, remains a target for influence but can also be a partner for change'.

This is an interesting note on which to explore the changing political contexts that have influenced community development, particularly in relation to the way we allow ourselves to be redefined and distracted by external agendas to the point that we can lose direction.

The political context

Beveridge and the post-war consensus on welfare

Popular consensus changed attitudes to welfare during the war years, and the welfare state, informed by the Beveridge Report (1942), was implemented in 1948, based on a collective responsibility for the well-being of all. This was a major landmark in social justice thought. Even so, such revolutionary thinking 'hid the giants Racism and Sexism, and the fights against them, behind statues to the Nation and the White Family' (Williams, 1989, p 162).

Uncovering the reality of relative poverty in 1965, Peter Townsend and Brian Abel-Smith (cited in Mack and Lansley, 1985) exposed the welfare state as failing in its ambitions. Television documentaries such as *Cathy Come Home* heightened public awareness of the reality of social problems. Out of these new insights into the damaging impact of relative poverty a Quaker initiative led to the Child Poverty Action Group (CPAG) being formed, co-founded by Peter Townsend. (CPAG continues to be a vital source of poverty analyses and campaigns relevant to community development, linking grassroots projects with wider collective action.) It is when we synthesise insights into poverty and its consequences with the campaigning to organise for change that we see movement towards social justice (Dornan, 2008).

The New Right and Thatcherism

Expansive welfare spending coupled with a global economic recession after 1973 led to a crisis in welfare provision, exposing a space for change. Neoliberal ideologies took hold through Thatcherism in the UK, Reaganomics in the USA, the Pinochet regime in Chile and the International Monetary Fund (IMF) and World Bank programmes in the developing world (Mayo, 1999). It was a revolutionary move to the Right. In order to understand the development of neoliberalism in the UK it is important to understand the way that these global forces were creating a world context for neoliberal globalisation to accelerate. Fundamental to its ideology is the concept of a free market. This is an unjust system that exploits the poor and vulnerable for profit. For instance, free trade, promoted by the World Bank, forces poor countries to cut public spending in order to repay loans. Developing countries are made to compete in a global market where producers from the rich countries of the 'first world' are still subsidised. Similarly, neoliberal emphasis on deregulation and privatisation of a state's economic activities create a niche for multinational companies to gain control over national economies. This benefits corporate interests, siphoning money out of local communities to profit big businesses, and in doing so makes some businesses wealthier than some of the poorest countries of the world. Kane likens this activity to that of 'a kind of international loan shark' (Kane, 2008, p 196).

These national and world changes created a moment in time for the politics that came to be known as Thatcherism to take hold. From the election of the Thatcher government in 1979, the full and unmitigated ascendance of New Right politics was in full swing by the mid-1980s. New Right rhetoric, blaming the victims of poverty for their own marginalisation, painted evocative stereotypes of the 'welfare scrounger' that divided the poor into 'deserving' and 'undeserving'. This was sewn into the minds of the people with such images as Norman Tebbit's 'on yer bike' message to abandon community in favour of employment, and the demonisation of single parents by Peter Lilley's rendition to Parliament of Gilbert and Sullivan: "I've got a little list, I've got a little list of young ladies who get pregnant just to jump the housing list". These divide–and–rule politics set people in poverty against each other and created a divided Britain. It was a clever and powerful ideology that captured the public imagination, paving the way for major policy change as working–class solidarity gave way to a widespread culture of individualism.

This conceptual paradox, one of *need* set against *greed*, made an immediate impact on communities. Social welfare became perceived as a burden rather than a collective responsibility and a moral right. Notions of collective social responsibility, which had formed the bedrock for the post-war welfare state, gave way to a competitive culture driven by consumerism. The 'Thatcher revolution', fuelled by social, political and economic change, was committed to a 'dismantling of the protective elements of state welfare, to breaking the power of the organised labour movement and to a reaffirmation of market forces that would bring poverty and unemployment to unprecedented levels' (Novak, 1988, p 176).

At the same time as a welfare revolution was being paved, a politics of *common sense* persuaded the British people to see the Miners' Strike of 1984–85 as an attempt to undermine democracy and liberty: miners became reviled as enemies of the state. Only in the course of time have the dirty tricks of the state been exposed as venting full power on the National Union of Mineworkers – the issue being not the economics of coal, but the right to organise (Milne, 1994). Margaret Thatcher perceived her hair's breadth victory as a triumph over collective organisation, and it gave her government a head of steam to bring in other major reforms. For instance, the Social Security Act 1986 promised welfare reforms unsurpassed since Beveridge, but the results were devastating, forcing vulnerable groups further onto the margins of society while the rich got richer (Cohen et al, 1996). This transfer of wealth from the poor to the rich created massive social divisions, with children replacing older people as the single group most vulnerable to poverty (Oppenheim and Harker, 1996). Under Thatcherism, social reforms devoured rights and reduced benefits for some of the most vulnerable groups in society. These risks of poverty were further exacerbated by class, 'race', ethnicity, gender, age and 'dis'ability, 'yet to suggest that poverty is evidence of structural rather than personal failing is to swim against the modern-day tide of individualism' (Witcher, quoted in Oppenheim and Harker, 1996, p vii).

As a society, we became complicit, allowing the most vulnerable to be exploited in the interests of the powerful. 'Between the 1980s and 1990s, the number of people who could objectively be described as living in poverty increased by almost 50 per cent' (Gordon and Pantazis, 1997, p 21). There was a massive transfer of wealth from the *poor* to the *rich*, with the income of the wealthiest tenth of the UK population being equal to that of the poorest half (Goodman et al, 1997). The indictment of this period is the way that poverty targeted children. From only one in ten children in 1979, by 1997 one in every three children in Britain was growing up in poverty (Flaherty et al, 2004).

The Third Way and New Labour

In the UK, the Third Way is associated with the politics of New Labour, the dawn of which was the landslide election of the Blair government in 1997.

The Third Way marked a distinct shift from Thatcher's 'no such thing as society'. Not long after his election, Prime Minister Blair wrote: 'we all depend on collective goods for our independence; and all our lives are enriched – or impoverished – by the communities to which we belong.... A key challenge of progressive politics is to use the state as an enabling force, protecting effective communities and voluntary organisations and encouraging their growth to tackle new needs, in partnership, as appropriate' (Blair, 1998, p 4). This new approach to government was informed by the thinking of Anthony Giddens (1998). New Labour combined strands of communitarianism: community as a life with meaning based on the mutual interdependence of individuals, and the role of the state in partnership with community in creating a quality of life. For the first time, we found the language of partnership with community, of bold anti-poverty statements, of a preoccupation with regeneration projects, of widening access to education. In this context, community development gained more policy recognition than it had known before. But radical community development was alerted to the increasing repositioning of Left and Right to the centre, removing the dialectical relations of traditional political parties to suggest that we are all on the same side in mutual partnership. Without this adversarial positioning, policies and practice became flawed by the absence of a structural analysis of inequality and injustice. The rhetoric of communitarianism, that of autonomous, flourishing communities founded on mutuality and reciprocity, took on an edge of state authoritarianism. Zero tolerance policing, punitive approaches to asylum seekers, and on-the-spot fines for anti-social behaviour were indicative of policy approaches that circumvented a bottom-up empowerment model to impose top-down interventionist approaches to community (Calder, 2003).

At Toynbee Hall, in March 1999, Tony Blair delivered a speech on the legacy of Sir William Beveridge, the unanticipated high spot of which was his own personal and political commitment to end child poverty within 20 years. The absence of 'poverty' from political discourse throughout Thatcherism created a smokescreen for what was happening in reality, so Tony Blair's public declaration to end child poverty brought an upsurge of optimism from the social justice lobby, and a raft of policies appeared on child poverty, unemployment, neighbourhood deprivation and inequalities in health and educational achievement. CPAG found itself for the first time working with a government that acknowledged the unacceptability of such high child poverty rates, and was encouraged by an abundance of anti-poverty policies directed at children and poor families. But, just below the surface, contradictions emerged between the interests of the state and the rights and responsibilities of parents. As Tess Ridge (2004) pointed out, a state interest in children as future workers leads to policies that are qualitatively different from those that are concerned with creating happy childhoods:

> Children who are poor are not a homogeneous group, although they are often represented as being so. Their experiences of being poor will be mediated by, among other things, their age, gender, ethnicity, health and whether or not they are disabled. In addition, children

will interpret their experiences of poverty in the context of a diverse range of social, geographical and cultural settings. (Ridge, 2004, p 5)

The pledge to end child poverty by 2020 was ambitious. Targeted anti-poverty strategies, between 1997 and 2001, moved the UK from the highest child poverty rate in the European Union (EU) to fifth highest (Hills and Stewart, 2005). This clearly left much room for improvement when ending child poverty is 'vital for the effectiveness, as well as the justice, of UK society' (Dornan, 2004, p 3). In spite of the generosity of the new tax credits, poverty for working lone parents, the majority of whom were women, remained high in relation to European levels, reflecting the gendered nature of poverty (Hills and Stewart, 2005). The links between women's poverty and child poverty are crucial to understanding that tackling women's poverty is fundamental to the success of any child poverty strategy. According to Ruth Lister's (2005) analysis these can be grouped around two main issues: those related to women's role as the main carers of children and managers of poverty; and those related to women's position in the labour market as working mothers. So, Blair will be honoured for putting child poverty on the political agenda, despite flawed analyses that failed to deliver his promise.

On a very different note, he will also be remembered for his alliance with Bush on the USA's 'war on terror', and the delusional justification of weapons of mass destruction. In 2001, he joined forces with the USA on the invasion of Afghanistan and in 2003 on the invasion of Iraq, flying in the face of popular opinion. In his first six years, Blair ordered British troops into battle five times – more than any other Prime Minister in British history. He was the Labour Party's longest-serving Prime Minister, the only person to have led the Labour Party to three consecutive general election victories, but his anti-democratic stance on war was to be his downfall and his legacy. He was succeeded as Prime Minister on 27 June 2007 by Gordon Brown.

When New Labour inherited a 'divided Britain', 'there was an increasing concern about so-called "worst neighbourhoods", with concentrations of poverty and worklessness and the associated problems of high crime and disorder, diminishing and dysfunctional services, empty housing and environmental decay' (Lupton and Power, 2005, p 119). In 1998, the newly formed Social Exclusion Unit (SEU) produced a report, *Bringing Britain together*, in which about 3,000 neighbourhoods were identified as having high levels of poverty, unemployment, poor health and crime, with poorer service delivery, poorer quality schools, fewer doctors' surgeries, fewer shops and high levels of litter and vandalism. This marked the beginning of a very different policy approach that focused regeneration on poor neighbourhoods, and in 2000 the National Strategy for Neighbourhood Renewal was launched. The New Labour vision was that 'within 10-20 years, no-one should be seriously disadvantaged by where they live' (SEU, 2001, cited in Lupton and Power, 2005, p 120). The main area-based programmes were the Single Regeneration Budget, Education Action Zones, Health Action Zones, New Deal for Communities, Sure Start, Excellence in Cities and Employment Zones, from which a plethora of initiatives emerged aimed at reducing worklessness and crime, improving skills, health, housing and environments, and lessening social divisions. These were informed by underlying concepts, such as exclusion, multiculturalism, social capital and community, within the overriding idea of *community cohesion* as a general principle for improving the quality of life in communities. Burton (2003), however, critiqued the divide between rhetoric and reality, outlining the tokenistic nature of the process: (i) unequal power relations in partnerships; (ii) top-down agendas; and (iii) inappropriate funding criteria as key issues that not only hampered community development, but destroyed the enthusiasm of local activists.

The need for critical approaches to community development is reflected in Gary Craig's reference to *ideological confusion* (1998, p 2). When we fail to be critical in practice, we are likely to find ourselves naively supporting policies that emphasise *participation* as a further erosion of rights in favour of responsibilities, rather than a process leading to social justice and equality. Gary Craig (2011), retrospectively analysing this period, concludes that we unwittingly colluded in the deconstruction of welfare, allowing, within the rights and responsibilities focus of the Blair–Brown government, our transformative concepts to be hijacked into policy that laid claim to social justice as the improvement of service delivery. During this period, critique and dissent became obscured in a frenzy of bureaucracy, short-term funding and skills-based approaches to practice that allowed community development to become distracted and diluted. Let us take a look at what was happening on the global stage.

Neoliberal globalisation

The process of neoliberal globalisation accelerated throughout the 1990s, increasingly projecting its free trade profit imperative across the world. Profit without constraints inevitably implies exploitation, and this began to take impact on people and the planet in crisis proportions. Neoliberal globalisation is the 'market-organized and imposed expansion of production that emphasizes comparative advantage, free trade, export orientations, the social and spatial divisions of labour, and the absolute mobility of corporations' (Fisher and Ponniah, 2003, p 28). In other words, we find ourselves in a world where capitalism has re-formed on a global level, exploiting the most vulnerable people and environments in the world in the interests of the dominant and privileged. It is a form of corporate capitalism where the most powerful systems of the West not only dominate the world economically, but invade other cultures with a western worldview that works on political, cultural, racial, gendered, sexual, ecological and epistemological differences. In the name of a free market economy, not only is labour exploited in the interests of capital (class), but the same structures of oppression that subordinate groups of people according to 'race', gender, age, sexuality, faith, ethnicity and 'dis'ability are being reproduced on a global level.

> Neoliberal globalization is not simply economic domination of the
> world but also the imposition of a monolithic thought (*pensamento unico*)
> that consolidates vertical forms of difference and prohibits the public
> from imagining diversity in egalitarian, horizontal terms. Capitalism,
> imperialism, monoculturalism, patriarchy, white supremacism and the
> domination of biodiversity have coalesced under the current form of
> globalization. (Fisher and Ponniah, 2003, p 10)

Wealth is increasingly transferred from poor to rich countries by exploiting the
labour and resources of the developing world in order to feed the consumerist
greed of the West. The consequence is increased social divisions both within
and between countries, with corporations becoming wealthier than poorer
countries and rich countries increasingly privileging the already privileged whilst
abandoning swelling numbers to lives in poverty. Globalisation presents anti-
discriminatory practice with increasingly complex, interlinking and overlapping
oppressions that are poorly understood and therefore infrequently challenged.
In this way, poverty becomes increasingly convoluted, and oppression becomes
distant and even more concealed. It is not possible to take a critical approach
to community development without having an analysis of the way in which all
communities are inextricably linked on this global dimension. For example, it is
Giroux's critique of the 'politics of disposability' (Giroux, 2006) as a central project
of neoliberal globalisation's profit imperative that has led to our understanding
of the full impact of an ideology of the market, and the way that our worth as
human beings is ranked according to our potential as consumers and producers.
The result is an increasingly divided world, one that is both environmentally
unsustainable and socially unjust.

The 'Big Society'

Moving back to focus on the UK, we need to keep in mind the global setting
for the emergence of the 'Big Society'. Perhaps Tony Benn's (2010, p 30)
comment on the state of democracy is useful at this point: 'We don't really have
a democracy. The gap between rich and poor is wider than when I came into
Parliament (1950), and globalization is handing power over to big corporations
and institutions. All the power is being sucked upwards'. And, worryingly, this
'power being sucked upwards' model equally applies to British government as
public schools increasingly become the spawning ground for MPs of Right and
Left, eliminating other routes to democratic election.

Much to the dismay of those of us committed to social justice, Gordon Brown,
the Labour leader, withdrew from the coalition debate after the inconclusive
general election of 2010, leaving the way clear for an alliance between David
Cameron, the Conservative leader, and Nick Clegg, leader of the Liberal
Democrats.

The 'Big Society' is the flagship policy of the Conservative Party, and has become the driver of the coalition government, aiming to decentralise state power and hand power over to communities and local people by:

- giving communities more powers
- encouraging people to take an active role in their communities
- transferring power from central to local government
- supporting co-ops, mutuals, charities and social enterprises
- publishing government data.

The concept of the 'Big Society' is about participatory democracy and community empowerment, whereas the Cameron–Clegg interpretation is anti-democratic. The paradox has been that the transference of power to communities has been accompanied by austerity cuts in public sector provision which will have a major impact on the poorest in general and on women in particular. The Trades Union Congress, in the most comprehensive analysis of public spending ever undertaken, *Where the money goes* (available at www.tuc.org), forecast that the public sector cuts in health, social and education services will hit the poorest 13 times harder than the richest, with most impact felt by women, children and older people. Vanessa Baird (2010) identifies a major contradiction by questioning the wisdom of prioritising community credit unions as anti-poverty strategies without setting this in juxtaposition with the need for redistributive wealth. The 'small state' is absolving its democratic responsibilities to the poorest in society by making austerity cuts in public services at the same time as making the poorest responsible for their own poverty.

The country was confused. What, precisely, did this mean in relation to everyday lives? Then the impact of major funding cuts was made public. The 'Big Society' was exposed as a metaphor for targeting the poor. In February 2011, as pro-democracy grassroots protests demonstrated the power of collective action throughout the Middle East, Cameron gave a public speech defending his 'Big Society', claiming it has nothing to do with financial cuts, it is about the social recovery of the 'broken society', it is about making people responsible, about mending broken families, about giving communities power by reducing public services, devolving state power and increasing charitable giving.

The 'Big Society' is strong on the rhetoric of empowerment but weak on an analysis of equality simply because it does not make critical connections between the economy and society. Anna Coote (2010), Head of Social Policy at the New Economics Foundation, predicts the undermining of social justice and the widening of inequalities:

> Effectively, the Big Society abandons the idea of collective action and shared responsibility on a broad scale through the state, focusing instead on encouraging local interventions by the 'little platoons' of civil society and businesses of all sizes. Individuals who are already

marginalised by poverty and powerlessness will be left behind by the Big Society, where everything hangs on how much power is assumed by which groups and businesses, to do what, for whom and how.

Such a naive analysis of the nature of power and its transference, as well as a lack of understanding of the fundamental essence of democracy, augurs ill for the coming years. The idea that society can be made stronger by getting more people to work together to generate more community organisers, neighbourhood groups and so on is good – we know that when people have control over what is happening in their lives health and well-being improves. Yet the beginning of this process has been to dismantle the established network of voluntary and community sector organisations by withdrawing funding, threatening to seriously weaken shifting power and responsibility for poverty, unemployment and inequalities to those people and communities most marginalised. This side-steps the very issue of the role of capitalism in creating disparities of wealth and power.

The 'small state' in handing over power to the 'Big Society' effectively labels communities as both the problem and the solution (Craig, 2011). Community development is a process of empowerment that leads to autonomous communities. Its role is not to provide an alternative to state services, holding communities to ransom for tackling poverty and inequality, ignoring the fact that this is predicated on an unequal playing field. Those communities most marginalised, disadvantaged and disempowered will not survive, whereas those most privileged, powerful and advantaged will flourish, creating even greater social divisions – flying undetected under the radar of structural inequalities that produce disadvantage. We need to change the way we think about poverty and privilege and address changes at structural levels as well as in local communities. In these ways, we could reduce concentrations of wealth and power. Participation is a partnership, with the state functioning as a protector of democracy to ensure fair distribution of resources, to maintain rights and to keep a balance of power between the powerful and powerless (Coote, 2010).

The New Economics Foundation offers us 10 ways to actively engage with the 'Big Society' in order to steer a course towards a truer participatory democracy:

1. Make social justice the main goal: develop a social justice framework to emphasise not only the 'big' but the fair and sustainable distribution of social, environmental and economic resources.
2. Build a broader economy: change the way that the economy and its markets work and their impact on social justice.
3. Build a bigger democracy: everyone needs an equal chance to contribute and benefit from the 'Big Society'. The aim has to be to transform not negate the role of the state, strengthen its connections with civil society so that devolved powers are used to promote social justice – so that there is participation in decision making at national and local levels.

4. Make sure everyone can participate: those with less advantage need support to build knowledge, skills and confidence, developing resilience and autonomy in poorer communities so that the 'Big Society' deepens democracy.
5. Make co-production the standard way of getting things done: changing the way we think about needs and services based on equality if we are to reduce need.
6. Transform the role of professional and other 'providers': change how they see themselves, how they respect others and act together in a more mutual way – 'a whole-systems approach' to the whole person.
7. Redistribute paid and unpaid time: the 'Big Society' calls for big demand on unpaid time – this should herald a slow move towards a much shorter paid working week of 21 hours. Thus equalising time and resources would have compensating measures, for example low wage increases, raising minimum wage – especially important for gender equality (women still earn an average of 30 per cent less than men in the UK).
8. Make it sustainable: in environmental, social and economic terms, to protect natural resources on which all human health and life depend, cutting carbon emissions and reducing our ecological footprint must be central to our purpose. The aim is human and environmental flourishing – health and well-being reduces need for services and constrains demand thus shifting values away from an economic order that depends on infinite growth with catastrophic consequences.
9. Measure what matters: not just short-term budget cuts but place values at the heart of the matter and measure against them – action research leading to in-depth understanding that leads to good future planning.
10. Make it part of a 'Great Transition': the economic, social and environment challenges that we face call for radical change – 'we need a bigger society, a broader economy and a bigger democracy' – a shift from an unsustainable path to devastation to a worldview where everyone and everything can co-exist in an ecosystem. This would change how we live and work, relate to each other and the natural world, organise our economy and society, and revere our environment. It calls for a movement for change that recognises that a different world is possible. (adapted from New Economics Foundation, 2010)

Silence and inaction are no longer options for community development if we are to steer a course towards participatory democracy within the current political climate. Engaging with this level of critique places us in a powerful position to work from local to global as a movement for change, speaking up for the common good.

Critiques of radical community development

In 1996, Ian Cooke called for a re-evaluation of radical community work in relation to the changing political context in order to get beyond 'the current lack of clarity and direction which hinders the further development of a coherent radical practice' (1996, p 7). He identified two major causes for a change in the radical agenda at the time: (i) the Conservative government's approach to a free market economy and the simultaneous acceleration of globalisation, and (ii) the decline of the Labour and trades union movement in favour of a more fragmented pressure group politics with the emergence of new social movements. Let me remind you that the key distinguishing feature of radical, as opposed to pluralist, practice is the political consciousness that unites people in collective action beyond the boundaries of neighbourhood to engage in wider structural change. Cooke, together with other key critical theorists (Allman, 1999, 2001, 2010; Hill et al, 1999), advocates a political analysis that unites a politics of difference within the centrality of class.

> If radical community work requires a mission statement for the nineties and beyond then we could do worse than the words of Sivanandan (1989): '... to open one's sensibilities out to the oppression of others, the exploitation of others, the injustices and inequalities meted out to others – and to act on them, making an individual/local case into an issue, turning issues into causes and causes into movements and building in the process a new political culture, new communities of resistance that will take on power and capital and class.' (Cooke, 1996, p 22)

At the same time as the debates around the future of radical community work raged, communitarianism (Etzioni, 1995, 1997) found expression in the political agenda of New Labour as a way of linking neoliberalism with *community* as a key component of its political project, locating a contradiction between its free market approach, which is a direct threat to community, and its emphasis on community and civil society. Robson refers to the 'rediscovery' of civil society within a communitarian ideology as 'the almost total neglect of Gramsci as an authority' (Robson, 2000, p 14). From a Gramscian perspective, civil society, far from being a collective spirited expression of citizenship as rights and responsibilities, is the site in which the dominant ideas of the ruling class infiltrate people's thinking by ideological persuasion – a more powerful force than state coercion. Robson feels that the communitarian definition masks the way in which a 'belief in the individual as a free and independent being with unlimited rights has been translated into a question of relative rights and unlimited responsibilities' (Robson, 2000, p 129). Now in 2011, we witness the full might of the state in co-opting civil society as an alternative provider of state services, eroding rights and magnifying responsibilities still further.

Robson (2000) faces us with the co-option of radical community work. Professionalisation has given rise to a new type of practitioner who has replaced critical Freirean concepts, such as *conscientisation*, with *sustainability* and *social inclusion*. This marks a subtle move that elevates material outputs over critical outcomes. At the same time, an emphasis on skills, training and managerialism has further obscured critical thought for surface-level activities that create the comfortable illusion of making a difference. Professionalisation has silenced us, obscuring our commitment to act for the common good. Berner and Phillips (2005) present an incisive debate on the fine line between an ideology of self-help and radical practice. Their fundamental premise is that *participation*, a radical concept and the foundation of participatory democracy, has been co-opted into mainstream theory and diluted in potential, together with other related concepts, such as *decentralisation* and *empowerment*. This is similar to Cooke and Kothari's (2001) critique that participation is the 'new tyranny', that key concepts reduced to buzzwords can dangerously flip transformative practice into placatory practice. Berner and Phillips warn that the shift to self-help obscures the social justice argument for redistribution of resources, failing 'to adequately serve the needs of the poor, succumbing to a neo-liberal wolf dressed up as a populist sheep ... the community self-help paradigm needs to be refined by a recognition that the poor cannot be self-sufficient in escaping poverty, that "communities" are systems of conflict as well as cooperation, and that the social, political and economic macro-structure cannot be side-stepped' (Berner and Phillips, 2005, p 20). These arguments also apply to the 'Big Society', that 'self-sufficiency, the idea that "left to their own devices" (and their current resources) poor communities would lift themselves out from poverty just fine, makes for an attractive myth but a regressive policy' (Berner and Phillips, 2005, p 23), although the 'Big Society' takes this a stride further by cutting public sector provision and pulling the rug from under the myriad of community organisations and networks that give substance to civil society at the same time as depositing full and unmitigated responsibility for human well-being at the feet of those with least resources.

Forces of exploitation and discrimination permeate communities, and if we overlook this then we fail to see the role of community development in the process of change for social justice. The depoliticisation of self-help places the responsibility for tackling poverty onto the very groups which are most targeted by oppressive forces, denying the reality of structural power that penetrates communities and perpetuates poverty. 'Empowerment means *changing* the relationship between the rich and the poor, not the false option of "breaking" it.... Empowerment cannot be depoliticized' (Berner and Phillips, 2005, pp 26-7). Empowerment is not the same as self-help: it involves a process of critical consciousness as a route to autonomous action, but it is not an alternative solution to the redistribution of unequally divided resources. Handing responsibility over to poor communities to 'develop themselves' is to provide a smokescreen for the forces of structural inequality by ignoring unequal wealth and power distribution, as well as to ignore heterogeneity and inequity *within* communities. It risks reinforcing 'the complacent view that the poor are poor because they have not helped themselves' (Berner and Phillips, 2005, p 27).

Civil society is a site of progressive politics that embraces different and often conflicting interests, but holds the future for participatory democracy and equality (Deakin, 2001). We have seen more rapid change since the latter part of the 20th century than could have been imagined prior to this. Absolutes have been dismantled: the Soviet Union, the Berlin Wall, Apartheid in South Africa with Nelson Mandela freed after 27 years' imprisonment to become president and world peacemaker. More recently the 'twin towers' at the World Trade Center in New York prompted the West's 'war on terror', and now we find ourselves in a world recession which has exposed the fragility of capitalism, all happening to the creaking of a planet in stress. Globalisation accelerates, helped by a technological revolution that has made communication immediate and boundless. Boundaries of nation states no longer offer any protection from global phenomena, and issues such as HIV/AIDS and climate change place social and environmental justice at our feet, rather than distant and in someone else's backyard. In turn, this connectedness creates greater possibilities for a participatory democracy movement.

As I write in early 2011, we are not revisiting 1968, but instead we are swept up in a grassroots revolution triggered by Twitter, one in which everyday truths outdistance hegemonic 'common sense' and result in global action against oppression and injustice. In ad hoc organic social networks, a different sort of big society is emerging in resistance. We are at a historic juncture, with democracy in crisis opening the way for a new world. The West's promotion of the ideology of the market has resulted in shifting boundaries between the state, the market and civil society, with community development unwittingly playing a role in dismantling the welfare state, leaving poor communities even more vulnerable (Craig, 2011). Pitchford with Henderson (2008) argues that even the term 'community development' has been muddied; it is not understood to be significantly different from either community involvement or community engagement agendas, therefore it has lost its distinctiveness as a process for facilitating social change. The incorporation of community development into government agendas, they say, has distracted us to the extent that we have lost our way and consequently have little sense of direction, let alone any clarity of overarching purpose. 'The case can and should be made for how community development can deepen democracy', but will not happen if practitioners' minds are colonised by top–down policy, resulting in 'herding communities into structures and forums they neither own nor relate to' (Pitchford with Henderson, 2008, pp 94-5). We need to refocus, but this calls for an alternative political project to engage the popular imagination (Craig, 2011). Meanwhile, the continuing dearth of community development literature based on analyses of power effectively eliminates the political dimensions of practice necessary for social justice to be understood in relation to culture and identity (Craig, 2008). We need more effective analyses of power, particularly in relation to whiteness and patriarchy. Without a strong theoretical base that pays attention to issues of 'race', class and gender as major sources of subordination, we will find it hard to survive as a distinctive occupation committed to social justice. More than this, in relation to our environmental justice commitment, we need to get to grips with the connectedness between poverty and sustainability issues (Blewitt, 2008). These times of transition call for a more critical approach to community development.

Critique and dissent are at the heart of deepening democracy, yet the colonisation of critical democratic spaces has all but eliminated critique and dissent from community development practice. As Danny Dorling says, 'Everything it takes to defeat injustice lies in the mind. So what matters most is how we think' (2010, p 320). How we live is not predetermined and a 'collection of movements will achieve the change we wish to see in the world' (2010, p 320), but first comes critical thought followed by grassroots action. Democracy is an engaged practice calling for participation, making debate, dialogue and deliberation central to community development's radical agenda. As Giroux (2009) warns us, a society that neither questions itself nor can imagine any alternative to itself often falls into traps of becoming complicit with the forms of power it condemns.

I am interested in the extent to which reformist measures can make any difference to a fundamentally corrupt system that is predicated on profit and exploitation. Similarly, Gary Craig (undated, p 6) also raises 'a major political question about the degree to which social justice is compatible at all with the operation of a market economy', as a free market economy reinforces the structures of exploitation and discrimination that social justice is committed to countering. Social justice, in relation to community development, needs analyses based on inequality, oppression and exploitation, and action based on participatory democracy. This is not the same as democratic elections, which are a part of democracy but do not define it. According to Vanessa Baird (2010, p 16), 'A deeper definition of democracy – literally "people's rule" – must also include freedom of speech, an independent judiciary, freedom from discrimination, and the rights to assembly, protest and to a fair trial'. This is in addition to human rights, to health, education and the means of survival. Community development will always have a role to play in critiquing the democratic state in order to keep these freedoms in place.

In relation to progressive politics in civil society, the International Association for Community Development, in partnership with the Combined European Bureau for Social Development and the Hungarian Association for Community Development, sponsored a conference in Budapest in 2004 with representatives from 33 countries coming together to explore building civil society in Europe through community development (Craig et al, 2004). The central thrust lies in the recognition that community development strengthens civil society through the empowerment of local communities in a participatory and democratic way by giving voice to those who are disadvantaged and vulnerable. A coherent, egalitarian ideological approach, set within the context of Europe, offers increased potential for alliances in collective action for social justice. This echoes Fisher and Ponniah's call for a universal approach to human rights that is based on new global values. 'The key to the development of new values lies in the capacity to produce democratic processes and institutions that will allow for a genuinely international or global dialogue that will articulate a "universalism of difference"' (Fisher and Ponniah, 2003, p 284). In this way, they argue for liberation through a form of participatory democracy that is built on a new solidarity, one that embraces diversity and grows out of civil society. Calder suggests that it would be more critical to approach community as a *project*, something yet to be achieved, 'not a thing, not a structure to be built, and then nailed down in stasis. It is, rather, a process [underpinned by participatory democracy] the political and moral precondition of a just, participative and genuinely inclusive public life' (Calder, 2003, p 6).

These themes will be revisited and developed at relevant points throughout the book.

Why empower?

Empowerment is a key concept at the heart of radical community development. It is the process whereby we develop the theory and practice of equality. Of course, in order to get to grips with this, critical insight into the way that power in society favours the already privileged, and the way that forces of disempowerment perpetuate these inequalities, is essential. Radical practice 'provides a starting point for linking knowledge to power and a commitment to developing forms of community life that take seriously the struggle for democracy and social justice' (McLaren, 1995, p 34).

Communities are contexts for liberation as well as domination, and there is a fine line between the two. For community development practice to achieve an emancipatory dimension, it must be capable of creating a body of practical knowledge grounded in everyday experience in the search for a more just and sustainable world. Our fundamental purpose is not simply to understand our world, but to use that understanding to bring about change. New paradigms, new worldviews, offer new possibilities for being in the world, and a radical agenda calls for a participatory paradigm, a participatory consciousness that contributes to what Reason and Bradbury (2001, p 10) see as part of a 'resacralization of the world'. In order to do this, we need analyses that help with insight into the nature of knowledge and power. The dominant hegemony, which shapes the way we think and therefore the way we act in the world, and in so doing creates a reality that privileges the already powerful, is one of the greatest obstacles to overcome.

Community development has become distracted from its commitment to social justice by allowing its radical agenda to be diluted by more reactionary theories that lead to ameliorative rather than transformative approaches to practice. This is linked to an ongoing tension in practice that emphasises *doing* at the expense of *thinking*; and *action* without *reflection* is uncritical. The result is a continuing divide between theory and practice that fails to achieve a critical praxis where action and reflection are a unity. In these ways, community development has become vulnerable to more diluted interpretations. Critical approaches to practice involve theory and practice in dynamic, building a body of knowledge based on concepts of justice, equality and democracy.

TWO

The story of a community

The previous chapter traced the history of radical community development, set the political context and explored some of the critiques relevant to the radical social justice agenda. Let us now move into practice and explore the ways in which critical approaches take shape.

Community development is grounded in people's everyday lives. A critical approach to practice calls for analyses of power at every level, and one way of beginning that process is the community profile. In Freirean pedagogy, this begins in the narratives of the people and is set within an analysis of poverty as structural discrimination.

Community profiling

> This struggle [for humanization] is possible only because dehumanization, although a concrete historical fact, is not a given destiny but the result of an unjust order that engenders violence in the oppressors, which in turn dehumanizes the oppressed. (Freire, 1972, p 21)

For Paulo Freire, the process of transformation for a just and equal world lies in theory and action that emerge from people's lived reality. The impetus for social change comes from grassroots, from oppressed people who engage in a process of critical consciousness to understand the world differently, and unite in collective action to create a better reality. We tend to accept the injustices of our world in unquestioning ways that give rise to false consciousness: seeing the world from a critical perspective involves questioning everyday experience. Both Gramsci and Freire believed that this would not happen spontaneously, that people external to the community provide the catalyst for critical consciousness. Community workers are popular educators working in informal educational contexts in community. Our role, through a diversity of projects, is to create the learning context for questioning that helps local people to make critical connections between their lives and the structures of society that shape their world. The process is one of action and reflection, and the specific skills and strategies needed for critical practice are addressed in Chapter Three. From this beginning, people generate theory in action. Every project that we undertake has this core of critical pedagogy running through it, giving rise to new ways of seeing the world that lead to new ways of being in the world. Community workers are privileged to be accepted into people's lives in community, and with this privilege comes a responsibility to develop relationships that are mutual, reciprocal, dignified and respectful. These underlying values emerge from an ideology of equality, and they shape every aspect of our practice, determining not only the quality of every encounter but the way that we plan, conduct and evaluate every project. The foundation of community development lies in listening, valuing and understanding people's particular experiences. It also involves analysing how these experiences are linked to the forces of power that are embedded in the structures of society, and understanding how these forces reach into communities to impact on personal lives. The ideas of Gramsci on hegemony as a process of coercion and consent offer insight into this process, and are discussed in Chapter Six. Foucault extends this from hegemonic sites of power to include power colonising our being and getting acted out in every action and perception at the micro-level of society to reinforce dominant power relations. (For more insight into this see the discussion of Gramsci and Foucault on p 161.)

Community is a complex system of interrelationships woven across social difference, diverse histories and cultures, and determined in the present by political and social trends. This calls for practitioners to have an incisive analysis of the changing wider political context and the historical issues that have helped to shape the present. One way into this understanding is through a community profile conducted in partnership with the community. Other types of profiling (social audits, needs assessments, community consultations) may have other political agendas and may not reflect the purpose of community development. The community development approach is based on an implicit assumption that 'the organisation and structures of society cause problems of powerlessness, alienation and inequality. To achieve greater equality and social justice, resources and power must be redistributed' (Haggstrom, quoted in Hawtin et al, 1994, p 35). A community development approach to community profiling is to have the voices of the people at its heart, and to weave together everything that is affecting people, including the way that they feel about their lives in community. This becomes more useful when it is set in comparison with other communities, in the local area, nationally and internationally.

Research is integral to community development praxis; it is the way in which practice is kept relevant to the changing social and political context. Research in community development is set within a participatory paradigm and its approach is referred to as *participatory, collaborative* or *emancipatory* action research, concepts that are closely allied but with subtle differences of emphasis. As a reminder of the social justice intention of community development, I prefer to use the term 'emancipatory action research'. It has a clearly defined ethical code and purpose that are consonant with community development practice. A more detailed definition can be found in Chapter Four. All research of this nature, including a community profile, needs to reflect feeling and thinking, theory and practice, local and global dimensions as an integrated whole in order to develop a critical praxis. Traditional approaches to research are based on positivism, and result in rational, scientific methods of measuring human behaviour that treat people like objects and deny the less tangible feeling aspects of being human. If we fall into a positivist approach to research that encourages research *on* people rather than *with* people, we will certainly overlook vital aspects of community life. For instance Hustedde and King (2002, p 338) refer to an 'increasing interest in the emotional life of communities as a neglected aspect of community development' and argue the case for a community's faith in the soul or spirit as critical to a flourishing community. This is a counter-force to a society built on western rational thought, and is akin to the more integrated approach to life of indigenous cultures:

> Soul is often linked to the beauty, mystery and forces of nature. In essence, soul is part of the world of creation. It can be part of the bonds of solidarity and capacity in community … it is about deep meaning and quality relationships. Soul thrives on paradox. It is about mystery – the presence of something profound that cannot be grasped by science or the boundaries of human language; it is something that's non-linear. The great wisdom traditions argue that soul is not about values and ethics but about a deeper reality that penetrates the illusion of the external world. We see soul when non-dominant cultures and people speak their value judgements (emotions) of compassion, forgiveness, understanding, and hope amidst despair. (Hustedde and King, 2002, p 340)

These qualities are of vital importance in the process of community development.

The community profile could provide you with your first project in a community, a chance to involve local people in researching their own stories, beginning the process of critical consciousness. If there is a history of community development in your community, you should check whether a profile has been carried out previously. As a local authority-employed community worker in Hattersley, a Manchester 'overspill' housing estate in Tameside, I found that although there was not a community profile as such, there was a massive amount of archive material. This came in the form of an extensive supply of newspaper cuttings and photographs collected by community workers and local activists, and it painted a picture of the creation of the community. Newspaper articles labelled Hattersley 'the forgotten town', and reported on early community action against the inadequate infrastructure for a community of 10,000 people, as well as the problems with damp housing. In the council offices, I found minutes of meetings and percentage (mid-term census) surveys that offered more formal evidence of Hattersley's development. Local authorities conduct research on communities, but do not always involve or inform community workers or local people. I was astonished to find a recent percentage survey had been undertaken, of which neither the community development team nor the community forum was aware. It was only by going to the council offices to ask about documentation on Hattersley that I discovered this valuable information. In addition, and to my further surprise, I found that Peter Townsend, the leading national authority on poverty, had been commissioned by Tameside Council on behalf of the Greater Manchester Boroughs to undertake a poverty analysis (Townsend et al, 1988). This was vital information for our work. When we examined the Townsend analysis we were shocked at how skewed the census data became with the ameliorating effects of the wealthier communities that surrounded Hattersley. With some gentle persuasion, the statisticians in the council offices disembedded the Hattersley data by using local enumeration districts (smaller units of analysis than wards). The picture that emerged was of a community that was amongst the most impoverished and disenfranchised in the country.

Structuring a community profile

The community profile enables you to make critical connections more readily if you juxtapose the voices of local people, statistical evidence, sociopolitical trends and community development interventions in a more structured way: (i) the individual; (ii) the group; (iii) the community; (iv) the structures/institutions of society; and (v) the wider society (regional, national, global).

This framework should be in place throughout any community activity. It not only helps you to weave the connections that take your analysis deeper, but in turn it provides a tool of reflection that you can use in practice, working with local people to frame specific questions that elicit a more critical picture of the forces impacting on community life. In these ways, you extend the potential of your practice to a more critical approach where people begin to question the nature of their lives and make connections with the structures of society that marginalise and oppress. (This is the essence of Freirean pedagogy and is discussed in more detail in Chapters Three and Five.)

Participation is a democratic principle and the basis of community development practice. It is important to ensure, in terms of anti-discriminatory analysis, that the early stages of participation represent the diversity of the community. By this, I mean that we need to understand the ways in which community life is heterogeneous: experience is shaped according to social difference. The term *difference* is a shorthand for the way in which our identity is formed from our class, gender, ethnicity, 'race', faith, age, sexuality, 'dis'ability and many other aspects of our being that affect our life experience. If the profile of a community is conducted from an external, or even an internal but single, perspective, it will not tell an accurate story of the lives of the people across all their difference and diversity. This is discriminatory practice. We may only hear the loudest voices or only notice those with whom we most identify, painting an inaccurate and distorted picture of community life. I give a deeper analysis of *difference* in Chapter Eight.

Where to look for information

Statistical data

Increasingly, current statistics are available via the internet and this offers a useful beginning. You will find demographic, housing and socioeconomic profiles as well as information on schools, policing and crime, transport and local government details – try www.upmystreet.com. For local authority information, including neighbourhood profiles and committee minutes, try www.open.gov.uk.

A national census is undertaken the year after the turn of each decade, and for information based on a ward analysis you will find details on demography including ethnicity, health, economic activity and housing/households, which are compared with overall data for the borough as well as the national average. For England and Wales, go to www.statistics.gov.uk; for Scotland, www.gro-scotland.gov.uk; and for Northern Ireland, www.nisra.gov.uk. For a history of your community and general background material, go to the Informal Education (Infed) website, www.infed.org, and access their 'Search' the web page. This website provides the largest collection of theory and practice papers in a single resource directly relevant to community development.

Involving people

First, you and your profiling group will need to have skills based on listening, valuing and dialogue. The voices of local people, in all their diversity and all their roles, are central to this project. Perhaps your profiling group could capture the essence of this by providing cameras and getting people to take photographs of what is important to them in their daily lives. You could work with a writing group to capture community life in story and poetry. Your team could develop research skills through the discipline of noticing, using journals based on noticing events, encounters and conversations as they happen (Mason, 2002). Maybe you could develop a display of photographs, archive material, stories and poetry that would stimulate other people to get involved in the research. For instance, we had a reminiscence group of older residents who worked together with local schoolchildren for a radio programme. The children began by introducing popular playground games, and this stimulated cross-generational discussion about local life and its similarities and differences over time.

How will you motivate people to act together? How will they perceive a community profile as relevant to their lives? Who will you contact and where will you find them? Are there active community groups already in existence? Are there key people you can contact? Should you hold a public meeting? How will you make sure the people who join you are representative and diverse? Communities are not homogeneous; there will be conflicting interests, sometimes marked by violence and hostility. For instance, how will you deal with sensitive issues like domestic violence, racism and homophobia? If these sensitive issues are swept under the carpet, we become complicit in their perpetuation.

The questions posed for the community profile should always be determined in mutual partnership with the community. By setting your own questions, you will inevitably be framing their world through your eyes. The process of constructing the profile, once you have established a working group, will be life-changing for the people involved and will form the basis of further community development practice. The important questions can be elicited through problem-posing. This is done by capturing an aspect of community life in drawing, photography, film, drama, music or writing. It focuses the group and stimulates discussion, the community worker facilitating the process by asking questions rather than giving answers. In other words, you create a learning context in which the group can explore its ideas about its own community more critically. Here are some ideas, using the structure set out above, with which to begin the problem-posing process.

(i) The individual

As community workers, we listen to the deepest feelings of the local community. Freirean pedagogy involves listening with compassion to people's fears, worries, hopes, resentments and joys. What are their deepest concerns? What most affects their lives? These emotions are the key to the motivation to act. The act of listening, of giving people your full attention, is empowering in itself. It takes people's experience seriously, creating a respectful and dignified experience.

(ii) The group

What unites people in their current experience? What are the different interests represented between groups? How active are groups in the community? What are the successes people have achieved by uniting in groups? We should always build on the strengths and value the experience of the community.

(iii) The community

What makes people feel a sense of belonging to the community? How do people feel about living here? What has united people in their history and culture? What diversity is there within local culture? Are differences celebrated? What are the skills that people have? What is the local economic base? Has this changed? Who does the unpaid work in the community? What are the resources that exist in the community? What are the resources that are, or could be, available to the community from outside? What are the collective concerns for the community? How positive or confident is the community to act on its own behalf?

(iv) A structural analysis

How do community statistics compare with the local authority, region, country or even world? How do diversity and difference in your community compare with the country as a whole? To what extent are the issues affecting your community in line with wider social trends? In what way do current policies benefit/discriminate against local people? How relevant and efficient is service delivery? What plans are in place for developments? How might these benefit or act against the interests of the local community? Do local people feel that they are taken seriously? What environmental policies and issues impact on the community?

(v) The wider society

In this section, think local to global. Who represents local people in local and national government? Are there other leaders who act on behalf of the community to influence decisions? What changes are there in dominant ideology, and how is it affecting the local community? What wider social trends are reflected in the community? What links does the community have with wider, European or global, movements and trends? What environmental policies and issues affect the local community? How is the process of globalisation affecting the community?

Presenting the profile

However you present your profile, the community must feel that it belongs to them, that it represents them in the most accurate way possible, that it is empowering and that they are proud of it. How will it become a working document? Will you have a community launch to celebrate its findings? Will this include a video, photograph and graphic display of the findings as part of a social event? Could part of it be displayed on a community noticeboard for a wider audience? How will you use it to stimulate action in the community? How will you use it to provoke critical thinking in the community? How will you integrate theory and practice? If you fail to weave theory and practice together, your work is likely to reflect unconscious prejudice and discrimination. One useful tool that might aid a critical approach to the profiling process is the model of critical praxis.

Model of critical praxis

The purpose of models is that they simplify complex situations. In their simplicity they can help us to understand significant interrelationships and, more than this, 'by constructing a model we gain additional understanding by virtue of the whole being greater than the sum of its parts' (Thompson, 2000, p 23). In this way, models play an important role in critical reflection by helping us to move towards a complete rather than a partial understanding. We are more able to locate the root sources of an issue, to develop relevant forms of practice and, in turn, through the process of reflection, to contribute to theory.

Dominant ideologies are powerful and persuasive, and it is important to remember that those of us who are struggling to free our own thinking are products of the same social and political context, and thus are subject to the same forces. Western thought is dichotomous and increasingly fragmented and alienating in nature (Reason and Bradbury, 2001). By this, I mean that we are taught to see life in relation to opposites: either one thing or another, for example rich/poor, Black/White, male/female. It is a hierarchical perspective that is built on superiority/inferiority, thus lending itself to domination and oppression (hooks, 1984; Spretnak, 1997). Contradictions and complexity are not within its scope.

Alternative worldviews, different ways of seeing the world, can help to move us towards a vision of wholeness: a reintegration of the self; strength in diversity; and a symbiotic relationship with the environment. This provides a model based on harmony rather than violence, on cooperation rather than competition, on need rather than greed. Today, we have much greater awareness of difference and diversity, giving insight into the experience of oppression in all its complexity. From here, the shift has to be towards interconnectedness across difference: the thread of humanity is held together by each individual and the quality of humanity is determined by mutual responsibility to this whole. A commitment to liberation and justice requires new ways of thinking about social reality from a critical perspective that embraces both social and environmental justice: 'future participation will mean a very different experience of the self, an ecological self distinct yet not separate, a self rooted in environment and in community' (Reason, 1994a, p 37).

The model of critical praxis I present (see Figure 2.1) is the result of my own reflections on practice over time. It worked for me by locating internal and external forces in community, and in doing so presented me with a more critical understanding of how these impact on local lives. This gives a much clearer insight into the ways in which community development has to work both inside and outside community in order to transform the root sources of oppression. A critical approach to community development calls for a framework within which smaller projects can be seen as contributing to a bigger whole. Otherwise, community workers can be either sucked into impotence and despair or respond with palliatives that are incoherent in the long-term quest for social justice. This is the spirit in which I offer the model of critical praxis.

The model aims to locate power and domination within a social and political framework, and gives an idea of the way in which subordination is reinforced. In juxtaposition to this is *critical consciousness*.

The two come together at the interface of *community* and *praxis*. The model indicates two major circuits: one I have labelled *hegemony* to denote the ways in which ideological persuasion leads us to unquestioningly accept the status quo, absorbing dominant attitudes and values into the core of our being; the other I have labelled *critical consciousness* to indicate an alternative way of seeing life based on equity and justice. These two circuits overlap in *community*. Let us follow my journey round the model.

Starting in ideology, I developed certain beliefs and values that were based on my experience and perceptions of the world (epistemology). These are always in process and have reformed many times. They are constantly re-examined in relation to my engagement with the world (ontology). As a community worker, I cannot make sense of my practice without having conceptual tools of analysis. Of these there are many, but I have chosen to name Freire, Gramsci, Foucault, feminism, 'Whiteness' and anti-discriminatory analysis as prime areas of thought which have profoundly influenced me in my search for a theory of transformative change. In much the same way, these theories would make little sense without my experience.

COP Dev. Praxis

Figure 2.1: Model of critical praxis

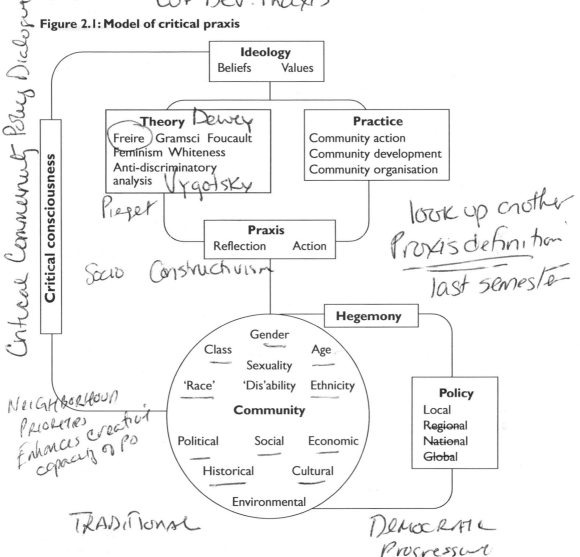

Critical Community Policy Dialogue

Piaget

Socio Constructivism

look up another Praxis definition — last semester

Neighbourhood priorities Enhances creative capacity of PO

Traditional

Democratic Progressive

Practice includes the stages of development in community, so here I have included *action*, *development* and *organisation* as reminders that community development adopts different approaches at different stages. These come together in *praxis*, the synthesis of *action* and *reflection*. Here, it is important to mention that this journey is not carried out in isolation. In *praxis*, my journey comes together with others in the quest for *critical consciousness*: making sense of the world in order to transform it is a collective experience. I share my thinking and ideas in dialogue with people in *community* as we move forwards in mutual inquiry and action. The dynamic between ideas and experience takes us deeper into the process of *conscientisation*.

It locates understanding in experience, rather than in a decontextualised intellect, and this is the basis of collective action.

Hegemony is flexible and in constant re-formation in relation to its context. On the model, the impact of local, national and global changes is seen in relation to *community*. If my praxis had developed in relation to community alone, failing to recognise the impact of outside forces, it would have been incomplete and much more likely to follow a self-help rather than a critical approach to practice. *Critical consciousness* is not possible without an analysis of *hegemony*. The two come together in *community* and are the basis of *critical praxis*. In this way, the journey towards critical consciousness is rooted in an analysis of the lived experience of people in their communities, within society.

Child poverty and social justice

> We live at a precarious moment in history. Relations of subjection, suffering dispossession and contempt for human dignity and the sanctity of life are at the center of social existence. Emotional dislocation, moral sickness and individual helplessness remain ubiquitous features of our time ... democracy has become ... subverted by its contradictory relationship to the very object of its address: human freedom, social justice, and a tolerance and respect for difference. (McLaren, 1995, p 1)

Social justice embraces a range of ways of being in the world that are not seen as *deviant* from the norm – young, old, 'dis'abled, single, lone parent, lesbian, gay, all faiths and none, and so on. If a just society is one in which people are treated with equal dignity and respect, where different cultures are embraced, where different abilities are valued, and where everyone is enabled to reach full potential, then injustice can be seen as a violation of these values.

Discrimination gets embedded in the structures of society through poverty:

> The ultimate cause of poverty is an imbalance of power. This imbalance plays itself out through the most powerful having a disproportionate control of the society's resources, at the expense of the least powerful. Poverty, the consequence, is a lack of financial resources, pure and simple. Other explanations that are from time to time offered, such as labour market problems, benefit inadequacy or behavioural explanations are the mediators which make powerlessness lead to poverty. Establishing the causal chain is critical: unless the causes are properly understood policy makers will not be in a position to design effective responses. (Flaherty et al, 2004, p 2)

The UK has one of the worst child poverty rates in the industrialised world, with 30 per cent, nearly four million, of its children growing up in lives defined by unnecessary deprivation. This not only robs children of achieving their full potential, but has immense costs for society as a whole. Fifty-nine per cent of these children live in families with at least one adult in work, 40 per cent are in lone-parent families and 38 per cent are in larger families with three or more children. Since 1999, when Tony Blair made his personal and political promise to end child poverty, only 550,000 children are in improved circumstances (*Poverty*, 2010a).

Community workers need a critical analysis of poverty and the way that it maintains social divisions if we are to contribute to change for social justice. We need to get angry about poverty and the suffering it creates in serving the interests of the privileged. This section offers you a discussion of the critical links between poverty and power in relation to community.

Debates have raged long and hard around *absolute* and *relative* poverty: *absolute* definitions are based on a minimum standard of living and a person's biological needs for food, water, clothing and shelter as basic rather than *relative* to a broader socially and culturally acceptable standard of living (Oppenheim and Harker, 1996, p 7). Often we hear arguments that justify inequalities as inevitable, an argument that Marcuse dismisses as 'the regulation of free competition among unequally equipped economic subjects' (Marcuse, 1991, p 1).

Peter Townsend's (1979) extensive study of *Poverty in the UK*, based on a major survey that he carried out in 1968-69, was hailed as a seminal contribution to understanding relative poverty and its impact on citizenship. Mack and Lansley (1985) built on the work of Townsend and brought the debate on relative poverty into public consciousness by asking a cross-section of people to prioritise life's necessities in order to reach public consensus on acceptable living standards, anything below which would define poverty. London Weekend Television commissioned MORI, survey specialists, to design and conduct the survey. 'The survey established, for the first time ever, that a majority of people see the necessities of life in Britain in the 1980s as covering a wide range of goods and activities, and that people judge a minimum standard of living on socially established criteria and not just the criteria of survival or subsistence' (Mack and Lansley, 1985, p 53).

There was a massive consensus across social classes to support this view, with more marked differences defined according to political affiliation: 'Conservative supporters are much more likely to blame the victim and much less likely to identify injustice' (Mack and Lansley, 1985, p 209). The surprising consequence of this research was the extent to which the general public supported the idea of redistributing wealth to create a more equal society. This is not the case today!

The concept of human rights is central to the poverty debate: 'people should have a right to an income which allows them to participate in society, rather than merely exist' (Oppenheim and Harker, 1996, p 11). Yet, child poverty in the UK remains hidden beneath the surface of prosperity, and social justice remains an illusion. As such, child poverty is an indictment of our times. During the 1980s, we became a more divided society than at any other time this century. From 1979, with the ascendance of New Right politics, the rhetoric of the 'welfare scrounger' took hold, and the UK witnessed a massive transference of wealth from the *poor* to the *rich*, reinforced by punitive policy changes. As marginalisation and exclusion escalated, poor people were told to tighten their belts and wait for the trickle-down effect, that rich people needed to get richer before poor people got richer. It was a good argument, but, of course, in reality nothing trickled down and the already privileged became even more privileged, as the poor got poorer. We need to be concerned about the persistent nature of the trend created at this time.

Under Thatcherism, child poverty escalated from 14 per cent in 1979 to 34 per cent in 1996/97 (Flaherty et al, 2004, p 145), and children replaced pensioners as the single group most at risk of poverty. This left the UK with one of the highest rates of child poverty compared with other countries facing similar economic trends. CPAG, formed in 1976 from a concern about the levels of child poverty, warned that 'the poverty devastating the life chances of children today will have future repercussions for us all' (Witcher, quoted in Oppenheim and Harker, 1996, p vi). The lasting impact of child poverty on adulthood is still poorly understood.

The employment position of the household is an important factor in determining the status of children, with over half of poor children in 1995/96 living in households with no adult in work. Incomes for households with children fell progressively behind those without children throughout the 1980s and 1990s, trends that were obscured for a long time, largely due to the handling of data that emphasised the cost of a child, rather than the risks of poverty to the child. In this way, trends accelerated by changes in household formation and re-formation – single-adult households, single-parent families and families without children – added to changes in employment patterns to mask the enormous impact that poverty was having on children (Gregg et al, 1999).

Growing up in a family in poverty is closely linked to poor educational achievement and reduces chances of employment. We also know that poverty creates ill health and premature death: for example, children of those in the bottom social class are five times more likely to die from an accident and 15 times more likely to die in a house fire than those in the upper social classes (Flaherty et al, 2004). Yet evidence points to the fact that escalating child poverty during Thatcherism was a political choice rather than an inevitability. Bradshaw (1999), investigating international trends, provides evidence that out of 25 countries only Russia and the USA had higher rates of child poverty than the UK. In 16 years, 1979–95, child poverty increased more in the UK than in almost all other industrial countries facing similar demographic and economic trends – in Europe only Italy had a sharper increase than the UK (Bradshaw, 1999).

Even a relatively superficial glance at the statistics reveals that children at risk of poverty correlate with social groups targeted by poverty, a critical factor in this analysis:

• lone-parent households
• low-paid households
• households without an adult in paid work
• minority ethnic families

- 'dis'abled children or those with a 'dis'abled parent.

Also, children who grow up in poverty are more likely to:

- have low birthweight leading to infant death or chronic disease later in life
- suffer from malnutrition
- under-achieve at school
- be suspended, excluded or truant from school
- have low self-esteem
- have low expectations
- experience unemployment and low wages
- for girls, become pregnant in their teenage years
- for young men, be at risk of suicide
- die prematurely (mortality)
- suffer from long-term debilitating illness (morbidity).

Growing up in poverty remains the biggest single determinant of life chances. It operates on 'race', class, gender, age and 'dis'ablist dimensions to perpetuate privilege and disadvantage in a rich country that has plenty to redistribute for the benefit of all.

> The true measure of a nation's standing is how well it attends to its children – their health and safety, their material security, their education and socialization, and their sense of being loved, valued, and included in the families and societies into which they are born. (UNICEF, 2007)

This UNICEF report on childhood in rich countries, produced in February 2007 (available at www.unicef.org.uk), ranked the UK at the bottom of 21 countries on an overall measure of child well-being, destroying the hopes of its future generations. The discriminatory nature of poverty ensures that the most marginalised stay in poverty. For instance, within a market ideology the concept of 'undeserving poor' has effectively become embedded in public consciousness. Killeen levels the accusation of a violation of human rights at successive governments for failing to redress this injustice, claiming that 'povertyism' sits alongside racism and sexism as a structural inequality, based on a belief that poor people are of less value (Killeen, 2008). This works in the self-interests of individualism and against the collective good: inequality is divisive and socially corrosive, reducing the quality of life for all (Wilkinson and Pickett, 2009).

The opportunity afforded by Blair by taking child poverty into the political arena has enabled anti-poverty activists under the End Child Poverty banner to increase public awareness and to assert pressure on the government to 'keep the promise'. The Campaign to End Child Poverty is an alliance of more than 150 organisations including children's charities, child welfare organisations, social justice groups, faith groups, trade unions and others, concerned about the unacceptably high levels of child poverty in the UK. In October 2008 the Campaign organised a demonstration: 10,000 people marched through London demanding that the 2010 target be met. It has not, but the Child Poverty Act 2010 embodied in law the Blair government's 2020 target to eradicate child poverty. Nevertheless, not to miss this opportunity, we still need to get our thinking inside the links between distributive justice and cultural justice, so that gender and 'race' are understood in relation to the traditional class struggle, not as competing with it, but as interacting with it to continue to privilege whiteness and maleness (Lister, 2008).

The global banking crisis that led to a global recession in 2008 continues to create rising unemployment, falling house prices, house repossessions and debt in the UK and elsewhere. As the recession hit home, commentators urged that governments should not cut public spending when the impact would hit poor families hardest (Brewer et al, 2009), when 'loss of employment is the single most significant cause of entry to poverty' (Sinfield, 2009, p 132). Yet, the coalition government, in implementing the 'Big Society', has targeted public sector spending to an unprecedented level, threatening massive unemployment in a largely lower paid and female public sector, as well as hitting poor families harder. It is particularly important to understand that policies need to prioritise 'child poverty and wellbeing in the here and now': deferred gratification does not compensate for the damage done in childhood. We need to get to grips with the unacceptable burden of poverty that we have placed on children today (Tomlinson et al, 2008).

The embedded nature of racism and the racist dimensions of poverty continue to place children from minority ethnic families at most risk. Whereas 30 per cent of all children are growing up in poverty, a different picture emerges when we look at ethnicity: 27 per cent of White children are growing up in poverty, whereas this figure escalates to 36 per cent Indian, 41 per cent Black Caribbean, 56 per cent Black non-Caribbean and 69 per cent Pakistani and Bangladeshi children, based on 2006/07 statistics (CPAG, 2008). Similarly, 'dis'abled children or those with a 'dis'abled parent are much more at risk of poverty, inadequate housing and social exclusion from public and community services (Flaherty et al, 2004). On top of this, concentrations of poverty are growing. London, with all its privilege and prosperity, has a child poverty rate of 39 per cent (Oppenheim, 2007). So you begin to see that when we dig beneath the surface, we begin to make more critical connections that provide us with a complex picture of the interlinking dimensions of poverty. The correlation between unemployment, poor mental health, homelessness, school exclusions, children in care/leaving care and high levels of youth suicide add further depth to that picture (Howarth et al, 1999).

We need to recognise what is happening in children's everyday lives, but also notice the ways in which these are social trends linked to structural injustice. Understanding the complex ways in which divisions of *difference* interact and interweave with poverty to reinforce prejudice and create inequalities is of vital importance to practitioners. When we make these connections we understand more fully the complex discriminatory dimensions of poverty. Campaigning, research and watchdog bodies such as the Campaign to End Child Poverty, the

Joseph Rowntree Foundation and CPAG are important in providing information on current action, policy developments and poverty statistics to keep our analyses up to date.

Currently, as the 'Big Society' unfolds and the impact of the austerity cuts implemented by the coalition government's emergency Budget take hold, we wait to see the full impact. There is a shift towards tackling poverty across new indicators: worklessness, welfare dependency, educational and health inequalities, family and community breakdown and multiple disadvantages (*Poverty*, 2010a, p 18). As things stand, the impact of the emergency Budget is likely to increase the number of children in poverty, hitting hardest at lone parents, unemployed households, families with three or more children and possibly families with a 'dis'abled child or adult (*Poverty*, 2010a, p 19). It is a 'national scandal' (Save the Children, 23 February 2011, available at www.savethechildren.org.uk).

At present, according to *Households Below Average Income* data, the statistics that CPAG are assessing help us to see comparative risk levels:

Table 2.1: Poverty trends: Households Below Average Income

	2007/08	2008/09
Children in poverty	31% (4.0m)	30% (3.9m)
Lone parents	52% (1.6m)	50% (1.6m)
Couples with children	25% (2.4m)	24% (2.3m)
All adults in household working	13% (0.9m)	13% (0.9m)
Workless households	80% (1.6m)	78% (1.5m)
Families with one child	26% (0.9m)	27% (1.0m)
Families with three or more children	43% (1.5m)	40% (1.4m)
No disability in the family	28% (2.7m)	28% (2.8m)
Families with a disabled child	34% (0.3m)	35% (0.3m)
Families with a disabled adult	44% (0.7m)	40% (0.6m)
Families with disabled adult(s) and child(ren)	44% (0.2m)	42% (0.2m)

Source: Poverty (2010a, p 19) (available at http://statistics.dwp.gov.uk/asd/index.php?page=hbai)

CPAG warn: 'policy needs to focus on eradicating the causes of poverty (tackling low incomes and reducing inequality) as well as ameliorating its effects, such as improving educational attainment. This complexity can be problematic, and a key task for policy makers is to distinguish between causes and symptoms accurately. If we cannot get this right, we risk engaging in dangerous politics' (*Poverty*, 2010a, p 20).

For community development to take a critical approach, we need to understand social trends in relation to structural injustices. Otherwise practice will address the symptoms and overlook the causes. In this sense, it is vital that these trends are set within wider issues of world poverty and its gendered and racialised dimensions.

UNICEF, in its report *State of the world's children 2005: Childhood under threat* (2005), provides evidence that more than one billion children, one in every two children in the world, are denied the healthy and protected upbringing defined by the Convention on the Rights of the Child (1989), and are reduced to growing up in poverty. These are consequences of neoliberal capitalism and its choice that profit is more important than justice.

Peter Townsend, as a critical commentator on world poverty and on behalf of UNICEF, talked about the UK escalation in child poverty as a 'neglect-filled Anglo-American model which unless there is massive investment in children we will head for economic catastrophe' (Townsend, 1995, pp 10-12). His prediction is now coming true.

Anti-poverty practice

Your community profile set within this level of analysis will inevitably lead to anti-poverty projects. Here I would like to introduce two, credit unions and participatory budgeting. In my own practice, we decided that a credit union would make a community-wide impact on poverty. Setting up a community credit union is a long-term project requiring not only the development of specific skills, but great perseverance and determination. Information on credit unions and a range of other local economic projects can be obtained from the New Economics Foundation (www.neweconomics.org). A discussion on credit unions and other local economic projects can be found in Twelvetrees (1998).

Women are at greater risk of poverty, and they are largely the ones preyed on by loan sharks. These predators arrive on the doorstep with much-needed bales of bedding, clothing, pots and pans – the stuff that is linked to women's role in keeping the home functioning and the children healthy. Offers of cash loans come next. Often short term, these loans carry extortionate rates of interest. In such ways, the women of the community are carrying the practical responsibility for keeping families together. It is the women who need to save, need to borrow and need support for their unrecognised contribution to the fabric of life. To illustrate my point, I will introduce Hattersley Credit Union. Unsurprisingly, it was the women of the credit union who rolled their sleeves up and transformed the idea into a reality. The men who were involved often wanted symbols of status, like lapel badges and titles. Women shared the vision and rose to the challenge. They developed skills they never dreamt they had. They staffed collection points, pored over the bookkeeping, and assessed people for loans. They were the ones who, in the end, challenged the men: "Stop strutting around looking important. Either roll your sleeves up and get on with it or get out!"

A credit union is founded on cooperation, mutuality and trust, encouraging its members to participate in policy making and to take an active interest in the day-to-day procedures. It is a not-for-profit organisation. After expenses have been covered and reserves have been topped up, any profit is returned to members in the form of a dividend. A credit union is owned by its members and it is run by an elected board of directors. All the roles are voluntary until it is able to employ people. It unites the community, encouraging regular saving to provide a common pool for loans. This is the principle of mutuality on which the system works – savings must remain intact when a loan is taken out, otherwise the pool is depleted.

In 1988, Hattersley was the first registered community credit union in the region. As confidence grew, the credit union women played a key role in travelling far and wide to other community groups to support them in establishing their own credit unions. Events and training days were held at Hattersley Community Centre with people attending from all over the region. On a wider scale, contact was made with Northern Ireland credit unions and each year, on International Credit Union Day, we held a social event for all members linking us into the global credit union movement. This process was immensely empowering. Communities in poverty usually believe that they are alone in their suffering, and the collective action generated by this anti-poverty movement brought confidence and optimism. Hattersley Credit Union not only offered the lowest unsecured loan rate in the country, but also did much to change the negative image of Hattersley, fostering a sense of pride in the community, a deeper consciousness of discrimination and collective action and campaigning on poverty.

Why is it that women are so active at grassroots level? Anne Witte Garland suggests that:

> ... since women are traditionally concerned with home and family and community, they're the first to recognise threats to them and to act on those threats ... men are more integrated into the system that creates the threats, and that since women have been excluded from that system historically, they have less to lose than men in fighting for it. (Witte Garland, 1988, p xii)

Hattersley has been ostracised by the surrounding communities since its creation. The 'slum clearance' label, an early polio outbreak and the Moors Murders brought about prejudice on a local level, which reinforced the discrimination of poverty. Yet, still the women rise and sustain the life of the community, just like the women of the mining communities, the women of Northern Ireland or the women of the communities hit by the 1991 riots; they are the ones 'who sustain[ed] the personal, public and political lives of these neighbourhoods' (Campbell, 1993, p 321).

Participatory budgeting has similar values but a different emphasis. Participatory budgeting leads to greater equity and increases well-being, it holds government to account, creating greater transparency by increasing levels of participation of marginalised people. In dialogue, local people debate and prioritise public spending projects, as true learning for democracy. First developed in Porto Alegre, Brazil, in 1989, this practical approach to collective decision making over collective resources has spread to more than 1,200 municipalities, not only in Latin America but also in France, Spain, Britain, Canada, Italy, Germany and India (Baird, 2010). Participatory budgeting, on a practical level, involves participation in deciding how to allocate collective resources, but its process is about redistributing power. Empowering local people to have influence over the way communities and societies are organised is a fundamental power shift that deepens democracy, sharing power in the interests of everyone.

In the UK, the Participatory Budgeting Unit is a project of the charity Church Action on Poverty, based in Manchester. Part funded by the Department for Communities and Local Government, it supports public sector and community groups to develop participatory budgeting processes in their local areas. In the first instance, local residents come together to identify, discuss and prioritise spending on projects. Importantly, it aims to strengthen the relationships between communities, local authorities and statutory agencies such as health and police services. Phil Teece of the Participatory Budgeting Unit tells a story that captures the power of participatory budgeting in the process of community development.

Giving people a voice: from Brazil to Manton

"Sue Cutts grew up in Manton, Nottinghamshire. Her father and grandfather were miners, and she remembers the close sense of community life based around the colliery. Everyone looked out for each other and there was a real spirit of togetherness and collective responsibility. The 1984–85 Miners' Strike changed all that. As the strike dragged on, money was short, and some of the men reluctantly returned to work. Neighbours and even families became divided. All of a sudden, the heart was ripped out of the community. Then the colliery closed in 1995, and economically and spiritually Manton went into decline. It was no longer a good place to live.

"When Teresa Rice, following her divorce, moved to Manton with her two young children four-and-a-half years ago, she didn't know anyone. Quite by chance, she came across the shop front office of Manton Community Alliance. This new community group – with a little help from an idea they borrowed from Brazil – had begun the rebuilding of the community. When Teresa wandered in to the Alliance's office to find out what they did, little did she know that she would soon be a volunteer, eventually a member of the board and a paid employee, and that she would know all about something called participatory budgeting (PB).

"Sue also became involved with the Alliance almost by accident. She was doing voluntary work at her grandchildren's school and was invited to join a local adult learning group. Through that, she became involved with the Alliance, and recalls that the first step on the road to community recovery was the reinstatement of what used to be the Miners' Gala. It was attended by 2,500 local people and demonstrated that there was something on which to build. She now chairs the board.

"Over the past seven years, Manton has been transformed through the efforts of the Alliance and their participative approach to community development, initially via participatory appraisal and then PB. It is an approach which centres on the importance of valuing the knowledge and experience of local people, empowering them to identify their own priorities, find solutions to the problems affecting them, and to make their own decisions about how public money should be spent.

"Participatory budgeting, a process 'invented' in Brazil and now practised across the world, is about giving all members of a community a voice and enabling them to listen to the voices and perspectives of their fellow residents. In Manton, the Alliance recognised that the key to community recovery was changing attitudes, and this required going out and talking to people in schools, pubs, street corners, homes, anywhere that people gather.

"Sue and Teresa explained that, for the first time, local people have been given the opportunity to express their views, the belief that those views are valued and, critically, the confidence to express them. Their passion and commitment to improving the community through the people that live there comes shining through when they talk about what it now feels like to live in Manton.

"They both talk about the impact of PB on the attitudes of older residents towards young people, and vice versa. Giving everyone a voice and encouraging listening has led to a greater mutual understanding and a willingness to cooperate together. Similarly, relationships between those that deliver services and those that depend on them have changed dramatically. As Sue says, 'One voice has become two and two voices have become four ... and together people now have a voice *that is heard*!' Teresa makes the point that collective rather than individual choices are so much more effective. Anti-social behaviour has reduced, the fear of crime has dropped, the physical environment has improved and more residents – one in four – took part in this year's PB event than voted in the last local election. But, most of all, the impact on people's dignity stands out. Sue was terrified when she first had to make a presentation to a public meeting, now she has the confidence to talk to anyone! She left school at 15 and now, in her early sixties, she is in her final year of a degree in sustainable communities at Sheffield Hallam University. Teresa had never been involved in the community before she moved to Manton, and now has a university-accredited certificate in participatory appraisal proudly displayed in her home. She says that PB has changed her way of thinking about democracy and she voted for the first time in the 2010 general election, 'Because my opinion counts and it is my responsibility to do so'.

"But let's give the last word to Sue, who captures the community spirit by asking, 'What would make the whole community better, not just my life? How can I improve the lives of others?'"

Community development is a mutual process. It begins in everyday lives, understanding histories, cultures and values, and listening to hopes and concerns as the beginning of a process of empowerment and change. A critical analysis of the way that prejudice and discrimination target specific groups through poverty, making them more at risk than others, and creating a system of domination and subordination, personally, locally, nationally and globally, is vital for this work. Identifying the forces that shape people's lives, we are able to make critical connections that form the basis of critical action. The community profile offers a strategy to gather this information together in a systematic way in partnership with the community. The critical connections that weave together through the profile provide a foundation for developing critical consciousness and practical projects, such as credit unions and participatory budgeting, that have global connections.

This is the basis of a critical approach to community development that weaves action and reflection, theory and practice, into a unity of praxis.

THREE

Doing community development

The most challenging context for practitioners is one in which people have been silenced into apathy; apathy lacks energy, and is a consequence of hopelessness. Anger, on the other hand, generates an energy that can be redirected into positive action. Working with Freirean pedagogy, we concentrate on critical consciousness as a vehicle for restoring hope from hopelessness, knowing that *relevance* is the key to unlocking the energy to act, and relevance is located in people's everyday reality. This chapter introduces the work of Paulo Freire, the Brazilian popular educator, who has made more impact than any other thinker on community development around the world since the 1970s. Here, I focus in particular on his emphasis on the stories of the people being at the heart of the process of change. I want to consider the skills and strategies with which to begin this process, while remembering to situate local action within the bigger political picture.

Introduction to Paulo Freire

Since the publication of *Pedagogy of the oppressed* in the UK in 1972, Paulo Freire (1921-97) has proved to be one of the visionary thinkers of our times for workers involved in the practice of social justice. The most significant contribution of his work is his insight into the political nature of education. For Freire, education can never be neutral: its political function is to liberate or domesticate. In other words, the process of education either creates critical, autonomous thinkers or it renders people passive and unquestioning. By failing to understand this, we fail to recognise the ways in which power and domination are woven through the fabric of our everyday experience. Freire achieves a synthesis of theory and practice that is fundamental to a critical approach to community development. His particular contribution, according to Cornel West (Preface to McLaren and Leonard, 1993, p xiii), lies in his 'genius ... to explicate in this text [*Pedagogy of the oppressed*] and exemplify in his life the dynamics of this process of how ordinary people can and do make history in how they think, feel, act and love. Freire has the distinctive talent of being a profound theorist who remains "on the ground" and a passionate activist who gets us "off the ground" – that is, he makes what is abstract concrete without sacrificing subtlety, and he infuses this concrete way of being-in-the-world with a fire that fans and fuels our will to be free'.

Critical pedagogy refers to education that is situated within an analysis of ideological and structural power. Paula Allman calls for a radical re-reading of Freire, stating that 'the publication of Gramsci's work in English has been one of the most important influences in preparing us for the rereading and radical use of Freire's ideas' (Allman, 1988, p 99; Gramsci, 1971; 1985). The complementary nature of the two lies in 'Freire's consideration of the political nature of education and in Gramsci's consideration of the educational nature of politics' (Allman, 1988, p 92). Freire cannot be ignored: his ideas echo through generations, continuing to inspire educators as well as generating passionate critique. 'Remaining steadfast till the very end to his cherished principles of radical humanization and democracy, Freire has, throughout his life, produced work that provides those who share his political–pedagogical philosophy with resources of hope and a strong sense of agency' (Mayo, 2004, p 2).

Freire's approach to critical pedagogy exposes the power and authority of the traditional educator in perpetuating domination. A popular educator is a critical pedagogue, working in community with values of humility and compassion, seeing the educational relationship as one of mutual humanisation with a loving commitment to people at its core. 'I could never think of education without love and that is why I think I am an educator, first of all because I feel love' is a remark attributed to Freire a few days before his death in 1997 (McLaren, 2002, pp 245-53). Community workers are popular educators, and as such every aspect of our work encourages the critical questioning of reality. Every educator–learner role defined in relation to critical pedagogy is mutual: it involves a co-learning/co-teaching approach in which the educator also learns and the learner also teaches. Rather than the traditional, authoritarian, top-down pouring of facts from teacher to learner, which assumes an unquestioning power relationship, popular education is a mutual search based on a 'profound love for the world and for people' (Freire, 1996, p 70). This is similar to Gandhi's emphatic declaration to the unemployed mill workers of Lancashire in the 1930s that he loved all the children of the world *as his own*. It is a worldview based on critical compassion. This mutual caring is the basis of dialogue, the foundation of a dialectical approach to learning that, in identifying the contradictions that permeate our lives, moves to transformative action. It calls for popular educators to act in solidarity to transform the ideologies and structures of oppression that continue to create suffering and subordination. Critical dialogue replaces the arrogance of the traditional educator with humility: 'For all their competence and authority, teachers must be humble to relearn that which they think they already know from others and to connect, through learning … with their learners' lifeworlds' (Mayo, 2004, p 93).

Freire in his life and times

Our lives are shaped by difference, culture, history and the politics of our times:

> Society not only controls our movements, but shapes our identity, our thoughts and our emotions. The structures of society become the structure of our own consciousness. Society does not stop at the surface of our skins. Society permeates us as much as it envelops us. (Berger, 1966, p 140)

In this sense, ideas can only be fully understood in relation to the thinker, contextualised culturally, politically and historically, and, in turn, are only useful if adapted to changing political and social times. For these reasons, it is important to understand the context from which Freire's ideas emerged. His early experience influenced his thinking profoundly. He was born in the town of Recife in North East Brazil in 1921 into a middle-class family. As a consequence of the world economic depression in the 1930s, his family was plunged into poverty. This experience had a great impact on him: as a child Freire could see the ways that social class barriers were still acted out in the face of starvation, and he was puzzled that people were silenced by their suffering. At the age of 11, he resolved to commit himself to the struggle against hunger so that other children did not have to suffer in the same way. Although malnutrition affected his early schooling, family fortunes eventually improved and he was able to qualify for Recife University.

Brazilian university education was modelled on that of the French, and it was through this system that Freire was introduced to the thinking of Althusser, Foucault, Fromm, Levi-Strauss and Sartre. After the rigours of his schooling, the academic life suited Freire but equipped him with little practical direction. In quick succession, he became a lawyer, a teacher of Portuguese and then an adult educator. In 1944, he married Elza, also a teacher. They became involved in the Catholic Action movement among middle-class families in Recife, locating critical contradictions between the Christian faith and privileged lifestyles. However, radical, democratic ideals were not well received in this petit-bourgeois context. 'It proved to be an extremely disheartening experience, as they uncovered strong resistance to the idea that bourgeois families should, for example, treat their servants as human beings' (Mackie, 1980b, p 3). They changed the focus of their work to the poor of Recife, which was a turning point in Freire's life, but not an easy transition. 'I said many beautiful things, but made no impact. This was because I used my frame of reference, not theirs' (Freire, quoted in Mackie, 1980b, pp 3-4). Sharing the lives of the people led him to name the *culture of silence*, the way in which political, social and economic domination lead to passive acceptance in those who are marginalised. His study of the ways in which oppression is experienced became the basis for his doctorate, submitted to Recife University in 1959, after which he was appointed to a chair in history and philosophy.

In 1962, Freire was invited to become director of the government's adult literacy programme in North East State Brazil. His radical pedagogy was based on the belief that every person is capable of engaging in critical dialogue when they perceive it as relevant to their life experience. Freire gained recognition, and was invited to become director of the national literacy programme. This placed him in a powerful position to influence both educational and electoral reform (Taylor, 1993). Freire's insight into literacy as a vehicle for political consciousness, the links between education and power, led him to be seen as an enemy of the state. So, when the multinational-backed military coup took place in Brazil in 1964, Freire was arrested, stripped of his professorship and imprisoned. He was seen as a threat to the status quo because of his intention to develop a national literacy programme that would increase literacy levels for the rural and urban poor, and so make them eligible to vote (Mayo, 2004). After 75 days, he was offered political asylum in Bolivia. Fifteen days later there was a coup in Bolivia, and he was, in turn, exiled to Chile where he continued his work at the Institute for Research and Training in Agrarian Reform.

This gave Freire the opportunity to experience his critical pedagogy from a different cultural, ideological and political perspective. He worked with 'the most progressive sectors of the Christian Democratic Party Youth ... finding himself in contact with highly stimulating Marxist thought and powerful working-class organizations' (Torres, 1993, p 123). After spending some time at Harvard as visiting professor, he moved to Geneva in 1970 as principal consultant to the Department of Education of the World Council of Churches. Throughout this period, Freire's influence spread, and his critical pedagogy offered a practical tool for progressive educators engaged in political/cultural projects in many countries. The concept of *conscientização* (conscientisation) gave fresh insight into the political nature of popular education as a tool for liberation. Freire gained worldwide recognition, speaking at conferences, acting as consultant to projects throughout the developing and industrialised nations, and advising governments. It was during the first six years of his long period of exile that his most celebrated work, *Pedagogy of the oppressed*, was written and brought him acclaim as a seminal thinker of his time (Mayo, 2004).

After his enforced 16-year exile, Freire returned to Brazil in 1980, following the amnesty of 1979. He began 'relearning Brazil' by reading Gramsci and also 'listening to the *popular Gramsci* in the *favelas*' (Torres, 1993, p 135). He spent at least two afternoons a week with people in their communities, listening to their experience and analysis and, in this way, developing a *critical praxis* out of lived experience. After this, Freire worked in the Faculty of Education of the Catholic University of São Paulo. He set up *Vereda*, an educational centre that brought together people from popular education projects. He also worked with the education section of the *Partido Trabalhista* (the Workers' Party), which led to his honorary appointment as President of the Workers' University of São Paulo, an organisation that fosters trade union and political education.

Paulo Freire's ideas have pioneered and epitomised the concept and practice of critical pedagogy. Although his original interest was in the relevance of people's education in developing countries, particularly through literacy, health, agrarian reform and liberation theology, he also worked closely with radical educators in North America and Europe, arguing that issues of exploitation and discrimination exist everywhere. The influence of Freirean pedagogy has spread far and wide, providing a major influence for those committed to a more fair and just world. The inescapable paradox is, as Torres puts it so well, that political pedagogy 'in industrialized societies is nurtured by notions of education and social change developed in the Third World' (Torres, 1993, p 137).

In 1986, Elza died, and Freire lost his long-time colleague and companion. He married Ana Maria Araújo (Nita) in 1988, a friend of the family and a former student, who shared his life and his work until his sudden death in 1997 (Mayo, 2004). Freire remained active to the end. In the last 10 years of his life he was Secretary of Education in São Paulo (1989–91) and taught at the Pontifical Catholic University in São Paulo. He also wrote prolifically and gave inspiring talks around the world. It was at the Pedagogy of the Oppressed Conference, initiated by Doug Paterson at the University of Omaha at Nebraska, that I was fortunate to meet Freire with Augusto Boal and Peter McLaren in March 1996 (and Ira Shor the following year, just weeks before Freire died). Both Freire and Boal were conferred with honorary doctorates by the university during the conference. This organisation, now Pedagogy and Theatre of the Oppressed, holds an annual conference in different venues in the USA, developing the work of Freire and Boal.

Mayo comments that 'in his later work, Freire stressed and elaborated on points that were already present in his early work ... a person in process, constantly in search of greater coherence' (Mayo, 2004, p 79). And although his later works are important, *Pedagogy of the oppressed* remains Freire's seminal contribution. His ideas continue to excite people with their ongoing relevance to oppression. Freire has always evoked extremes of passion, and I address some of the critiques of his work in Chapter Eight. His ideas were shaped by, and need to be understood in relation to, his cultural and political times. New understanding of the concept of multiple, interconnected oppressions has challenged his oppressor/oppressed analysis as simplistic, obscuring the complexity of the process. Nevertheless, Freire's profound insight into the nature of oppression still offers the conceptual tools with which to develop our ideas, and this begins with a critical re-reading of his work from our many new understandings. 'We can stay with Freire or against Freire, but not without Freire' (Torres, 1993, p 140). This call for a critical re-reading of Freire is echoed more and more by those critical pedagogues who see the transformative potential of his work to engage with issues of 'race', gender, age, ethnicity, 'dis'ability, sexuality and so on in all their complex intertwinings – Ira Shor, Peter McLaren, Paula Allman, Peter Mayo, Keith Popple, Kathleen Weiler and Antonia Darder, to name but a few.

Freire's work embraces an eclectic range of thinkers: he was influenced by Antonio Gramsci, Eric Fromm, Karl Mannheim, Jean-Paul Sartre, Herbert Marcuse, Mao, Che Guevara, Franz Fanon, John Dewey, Lev Vygotsky, Martin Buber, Teilhard de Chardin and Jacques Maritain, among many. From a feminist point of view, he was one of those rare male thinkers who embrace emotions, intellect and faith to provide us with a more integrated approach to praxis. He gave us confidence to believe that we can develop theory in action, based on the underlying belief that we all have the right to be fully human in the world. In other words, people, when they are thinking critically, are capable of analysing the meaning of their own lives. Freire's great strength is the way that he locates critical pedagogy within an analysis of power and the way that it becomes woven into the structures of society. In this way, Freirean pedagogy is not segregated from life in the false structures of a classroom, but is all around us in the places that people live their lives; an engagement with people in context.

Freire, from his early days in Brazil, recognised the vital energy produced by using popular education for critical consciousness, because it has relevance in people's lives:

> People will act on the issues on which they have strong feelings. There is a close link between emotion and the motivation to act. All education and development projects should start by identifying the issues which the local people speak about with excitement, hope, fear, anxiety or anger. (Hope and Timmel, 1984, p 8)

People make critical connections when they link cultural, political, social and economic issues with their everyday life experience. This counters the apathy and disaffection symptomatic of a *culture of silence*. Such insights into the nature of oppression, and the ways in which the traditional education system functions to maintain the obedience of paternalism, informed the development of Freire's pedagogy, a form of learning based on questioning answers rather than answering questions, in a process of 'extraordinarily re-experiencing the ordinary' (Shor, 1992, p 122). The cornerstone of his theory is that every human being is capable of critically engaging in their world once they begin to question the contradictions that shape their lives.

I witnessed Freire's critical pedagogy in action in Nicaragua in 1985, a living example of participatory democracy in process. The local Nicaraguan people I met in their own communities, often geographically isolated, felt politically engaged in the development of a participatory democracy. Their national literacy campaign, to which Freire acted as consultant, reduced illiteracy from 50 per cent, one of the highest in Latin America, to less than 13 per cent within five months (Hirshon, 1983, p xi). Antonia Darder, born in Puerto Rico, talks about the Nicaraguan literacy campaign as one of the Sandinista government's major 'ideological enterprises' (Darder, 2002, p 205). She reflects on her own political awareness as a schoolgirl being triggered by some of the most progressive Freirean thinkers in her country. Freire's ideas inspired such radical training texts as Hope and Timmel's *Training for transformation* series, developed out of practical experience in Zimbabwe in the 1970s (first published in 1984), copies of which were like gold dust to UK community workers of the 1980s. People travelling to Africa would bring copies home, until eventually there was a supplier in the UK. Freire's reach has been global, influencing the practice and analysis of many local projects, such as the Gorgie-Dalry Adult Learning Project in Edinburgh (Kirkwood and Kirkwood, 1989) to West Bengal, where Freirean approaches to literacy developed by Satyendra Nath Maitra from 1978 onwards brought popular education to adult literacy through folklore using puppetry, song, short story and popular culture that were adapted in reading primers. This approach developed across India to have wider influence. Asoke Bhattacharya of the Indian Paulo Freire Institute, Kolkata, tells how Freire has touched the lives of women in West Bengal:

Freirian critical literacy in West Bengal: Malati, Minati and Amina

"I had just taken over as the Director of the Adult, Continuing Education and Extension Centre of Jadavpur University, Kolkata, India. Only a few kilometres from the university campus, in the South 24 Parganas, we were looking for suitable villages that could be adopted for taking up literacy programmes, with the help of young people. I visited the Gram Panchayats (Kalikapur 1, Kalikapur 2 and Pratapnagar) very near to the Sundarbans, the famous mangrove forest of India. The saline soil did not yield more than one crop and the people were generally very poor and literacy levels were very low.

"Malati, a widow, came to meet us to request a literacy centre near her village. 'Why?', I asked. 'Since the death of my husband, I have to support my family by selling vegetables at the market. Due to my poor knowledge of counting, I am in a fix when purchasing my merchandise from the wholesalers and selling them to my customers. Very often, I make a loss. Please help me to learn the art of counting so that I can survive.'

"Minati told me that she remembered when she was admitted to the village school early in her life. But then she was married off, and had to discontinue her studies. She comes to the city to work as a maidservant in the houses of the Babus and finds it difficult to board the correct bus as she cannot read the bus routes and numbers. Literacy is necessary for her everyday life.

"Amina, a muslim woman of around 25 years of age, had been married off quite early in her life. Her husband's family was very conservative, but she was insistent that she would come to the literacy centre. She wanted her daughter to go to school. Amina's father's home was far away from her married home, but sometimes she felt like contacting him when her in-laws tortured her mentally and physically. Literacy was necessary for her for to communicate with her family, as well as for improving the quality of life of her child.

"The work of the literacy centres started in earnest. The course was for six months. Classes were held three times a week in the afternoon between 3pm and 5pm when the women had some free time. Appropriately, there were female educators trained to do the job properly. My job was to convene monthly meetings to monitor progress. The women enrolled were mostly within the age group of 15 to 35, although some elderly women like Malati were also there. The approach to the world of literacy was based on Paulo Freire's critical pedagogy and primers were prepared by the State Resource Centres. One day, Mira, the supervisor, came to my room and informed me that six months were over and that she about to do an evaluation test. I readily agreed to go to the centre for this important event. After the test, Mira handed me the evaluated papers. Malati had correctly answered all the sums. Minati read out clearly and correctly from an unseen text. Amina had written a letter to her father.

"I had another surprise in store: Mira had arranged for a debate on the motion 'Joint family is no longer feasible'! Only a few months ago such a topic would never have been discussed openly there. Most of the young women spoke in favour of a unitary family. They wanted to have their say in running the family. They spoke firmly and placed their arguments convincingly.

"Tears came to my eyes; I was witnessing the birth of a new society. The *culture of silence* was broken. Paulo Freire was the architect of this new world!"

Asoke illustrates the power of critical literacy on questioning the status quo and the implications this has for cultural change.

Finally, it is important to mention Myles Horton and the Highlander Folk School in Tennessee. Freire and Horton, from two vastly different cultures, had a similar vision of the role of popular education in the process of empowerment. The idea for Highlander was stimulated by Horton's visit to Denmark to study the Danish Folk High School movement. The following year, 1932, he started Highlander with Don West, with the broad idea of using popular education for social and economic justice. He was its director until he retired in 1972. In the early 1950s, Highlander focused its attention on racial justice, and from then it played a key reflection and action role in the emerging civil rights movement, with connections with prominent Black activists such as Rosa Parks and Martin Luther King, Junior. A key community initiative was the development of citizenship schools, which concentrated on Black literacy as a route to political power. Horton and Freire eventually came together in December 1987, and Freire felt that their meeting brought him through his despair over Elza's death. The talking book they did together, reflecting on their lives and their experience of radical education, united their shared beliefs, and was published as *We make the road by walking* (Horton and Freire, 1990). A week after they met to discuss the manuscript, Horton died. Freire went on to become director of public education in São Paulo.

Freire's commitment is to the oppressed everywhere, not only in developing countries; the concept is 'ideological and political, not geographic' (Mackie, 1980a, p 119). His powerful ideas have extended beyond the limits of literacy to areas such as community development, social work, liberation theology and participatory action research (Reason and Rowan, 1981; Reason and Bradbury, 2001). Indeed, Freire's connection with the liberation theology movement continued throughout his life and 'in a conversation with Carmel Borg and [Peter Mayo], the then São Paulo cardinal, Paulo Evaristo Arns, stated categorically that, in his view, Paulo changes not only people's lives but also the Church' (Mayo, 2004, p 6). His vision was one of transforming humanity to a state of mutual, cooperative endeavour defined by liberation and participatory democracy.

Many criticisms have been levelled against Freire's pedagogy: he has been seen variously as a dangerous revolutionary, an eclectic philosopher or as a literacy expert. He has been accused of interrelating such a diversity of ideas in his work that it reaches the point of analytic impossibility, and of coming from an unacknowledged Christian and Marxist perspective (Leach, 1983). Nevertheless, Freire's thought is compelling:

> A word of witness has its place here – a personal witness as to why I find a dialogue with the thought of Paulo Freire an exciting adventure. Fed up as I am with the abstractness and sterility of so much intellectual work in academic circles today, I am excited by a process of reflection which is set in a thoroughly historical context, which is carried on in the midst of a struggle to create a new social order and thus represents a new unity of theory and praxis. And I am encouraged when a man of the stature of Paulo Freire incarnates a rediscovery of the humanizing vocation of the intellectual, and demonstrates the power of thought to negate accepted limits and open the way to a new future. (Richard Shaull, Foreword to *Pedagogy of the oppressed*, Freire, 1972, p 11)

Let us now explore an example of a Freirean approach to community development practice.

Empowerment and the use of story

Paulo Freire emphasises that transformative theory begins in lived reality, in the stories of the people, in relations of trust, mutuality and respect, and that dialogue is the basis of this praxis. It is in these relations of trust that we share stories that are told from the heart. Community development is committed to social justice through a process of critical education that begins in personal empowerment, and follows through to collective action for a more just, equal and sustainable world. The strong ideological base on which our work is founded frames the lens through which our practice is shaped, and is a key component of critical praxis. A stumbling block in the process of collective action is the move from personal, group and project stages to the full collective force that is needed for transformative change. This places the use of story at the heart of the deeply personal and the profoundly political. Power and empowerment, poverty and privilege, nature and humanity are all inextricably linked by the interdependent web of life on earth, and the beginning of change for a just and sustainable future begins in the personal. It is this personal/political dimension that I want to focus on by linking the use of story to collective action for change.

> A real narrative is a web of alternating possibilities. The imagination is capable of kindness that the mind often lacks because it works naturally from the world of Between; it does not engage things in a cold, clear-cut way but always searches for the hidden worlds that wait at the edge of things. (O'Donohue, 2004, p 138)

If the stories of the people are the beginning of the process of transformative change, where does story link to the process of empowerment? Steedman (2000, p 72) says, 'The past is re-used through the agency of social information, and that interpretation of it can only be made with what people know of a social world and their place within it.' Life is a fiction. We tell and retell the stories of our lives differently according to our audience, our recollection and our insight; thus stories become shaped by time and space and understanding, and the telling of stories can be, in turn, the vehicles of our understanding. But, for this process to follow through to its collective potential, personal stories need to be set within a theoretical analysis that offers critical insight for action.

In relation to personal empowerment, Mo Griffiths talks about the 'little stories' that link voice to narrative, making that vital connection between the deeply personal and the profoundly political 'by taking the particular perspective of an individual seriously; that is, the individual as situated in particular circumstances in all their complexity [and linking this] to grander concerns like education, social justice and power' (Griffiths, 2003, p 81). Voice is an expression of self-esteem; it is rooted in the belief that what we have to say is relevant and of value. If we are not heard with respect, our voices are silenced. My point is that the simple act of listening to people's stories, respectfully giving one's full attention, is an act of personal empowerment, but to bring about change for social justice this process needs to be collective and needs to be located within wider structures.

There was a revival in the ancient tradition of storytelling linked to the political activism of the late 1960s, emerging from the civil rights and anti-Vietnam struggles (Little and Froggett, 2010), and they were also at the heart of the women's movement, where the myriad of little stories captured understanding of difference and diversity and formed the basis of building theory in action as collective narratives for change. The telling of stories is the articulation of experience, which in its articulation presents possibilities for reflection and analysis. In this process, personal stories link to collective experiences which become capable of challenging dominant ideology. Storytelling, used in these ways, can be seen as a democratic force embodying a radical agenda. Chris Cavanagh talks about the way in which story is so much a part of our lives that we overlook its significance and power:

> Stories define societies, cultures, communities. They act as social-cultural glue. Our histories are all, of course, stories and there has been much scholarship in the last twenty years that looks critically and sceptically at who wrote the various canonical histories and for whom and in what interests they were written. Postmodernism (in its progressive aspects) and post-structuralism have injected a healthy scepticism about the grand narratives to which we grant normative power. Popular education is a practice that structures and applies this post-structural scepticism in a democratic and rigorous fashion to enable people to tell new and better stories — recovering personal

and community histories that have disappeared or were subjugated and subordinated to the dominant (or hegemonic) narratives. It also develops our collective capacities to imagine different stories about where we might be going in the decades we might yet have to live – assuming we survive the imminent crises of peak oil, global warming, extreme neoliberalism and the ever-present militarization of our beleaguered world. (Cavanagh, 2007, p 45)

Storytelling is central to the process of community development, encouraging participation through listening and understanding. Belonging and confidence grow as people are listened to, valued and taken seriously. Autonomy and action gather strength in a collective process of change for equality and justice. In this sense, storytelling has many parallels with forum theatre, where an individual experience is acted out and audience participants change the experience to give possibilities for practising that change in the world (Boal, 2008). In discussing the use of storytelling around the world, Little and Froggett (2010) note that the West's preoccupation with identity and the self is not so central to non-western narratives, where culture and community come before self. This observation helps us to understand story as a possibility for reconnecting western people to a fractured whole, with community as the key connection. Storytelling, I believe, dislocates the centrality of the speaker, offering a form of democratic possibility that is beyond the resistance of personality; it is a form of communication that is less fearful, less radically associated, yet capable of transformation as it stimulates critical consciousness. Take the potential of working with this story of women as community activists caught up in the Troubles in Northern Ireland from Avila Kilmurray, Director of the Community Foundation for Northern Ireland.

Women in war: Memories of the 1970s, Derry, Northern Ireland

"'Of your five senses which is the most important when the shit hits the fan?' The question hung in the air apropos of nothing in particular. Kate paused, returning her glass to a table that was already littered with accumulated debris. The five senses, she pondered, as she tried to conjure them up. Sight, taste, touch, smell and hearing – was that them? 'Well, touch, I suppose – what you do, I mean, how you impact on people. That's important, isn't it?'

"'Hmm, I reckon it has a place, but personally I don't rate it,' replied Sorcha, a long-term local activist and her drinking companion for the evening. 'No, hearing and sound are your high fives. What you hear and what you say.' She nodded knowingly as if agreeing with herself. 'I can sum it up in two. First of all sound – keep the head down and the ear to the ground. Listen for those nuances, half remarks, jokes with a jag to them, and most importantly, listen out for what's not said at all. And then your mouth – keep a guard on it; in fact, whatever you say, say nothing.'

> "'Speech isn't a sense,' protested Kate. 'No?' queried her friend. 'Well whatever it is, it's good advice in this part of the world, where as they say, just because you're paranoid doesn't mean to say that they're not out to get you.'
>
> "Kate regarded Sorcha uncertainly. What she said went against all her training that had argued for careful preparation, rational planning and effective follow-through on delivery. Instead, what she was hearing was all about survival. Sorcha smiled at Kate's obvious bemusement. She raised her glass in a closing-time toast. 'Slainte go saol agat, and long life to you.' It was a salutation worth the having in a city at war.'"

Stories such as these offer the basis of analysis for critical consciousness and social change. Sharing stories embodies trust, respect, dignity and all the other qualities that frame this approach to practice, and out of the process, trusting relationships are formed. The act of listening from the heart is the foundation of dialogue:

> Paulo somehow connected his whole being, his reason and emotion, to the whole being of another.... His ability to listen, not just to hear the other person, but that way of listening mentioned in the [*Pedagogy of freedom*] – also noticeable in his look signaled the moment when he accepted and gathered within himself what he was hearing from the other.... In Paulo, to touch, to look and to listen become moments of me and you in dialogue about something which he and the other person wanted to know. (Ana Araújo [Nita] Freire (1998) 'Paulo Freire: To touch, to look, to listen', *Convergence (A tribute to Paulo Freire)*, vol 31, pp 3-5, cited in Mayo, 2004, p 80)

Feminist pedagogy, like Freirean pedagogy, is rooted in everyday stories as the beginning of a process of personal empowerment leading to a critical understanding of the nature of structural oppression. This is based on the notion that the deeply personal is profoundly political. But feminist pedagogy emphasises difference, and the complex interlinking, overlapping matrix of oppressions that shape us all according to 'race', class, gender, age, ethnicity, sexuality, 'dis'ability, religion, and so on, rather than a simplistic dichotomous analysis of oppressor/oppressed.

From a feminist perspective, any form of emancipatory practice needs to examine the power relationship in the collaboration. For example, I continually ask myself whether I am focusing my middle-class, White, female, heterosexual, Northern English, Quaker gaze across difference and putting my interpretation on other lives as an outsider looking in (Weiler, 1994, 2001).

Let me give you an example of what I mean in relation to my own practice. Wendy and I found our lives woven together in 1985 when I began work as the community development team leader and community centre manager in Hattersley, Wendy's community. Wendy, who had been a community activist for a number of years, was elected chair of Hattersley Forum at the same time. This was the beginning of a seven-year partnership, and our friendship continues across the 100-mile divide that was created when I moved to Lancaster. The idea of using story in the process of empowerment as useful to emancipatory practice is captured in the following story, and in its fragile conception, when Wendy powerfully and immediately identified my 'outsider' gaze.

In the beginning, the idea...

"The summer sunshine beamed on us. I drove, Wendy by my side, Celia and Mary in the rear, out for the day in the rugged Derbyshire countryside. Our reunions, this little group of women who had pioneered Hattersley Women for Change in the 1980s, happened at irregular intervals out of a shared history and a fondness for each other. This would be the last, the end of an era, as we were destined to find out a few months later, when Celia died. Today, my head was full of ideas for a partnership with Wendy, based on collaborative action research, a continuation of the political activism we had shared. We stumbled down the slope together to the wishing well, to witness where baskets of provisions had been left for the plague victims several centuries before, Mary and Celia too infirm to make the little detour from the car. While we were alone, I gingerly broached the subject, trying to inject it with enthusiasm. 'I've got an idea for some important work we could do together...' Wendy looked ill, drawn, preoccupied, and inwardly I had nagging doubts. Was this really an opportunity for a reciprocal venture, or was I using my friendship with her to further my own academic interests? At that stage, I was acutely aware that the experiences we shared in common as women had vastly different outcomes, some of which led to her being so unwell. I had tried to avoid pre-formulating my ideas, asking Wendy to climb aboard my wagon, on my terms, and I stuttered, trying to communicate my good ideas in the face of her lukewarm response. She'd give it some thought, she said.

"Some weeks later, we negotiated the miniature wooden bridge in dimmed light to the sound of running water and found a secluded table where we could talk. This theme pub, built at the end of the new motorway that led to Hattersley, was a landmark for passing motorists, a sign of consumerist luxury never dreamt of in my days there. Tentatively, I revisited my ideas. In my mind, this research would focus on the story of Wendy's life. It didn't occur to me that, in my intention to call the research collaborative, I had clearly perceived the collaboration to be in the product; I failed to notice that I was levelling my middle-class gaze at her working-class story. She looked at me, 'Are you suggesting that I should be the one left standing in my underwear in public! I don't think so! You join me, and we'll stand in our underwear together.' In those words, she located the inherent contradiction in my ideas. I, in turn, felt exposed! This was Wendy, identifying and dislocating my power in relation to her, and presenting me with a critical insight into my own assumptions. I was shocked into silence!"

Wendy's challenge located and named my power and privilege, acted out within our relationship. In Freire's terms this comes into the concept of 'denunciation and annunciation', naming power in order to dislocate and change relations. From that time on, Wendy's challenge to my consciousness and my openness to reflect on it has resulted in a much more mutual, comparative approach to our life stories in order to identify the power structures that have shaped our different experience of the world.

A sense of who we are in the world

If story has a powerful potential in the process of critical practice, it is important to have a theoretical understanding that explains how it might work most effectively. Griffiths (2003) supports the idea that 'little stories' restore self-respect through dignity, mutuality and conviviality, but stresses that this is not transformative until it becomes a collective process. Darder talks about the way she provides learning contexts in which she resists giving answers, but encourages people 'to reach into themselves and back to their histories' (2002, p 233). Using reflective writing to explore the inner depths of memory and history, she works with her students to analyse their stories from theoretical perspectives. The focus of each reflection moves in a connected way to excavate the deepest life experiences. Take, for example, Darder's idea of *problematising* 'reading' with her students. Reflections begin with the first memory of hearing stories told by people who love us, extending by degrees to reflections on learning to read in school. By reaching inside themselves and their histories, she uses this approach with her students to develop reflection and story as a discovery of who they are and what has shaped them in their world. This is the beginning of *critical consciousness*. These stories are critical pedagogy in action, leading to personal autonomy and a collective will to act together for change.

In these ways, we begin to build theory and practice around the role of story in developing the self-esteem that leads to autonomy and the confidence to act. Most importantly, we understand the significance of beginning in the deeply personal stories that have constructed people's reality in the overall process of collective action for social justice. Stories give voice to experience, and in turn provide a structure for reflection on the world. The insight gained from this reflection reveals the political nature of personal experience and leads to critical consciousness and critical action. More than this, the sense of identity that emerges leads to personal autonomy.

Doyal and Gough (1991) suggest that autonomy of agency is a basic human need that leads to critical autonomy, and they see this as the prerequisite to critical participation in society, the basis of collective action. Expressed diagrammatically, this offers a clear structure to the development of critical practice (see Figure 3.1). It suggests that identity politics, so central to community development practice in the 1980s and early 1990s, plays a vital part in discovering the pride and confidence in who we are that is so necessary for community activism. But, for personal empowerment to become a liberating force, our consciousness must be critical; we need to understand ourselves in relation to the structural forces that

Figure 3.1: Critical autonomy and collective action

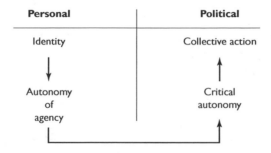

shape us if we are to empathise with others and act collectively for a fair and just world. These theoretical insights link the practical strategy of reflection as story with a political discovery of who we are in the world.

Richard Winter, in his work on patchwork texts, remarks that story often starts from a personal interpretation, an 'exploring inwards':

> ... but if fiction is to be the basis for a process of reflection that is to be sustained, we need a format where questioning and exploring beyond one's initial set of ideas is made explicit and is built into the writing process itself, as well as into the discussion of the writing.... In order to sustain the reflective process, a format is needed which is flexible enough to allow different ways of writing to be combined, a format which allows the writer to move easily between description, imaginative creation and analytical commentary. (Winter et al, 1999, p 65)

He suggests that we can create a plurality of voices without false claims to a single truth: that we can present a unity of narrative out of this diversity if we are explicit about uncertainty and present possible, plural truths. In other words, it is possible to link the personal and the collective without reducing or silencing the diversity of different experiences. It is also possible to engage with paradox and contradiction as a more complex 'truth', a counter-force to positivism, as suggested by O'Donohue (2004). You may wish to link these ideas to the feminist critiques of Freire and the argument for a Freirean-feminist-anti-racist pedagogy presented in Chapter Eight.

Community development always focuses on the stories of the people as the basis of action and reflection. My purpose is to locate this more rigorously as a central component of critical praxis and to define it more clearly as a way of integrating research with people in community into our praxis. I see it as a form of Freirean *problematising*, using story as a vehicle for critical consciousness.

Without an analytic commentary linking the personal to the political, stories remain subjective and without criticality. The following section offers practical suggestions for working with story in practice, using story as a tool of empowerment leading to autonomy, critical consciousness and change.

Practical ideas for using story with community groups

Chris Cavanagh works at the Catalyst Centre in Toronto running programmes for popular educators. Our paths crossed when we were both involved in the Pedagogy and Theatre of the Oppressed management board's planning retreat in Portland, Maine, a few years ago. We are all born storytellers, and Chris uses this as the basis for his focus on storytelling in the practice of social justice. He has developed a seven-stage structure for developing storytelling skills as a popular educator (Cavanagh, 2004, p 13):

1. *Listen:* Listen for the ways in which people tell a story. Listen to the choice of metaphors, adjectives, punch-lines, character. Listen to their body-language. Listen to your body-language. Listen to the things unsaid. Listen to the moods. Listen to how you don't listen.
2. *Choose:* Choose stories that mean something to you.
3. *Structure and pattern:* All stories have structure and pattern. Some have a beginning-middle-end. Some are: accumulative; circular; journey and return; descent and ascent; circles within circles; set-up and punch-line.
4. *Visualize:* See the story – run it like a film. Map it out on paper. Story-board it. Memorized words and phrases are easier to forget than images.
5. *Tell:* Rehearse. Tell it to a mirror. Tell it to the stars. Tell it to kids – they are kind and unforgiving critics. Don't forget about eye-contact.
6. *Reflect:* Ask for feedback, negatives and positives. Listen to both without getting defensive. An opinion about your telling is merely advice that can be taken or ignored or taken in part. Listen to yourself tell. What did you leave out? What did you like? How do you feel when you're finished telling?
7. *Research:* Look for other versions of the story you told. Hold a story in your head as you go through the day and look around to see where else that story exists. Read books about storytelling and narrative and myth. Write your thoughts. Talk to your friends about your thoughts.

In these ways, we can develop more confident structured skills in the use of storytelling as a vital component in the toolkit for transformative practice. Chris talked to me about his own story and how that was changed by a story given to him by his friend, dian marino.

The Master Archer

"Years ago I paused in my life of ceaseless activism, travel and troublemaking. I had been doing popular education work in Montreal and Nicaragua, across Canada and the USA and including forays into Southern Africa. I felt a need to reflect and better figure out what I had been doing that was right and, of course more importantly, what I had been doing wrong. I enrolled in a graduate program where a close friend taught and with whom I had already developed some powerful understandings (or hegemony and resistance, of art and play). It was a self-directed program in which students designed their own curriculum – something that suited me very well."

Each year, dian marino would begin the semester with an introduction to the incoming students that began with the following tale:

"There was once a general of war who was tired of fighting. He had spent his whole life perfecting his skill in all the arts of war, save archery. Now he was weary and wished to end his career as a fighter. So he decided that he would spend the rest of his days studying archery and he began to search far and wide for a master to study with.

"After much journeying he found a monastery where they taught archery – he entered the monastery and asked if he could live there and study. He thought that his life was now over and the remainder of his days would be spent in study and meditation behind these monastery walls. He had been studying for 10 years, perfecting his skill as an archer, when, one day, the abbot of the monastery came to him and told the former-general of war that he must leave. The former-general protested saying that his life in the world outside the monastery was over and that all he wished was to spend the rest of his days here. But the abbot insisted, saying that the general, now a Master Archer, must now leave and go into the world and teach what he had learned.

"The Master Archer had to do as he was told. Having nowhere to go when he left the monastery he decided to return to the village of his birth. It was a long journey and as he neared the village he noticed a target on a tree with an arrow dead-centre in the bulls-eye. He was surprised by this only to notice more bulls-eyes on trees and, in the centre of each, an arrow. Then, on the barns and the buildings of the town he saw dozens, hundreds of arrows in bulls-eyes.

"The peace he had attained in 10 years of monastic life had left him and he approached the elders of the town, indignant that after years of devoted study he should return to his home and find an archer more skilled than he. He demanded of the elders that the master archer meet him by the edge of town in one hour. Waiting by the mill the general could see no one coming to meet him though he noticed a young girl playing by the river. The girl noticed him and came over.

"'Are you waiting for someone?', asked the girl looking up at the former-general.

> "'Go away', he said.
>
> "'No, no', said the girl, 'you look like you're waiting for someone and I was told to come and meet someone here.'
>
> "The former-general looked unbelievingly at the little girl and said, 'I'm waiting for the Master Archer responsible for the hundreds of perfect shots I see around here.'
>
> "'Then it is you I was sent to meet. *I* made all the shots', said the girl.
>
> "The former-general looked even more sceptical, convinced that this girl was trying to humiliate him. He said to the girl, 'If you're telling the truth then explain to me how you can get a perfect shot every single time you shoot your arrow.'
>
> "'That's easy', said the girl. 'I take my arrow and I draw it back in the bow and point it very, very straight. Then I let it go and wherever it lands I draw a bulls-eye.'"

This story has had an enduring impact on Chris's life: "It contains truths that continue to guide my life, truths for which the people and communities with whom I work have a desperate need."

> "My experience of authoritarian education (primary and secondary school) inspired in me a profound resistance to such education. Such that 'discovering' popular education (which, for me at 19, was coming across *Pedagogy of the oppressed* by Paulo Freire) was tantamount to a personal revolution. I chose then as I have continued to choose for over 30 years to practice and learn and share popular education. The primary context for doing this has been community development (which has included human rights work, international solidarity, anti-poverty work and much more). Perhaps dimly at first but rather quickly becoming more clear what I was most passionate about was facilitating people's capacities for self-organising, for advocacy for social justice, for dissent and active (and creative) resistance to injustice and inequity and for making transformative meaning from their experiences and reflections. It was this last dynamic that became clear when dian shared her story with me. And story moved into a central place in my praxis.
>
> "These wisdom tales have been swapped back and forth among earth's peoples for millennia. So does that make them all common property? In a sense it does. We are left with the messy world of politics, culture and the very, very complicated relations of inequality, oppression, struggle and so on. What is most true to me about telling stories is that there is always a context from which the stories came, in which they were learned and in which they are being told. And it's that context that concerns me most."

Stories hold the potential for radical change in everyday life; they are the linchpin between past experience and imagined futures. When you have developed the skills in becoming a storyteller yourself, you are more aware of the ways in which to use these in your community development toolkit. I find a very simple structure that works with groups is:

1. Start with your own stories to put everyone at ease, keeping it relevant and focused.
2. Begin in a spontaneous, unstructured way, building on critical incidents from everyday life, developing listening as part of the dialogical process. Use one story to build on another, building trust and confidence in the group, leading to 'multiple paths of exploration' (Treleaven, 2001, p 268). Do not analyse unless it evolves spontaneously from within the group.
3. Choose a relevant issue, so that no one feels daunted and everyone has something to say: a conflict, a misunderstanding, a missed opportunity, a moment of joy, compassion, hope, fear, anxiety, inspiration, danger, a new beginning, and so on (Bolton, 2005).
4. Gradually develop a more structured approach, as people offer their stories for analysis. Develop skills of respectful questioning and sensitive feedback in the group, together with the idea of connected knowing – profound empathy with experiences and ideas that are different from our own (Belenky et al, 1986). As a group, experiment with identifying experiences of power relations linked to dominant narratives.
5. Experiment with writing fictional counternarratives, reconstructing the original story in new ways.
6. Share these counternarratives and explore how they could influence new directions, new futures. What action needs to be taken to bring change about?

The basic skill is *dialogue*, a mutual and reciprocal form of communication in which the act of listening in a holistic way is valuing, and therefore liberating. Without humility on the part of the practitioner, dialogue cannot happen. Communication is a key skill in community development that involves an understanding of power in relationships. (For more insight into this, see Chapter Eight where I link Foucault to Peggy McIntosh's practical reflections on Whiteness and maleness as assumed power in everyday experience.) To be more fully open to others in listening to and telling our stories we need to develop skills in 'connected knowing' by suspending our own truth in order to more fully hear the truth of others (Belenky et al, 1986). As we learn to practice our values in action in these ways, *dialogue* becomes a key tool in emancipatory practice. This is the foundation of praxis. The next stage in the process is problem-posing, or *problematising*, presenting an everyday reality in a symbolic form – photograph, story, cartoon, drama, music – in which it generates debate and alternative perspectives. Here, I have concentrated on the use of story in community groups as a form of *problematising*. Group discussion gradually shifts from the initial focus and assumes a more critical analysis of the situation. Developing the skills to connect the personal to the cultural and political context is central to critical practice. Without this, each personal case becomes pathological: the emphasis placed on the inadequacies of the individual rather than the inequities of the system. Our challenge is to find a strategy for locating 'little stories' in the bigger picture. Action research, embedded in an emancipatory ideology, offers us the potential to look deeper under the microscope of the personal while framing it within the wider political picture. Thus, 'little stories' give depth to bigger pictures, and the personal is understood as political.

> You can begin to trace the pattern of story as a reaching inwards to explore the self under the microscope of a self-reflexive narrative, to discover the ways in which 'the social is embedded in ... skin and bones'. (Berger and Quinney, 2005, p 265)

As Giroux et al say (1996), counternarratives not only counter grand narratives, but they also challenge the hegemonic narratives of everyday life that manipulate people to think and behave according to a dominant set of cultural beliefs. In these ways, counternarratives are 'little stories' that have transformative potential. But to sustain the process through to a collective level, Winter et al (1999) offer some helpful hints to get beyond the 'little story' to a 'multi-voiced' patchwork text. As mentioned on p 67, this approach calls for a sustained reflective process and a flexibility of format which allows for flow between 'description, imaginative creation and analytical commentary' (Winter et al, 1999, p 65). The 'little story' (as conceived by Leotard) is a starting point for developing a plurality of voices, 'the imaginative shaping of diverse elements into a unity ... derived from an irreducible diversity' (1999, p 66). Think of a radial structure, a collage, a montage, a documentary or a film that begins with snatches of seemingly unrelated scenes which force us to reflect: 'how are these different matters going to turn out to be linked?' (1999, p 67). This helps us to move towards a collective analytic narrative which holds the key to collective action. Community development practitioners unlock the key to the innate passion and enthusiasm that grows with confidence and self-esteem as people begin to believe in themselves. This sense of personal autonomy is a prerequisite of collective action (see Figure 3.1).

A Freirean-feminist-anti-racist approach to story as personal empowerment in the process of collective action for change

- *Community groups*: grounded in an ideology of equality, providing the initial context for the practice of social justice, that is trust, mutuality, reciprocity, respect, dignity, empathy in action.
- *Writing and telling*: using story as reflection, as *problematising*, as noticing, as fiction, as a skill for community workers.
- *Listening*: from the heart and mind, taking experience seriously as the bedrock of action/reflection, grounded in theory; story as the basis of empowerment.
- *Noticing*: 'extraordinarily re-experiencing the ordinary' (Shor and Freire, 1987, p 93); feminist claiming of feelings and emotion as legitimate knowledge, alongside

> the intellect, as a more holistic epistemology; exploring whiteness and maleness as assumed power.
> - *Empathising:* understanding difference – locating the interface of unity and difference in a complexity of oppressions.
> - *Making critical connections with the bigger picture:* identifying emergent themes; framing the story within analytical/critical comment – historical, cultural, political, social; moving from the personal to the political.
> - *Action plan:* coming to new ways of knowing (epistemology) and determining action for new ways of being (ontology).
> - *Collective action for change:* moving from groups, to projects, to movements for change; developing alliances and networks that have a local/global potential.

This model encapsulates the ideology, theory and action of community development in a framework that moves from the deeply personal story through to collective action for change.

Beginning the process

Narratives of liberation are anchored in people's stories. In this sense, what stories we decide to tell, and the way in which we decide to tell them, form the basis of critical pedagogy (McLaren and Leonard, 1993). Stories bring our work to life in theory and action. In a process of becoming critical, they are told in informal chats on street corners, shared in dialogue in groups, analysed in more structured ways as experience develops, and in more collective ways as the process develops. Mae Shaw from the University of Edinburgh tells a story about participatory democracy in action that captures the top-down/bottom-up tensions in a society built on *participation* as tokenism. She warns of the dangers of reversing the process of critical autonomy (see pp 66-7), of destroying self-esteem if community development becomes uncritical and unreflexive, capturing these points in the story of June and Betty.

What's a stakeholder?

"June had been an activist for over 30 years – not that she would have called herself that. It was just that she tried to speak her mind when she thought something was wrong. The first time she got involved in 'community action' as she later came to know it, was when she had post-natal depression: an odd time to start doing something like that when she felt that she could barely get through the day. The local health visitor had got a few of them together – the PiNT group – so they could support each other. They were encouraged to talk about how they were feeling, something June had never had trouble with until she was expected to do it in the company of relative strangers. She went to the group mainly because there was a crèche available and she was so tired: Donna hadn't slept a full night for the past six months. The thing was, though, that once they all started talking it became dead obvious that, while some of them certainly had 'self-esteem issues' as the facilitator put it, their main problems were their houses, their incomes and their men.

"Once they got going, they also began to understand that neither self-help, counselling nor medication were going to change the things that needed to be changed. They were going to have to start using their frustration and anger as a weapon rather than a medical symptom. First, they got a petition going about dampness in their houses, they gathered evidence and took a deputation to the Housing Committee. This was quite nerve-wracking but also quite exciting and they were so impressive that the Committee was bowled over. It didn't take long to realise, however, that, despite all the nods of approval and promises of support, nothing had actually changed – nor was it going to. This was a bit of a setback. It's hard enough keeping enthusiasm going in a group when everybody has to contend with children and jobs as well. Nevertheless, once they got together to talk about it, they went from disappointment to resignation to resentment and then right back to anger. It always amazed them how ideas bounced around, got some shape and then, almost miraculously it sometimes seemed, out of all the muddle they suddenly had a practical strategy.

"One day a drama worker new to the area contacted the group – now called the Women's Action Group – to see if they would like to be involved in thinking about turning some of their experiences into a play. They weren't sure what this meant, but were happy to give it a go. For some reason they began talking about their children and from that they went on to their experiences of childbirth. As they talked, they began to identify things in common that they had just taken for granted at the time: the indignities of the enema and pubic shaving for a start. They laughed about it, but they also wondered why childbirth couldn't have been at least a more human experience if not a very pleasant one. The play was quite good and they began to tour it around community centres and have discussions with other women about their experiences too. At one of their events they even managed to get a couple of hospital consultants along as 'guest listeners'. They thought they were having a small but important effect on the medical establishment – and on encouraging other women to expect more for themselves when it came to childbirth.

"By this time they were getting quite well known and their numbers were growing. So, when the local hospital was threatened with closure, they were the first to get involved in a campaign to save it. They found that their drama experience had given them the skills to act out little sketches to make their point in a more entertaining and fun way. Other groups gradually joined in and an alliance of different groups against the closure was formed. Some of the women weren't too keen on that and didn't carry on, but several did and became quite prominent. June, for example, was always in the papers and even on the television once. The campaign kept going strong for a while but it petered out when it was clear that they weren't going to win. When she ranted on at home about how stupid it was to close a local hospital that was so necessary and so well used, June's husband would say 'Okay, now get off your high horse'. 'No', she'd say, 'I can see better from up here.'

"When the area was designated first as a priority treatment area, then as an area for special measures, positive discrimination, community empowerment and finally social partnership, June did her bit each time. She'd always believed that communities doing things for themselves was only half the story. Her dad had been a member of the Labour Party in the 1940s because he'd seen a generation lost one way or another to the War and thought that the government should provide decent services 'fit for heroes'. He had no doubt that if the state guaranteed decent public services, most people would respect them and he'd drummed this into June. She had never believed that the image of 'social security scroungers sponging off the state' was fair. In any case, stigmatising people didn't make them any better.

"She was quite positive first of all about the potential benefits to the area from the various participation programmes and started off representing the women's group. Her view was that it was better to be on the inside trying to change things than outside looking in with no influence. She managed to persuade the group of that when they questioned whether this was the best way for them to spend their limited time. As things developed, though, she saw less and less of them. She was now on various sub-committees and went on fact-finding trips here and there – even to Paris, once. She got to know people in other places – and they got to know her. She'd become quite confident about public speaking and was getting regular invitations to talk at meetings elsewhere and even at one or two big conferences. By now, she spent more time outside than in the area and was becoming aware that, despite her endless activity (which she quite enjoyed, actually) very little was changing. In fact the area seemed to be getting worse. Nevertheless, she tried not to scupper the new participation initiative that was just about to be launched because otherwise the area wouldn't be allocated the 'special targeted funding' as she was told in no uncertain terms when she suggested at the 'consultation' that the priorities in the area might be different to those of the council.

"On her way home from the consultation meeting, she met Betty who had been there too. Betty had been in the women's group as well and they'd remained friends when it folded a few years ago. In the meantime, Betty had got involved in an older people's reminiscence project – going to care homes in the area to record people's memories of past campaigns. This had stimulated a real interest in looking at how the area had changed and how much they'd all contributed to the change. They'd campaigned about everything and now they were worried that the services they'd fought for were under threat, as they'd been many times before. But this time there didn't seem to be any real local protest.

"Betty and June shared a complete faith in the benefits of the welfare state, although they didn't always like how it operated. For example, Betty was a bit more cynical than June about the way the community was always expected to participate – usually on 'their' terms. Nevertheless, she knew it was right that local people should have a chance to make their views known. There were certainly different groups in the area that wouldn't necessarily agree with each other but nevertheless they had to live together one way or another. That's what she always felt when she read newspaper stories that tried to create a kind of 'them and us' impression – the good community and the bad community, as if they were from different planets. She and June had just been talking about a neighbour of hers who'd had a recent break-in: 'the

> lad who did it was out of his head on drugs; turned out to be the son of Afsana who runs the Post Office. She's mortified. She's been trying to get him onto a programme for ages, but there are so few places available.' Both of them had teenage grandsons with no jobs and they were always worried about them getting into trouble, so they really sympathised. 'We'll need to do something!' they wearily agreed.
>
> "They had got to the shopping centre and were about to go opposite ways when it came up! June said, 'Did you get a letter from the new Community Engagement Agency last week?'
>
> 'No.'
>
> 'That's strange, it was sent to all stakeholders in the area.'
>
> 'What's a stakeholder?'"

A story such as this carries the seeds of critical analysis for further action on many different levels, and can be used to problematise the process in order to move forward with insight and understanding. The initial challenge for community workers is to make contact with people wherever they happen to be, in their homes, at the shops, in the pub, launderette or in already established groups. By identifying issues and interests that are relevant to people's everyday experience, coming together becomes less threatening. Community groups will contain all the raw emotions of life, but a culture of respect evolves out of mutual respect, and this is the setting where critical issues are explored, and where action is decided. Overcoming the apathy or anger generated by social exclusion is a crucial skill, and *relevance* is the key to this transition. The loss of self-esteem, which gives rise to apathy and anger, can be transformed into confidence and a sense of personal autonomy early on in the process if your practice is founded on the values that form the foundation of community development but it has to be maintained so that personal autonomy grows into collective autonomy, harnessing the dignity, hope and passion for change that community activists bring to the process. This is the basis of Freirean pedagogy, and more of this approach can be found in Chapter Five. As well as an evolving critical consciousness, community action can also be triggered by a shared crisis: a death, a suicide, an external threat to the community, all factors that unite people to act together. This in itself generates energy out of apathy and gives you the opportunity to bring people together from a critical perspective.

FOUR

Organising in the community

> Education, or the act of knowing as Freire calls it, is an ongoing research
> programme into aspects of people's experience and its relationship to
> wider social, economic and political factors. (Kirkwood, 1991, p 103)

An integrated praxis grows through the ongoing dynamic of research, critical
education and community action in symbiotic relation. It is a process of
conscientisation through *dialogue* (Freire, 1972).

Dominant ideology is absorbed into the very fabric of people's being, influencing
the way we see the world and engage with it, creating a false consciousness that
does not question reality. Community development practice emerges from a strong
value base founded on an ideology of equality; our trust in people, in turn, restores
people's faith in themselves. In order to be a critical practitioner, it is necessary to
be reflective and self-reflective, an inner and outer process of research. In the inner
process, we need to be reflexive: to question our reflections, and take them to a
deeper level. This is the way we challenge our own inner attitudes and prejudices.
In the outer process, we need to create critical spaces where we can engage with
others in building a body of knowledge that takes our collective understanding
to more complex analytic levels. Critical thought is discouraged in a world that
is founded on capitalism, one in which the interests of the powerful are served by
the subservience of the many. Herbert Marcuse, whose thinking was formed in
the 1950s and 1960s, identified structures of domination and social control that
produce an advanced state of conformity: 'Independence of thought, autonomy,
and the right to political opposition are being deprived of their basic critical
function in a society which seems increasingly capable of satisfying the needs of
the individuals through the way in which it is organized' (Marcuse, 1991, p 1).
Marcuse talks about false consciousness being the conceptual repression of
understanding life experience: 'a restriction of meaning' (1991, p 208). In this
chapter, I look at the process of critical consciousness in collective, public spaces
as the basis for organising in community.

Emancipatory action research (EAR) as the glue that binds critical praxis

Research is essential to the community development process. It develops
knowledge in action, and keeps it relevant to the changing political context.
But, the approach to research that we adopt has to fit the ideological base of
community development.

I am suggesting to you that emancipatory action research (EAR) is the glue that binds community development theory and practice as a unity of praxis, keeping it critical. By this, I mean that EAR is relevant to building theory in action and action from theory. Stephen Kemmis (2009) talks about a 'unitary praxis' as an approach to life in which we 'aim to live well by speaking and thinking well, and relating well to others and the world.... If we accept this view, then we might say that action research should aim not just at achieving knowledge of the world, but achieving a better world.' For EAR to work in this way there are some important issues to consider. Most importantly, in order to reach our transformative potential, we have to be critical at every stage of the process. First, EAR is a process of participation where all people involved come together as co-participants in action for social change. This, as you can see, involves dismantling power relations that are associated with traditional research in favour of a mutual, reciprocal inquiry of equals. For work of this calibre to develop, we need to create critical spaces for dialogue, involving all co-participants in co-creating knowledge for our times. These are counter-hegemonic critical spaces where power relationships are deconstructed according to our analyses of power in order to reconstruct democratic relations with new possibilities for a world that is fair and just. This concept of a democratic public space is a vital context for community development as a site for critical dialogue and participation in the process of participatory democracy (Habermas, 1989). Public space is place where not only people who identify with a group can participate and interact, even as strangers, but also the space where there is a connection between groups that provides the glue that binds a diversity of people together in community. Community centres have often served this function. But we need to identify new spaces, including the virtual spaces offered by social networking, in which we can engage with critique and dissent, identifying new truths, and developing the courage to 'tell unwelcome truths' in the wider world as part of our action (Kemmis, 2006). It is what Freire had in mind when he talked about denunciation and annunciation, critiquing what is, opens the space to transform the present into a better future. In these ways, EAR contextualises personal lives within the political, social and economic structures of our times (Kemmis, 2006). And, to have a sustainable impact on social change, it needs to extend beyond individuals and groups 'to build systemic pictures of what is going on, and systemic intervention strategies, developing multiple inquiries that engage whole systems in ongoing cycles of inquiry' (Burns, 2007, p 18).

For too long, I have talked about the divide between theory and practice in community development. It not only leads to inadequate practice, but also leaves us vulnerable to misappropriation. Inadequate practice in this sense refers to that which has no capacity for change based on social justice. I have often drawn on Rennie Johnston's concept of 'thoughtless action' (cited in Shaw, 2004) in relation to this. If our action is 'thoughtless', how can we claim to be contributing to the process of social justice? This is a bold commitment, and practice of this quality needs to be accountable, vigilant and analytic. In order to ensure a critical and systematic approach to practice for social justice, we need to develop a living praxis, one in which theory in action and action from theory are in symbiotic relation in our everyday work. This is what is meant by a unity of praxis in Gramscian theory, what Kemmis (2009) refers to as 'action that comes together and coheres in the context of a way of life'.

Community development is a cyclic process of action and reflection, both of which inform each other. Imagine the juxtaposition of epistemology and ontology, that is, the way we see our world, the way we make sense of it, directly relating to the way we act in the world. A wise approach to practice is to engage with curiosity and questioning, constantly asking what is going on, who is being affected and why. And in relation to our practice interventions, we similarly ask questions that help us to elicit evidence of change, that is, if we claim that our purpose is social justice and environmental sustainability, what evidence is there that we are making a difference? Having stated my position, I now want to look at what this means in relation to becoming more critical in everyday practice. The aim to create a 'better world' (Kemmis, 2009) seems to me to fit into our claims for principled practice based on social justice and environmental sustainability. It is a world in which with others our intention is to live a good life by relating well to others and the world – a life based on connection with people and planet as a life well lived.

Not only did the availability of Paulo Freire's seminal work *Pedagogy of the oppressed* (first published in English in the USA in 1970 and in the UK in 1972) have an immediate impact on community development, but Freire's thinking was also instrumental in the participatory action research movement, which challenged the controlling assumptions of traditional research and its role in reinforcing the dominant interests in society. The pioneering work of the new paradigm research movement came to fruition with the publication of *Human inquiry* (Reason and Rowan, 1981), bringing together an eclectic range of methods within an action research approach based on working with people in reciprocal, mutual relationships to co-create knowledge in cycles of action and reflection. In this sense, it is a liberatory practice in its own right that fits well with community development.

EAR is an approach that is overtly committed to social justice:

- grounded in an ideology of equality;
- adopting a methodology that is emancipatory, working *with* not *on* people, power is redistributed;
- using non-controlling methods, open to multiple ways of knowing, experience is explored beyond the written word through dialogue, story, music, drama, poetry, drawings and photographs in a search for multiple truths;
- action for change emerges from new knowledge.

This approach to research involves four interlinked stages in the process of transformational practice:

- critiquing the status quo
- identifying key sites of intervention
- creating new ways of making sense of the world (epistemology)
- creating new ways of being in the world (ontology).

This is an evolving praxis, a living process of co-creating knowledge in action and action as knowledge.

Co-creating knowledge

Based on the idea that 'every idea has an owner and that the owner's identity matters' (Hill Collins, 1990, p 218), we all become agents of knowledge, seeking truths that emerge from dialogue based on lived reality. Hill Collins notes that dialogue has its roots in cultures of an oral tradition and is the antithesis of western dichotomous thought which makes sense of life by creating power relations based on subject/object. She sees an African worldview as much more holistic in search of becoming more fully human with dialogue as central to that process. This links to the African concept of *ubuntu*, discussed in Chapter Five, to Belenky et al (1986) on dialogue as connectedness rather than separation, and also to bell hooks' comment on dialogue as talk between two subjects, rather than subject and object: 'It is a humanizing speech, one that challenges and resists domination' (hooks, 1989, p 1312).

EAR offers an approach to co-creating knowledge in the interests of everyone as a mutual and equal endeavour committed to a fair and just world. Within this approach, education and action, the investigation of social reality with critical consciousness, in cycles of action and reflection become 'prerequisites for participation' (Tandon, 2008, p 288).

Traditional approaches to research with human beings give power to the researcher as an external expert carrying out research *on* people rather than *with* people. One of the key concepts here is *cultural invasion*: the 'imposition of the values, belief systems, ideology, cultural norms and practices of an imperialist culture on those it has colonized and oppressed' (Southgate, 1981, p 53). It is ideological hypocrisy for community development to resort to research methods that are based on unequal, culturally invasive relationships.

One of the most formative contributions to my thinking was Rowan's 'Dialectical paradigm for research' (Rowan, 1981). In his attempt to synthesise old and new paradigm research, he analyses three concepts: *alienation, social change* and *the research cycle.* 'Alienation' refers to the treating of people as fragments, as a result of which they are not perceived as an essential part of a whole. In other words, studying the way people behave without relating it to the whole person, let alone their social and political context, is a dehumanising act. People function as whole beings within a context, and we need to understand the context in order to understand people. I am, therefore, suggesting that research that is taken on without critical, ethical analysis is likely to be incomplete, oppressive and alienating. It is likely to be based on assumptions that reinforce discrimination. If we are seeking a style of research that is compatible with anti-discriminatory ideology, we need to be sure that it contributes to the process of liberation from oppression. EAR involves everyone in the process of change, demanding 'that the investigator be as open to change as the "subjects" are encouraged to be – only they are now more like co-researchers than like conventional subjects' (Rowan, 1981, p 97). This is a model of research that is based on collective action, with all participants acting in the interests of the whole. It begins as a response to the experience of the oppressed and is a mutual, reciprocal process of discovery 'where the researcher and the researched both contribute to the expansion of the other's knowledge' (Opie, 1992, p 66).

The cycle model as a model of process

Rowan's research cycle model, which I have adapted in Figure 4.1, offers a clear diagrammatic structure for stages of the process of community development, taking an EAR approach that is central to critical praxis.

The cycle model is particularly useful in integrating reflection and action in the process of community development. Although it is possible to enter the cycle at any stage, for ease of explanation I will begin at *Being*, the stage at which we become aware of a need for change. Perhaps an issue has arisen that calls for new thinking. The cycle has an inner and outer flow. As we move into the stage of *Thinking*, the arc indicates an inward process of seeking. It is a collective

Figure 4.1: The cycle model

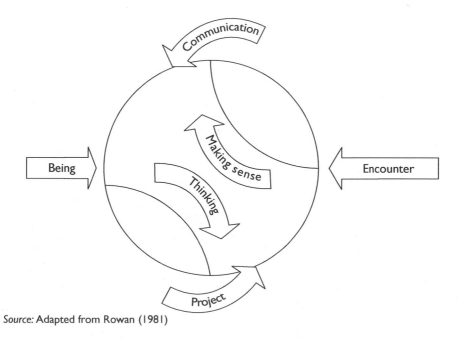

Source: Adapted from Rowan (1981)

process that gathers people together, sharing ideas and experience, and finding out relevant information. At some point, thinking is not enough and we need to move outwards to the stage of *Project*, involving others as the process moves on. At this stage, we formulate a plan of action, which moves from the contradiction of the existing situation towards new practice. Continuing the outer movement, we move towards *Encounter*, the stage at which we engage in action with the wider community. The model is flexible: it is possible to flow back and forth between stages, until we are satisfied with the relevance of our work. But there is a point at which action needs to move inwards from *Encounter* to a stage of *Making sense*. This is the stage at which 'experience turns into meaning and knowledge' (Rowan, 1981, p 100) and where a balance between achieving understandable simplicity and complex connections has to be reached. Following the arc outwards to the stage of *Communication* with new understanding emerging from practice, we are generating knowledge in action and need to share it so that others can learn from the experience. Community workers need to share experience by writing up projects for publication in books and journals; having dialogue with other communities; sharing ideas and experience at conferences and meetings; and using the media more effectively. In doing so, we contribute to an increasing body of community development knowledge.

At each point in the cycle I have adapted categories of questions that check the quality and validity of the process, helping it to become more rigorous and insightful, and also to check that we are doing what we claim to be doing. This is a collaborative process, and these questions should be decided on by all those involved:

(i) *Methodology and methods:* What is the approach to this research? How is information gathered? How does it fit with the value base of community development?

(ii) *Process questions:* Who has initiated the research? Who has defined the problem? Who is involved? How is the power and decision making shared?

(iii) *Power questions:* Is the social/political/economic context being taken into account? How is this research representative of the diversity of the community?

(iv) *Dialectical questions:* Is just one answer being sought? Is the situation being explored from more than one angle, based on multiple truths?

(v) *Legitimacy questions:* Is there pressure to avoid certain problems? Who is funding the research? Are there preconceived outcomes?

(vi) *Relevance questions:* How will this research benefit people? Will it benefit some people more than others? Is it relevant to the people who took part? How does it contribute to social and environmental justice? How does it address 'race', class, gender issues?

(influenced by Rowan, 1981; and Reason and Bradbury, 2001)

All too often community development is limited by failing to share theory and practice in a wider context. It is part of the '*doing* rather than *thinking*' syndrome that results in all too few projects contributing their experience to a larger body of knowledge. The result is that theory is impoverished, and, as a result, fails to develop the necessary analysis for practice to achieve its potential for transformative change. So, I am proposing that research is an integral and essential part of the process of change, and that EAR is the approach that is consonant with community development ideology. The cycle model structures our often chaotic and tangled process in clear, diagrammatic form, representing balance and directional flow. This does not mean to say that it denies any of the complexity of the process; quite the opposite. It is of great value in offering structures within which to contain and disentangle the knots. For the community worker, I feel it represents stages of the process in relation to the whole. It reminds busy workers that practice is only effective when it is part of a balanced process of reflection, action, inquiry and communication: 'seeing research as a set of phases can also help make clearer some of the problems facing community development in its work of developing alternative ways of doing research' (Graham and Jones, 1992, p 236).

The cycle does not remain isolated. It becomes part of multiple cycles in an interlocking model. These can be used sequentially to go deeper into an issue, producing a spiral, or they can be used concurrently so that the same issue is developed from diverse perspectives. An example of a spiral from my own practice would be the way that a group of women writers got involved in Hattersley Women for Change, which in turn developed Hattersley Women's Room. An example of a concurrent model would be the way that Keeping Hattersley Warm, a home insulation project, had sideways links with the precinct action group, the residents' association, and a gardening/allotments project, all of which focused on different aspects of improving the quality of the environment. When developed in conjunction with reflective questions, the cycle model becomes more rigorous, and at each stage we are reminded of the anti-discriminatory, reciprocal and empowering essence of this approach. 'By making each cycle fully rigorous in its own terms, we can achieve a recursive validity of a cumulative nature – yielding a deeper and more extensive truth than that given by a linear approach' (Rowan, 1981, p 105).

This collaborative approach to research sits well with community development practice and plays a key role in critical praxis by uniting theory and practice in emancipatory action. It calls for an ideological change of consciousness on the part of the researcher where the skills involve being fully present, to 'suspend thinking and to stay aware of your experience in the ever-flowing present' (Reason and Rowan, 1981, p 122). Rather than the claimed neutrality of the traditional researcher, the emancipatory action researcher is involved in the process as a co-researcher in partnership with the community. To be fully present is not as simple as it sounds. It requires the community worker to operate at critical and self-critical levels of awareness, otherwise 'all we are doing is opening ourselves to our most unthought-out prejudices and emotional reactions' (Rowan and Reason, 1981, p 123).

One of the most challenging concepts to emerge from this approach to research is that described by Heron as a state where there is full interpersonal reciprocity at each stage of the research action – where the researcher becomes co-subject and the subject becomes co-researcher in a truly Freirean way (Heron, 1981). This not only integrates the researcher in the process, letting go of any delusions of neutrality, but it also relinquishes power over the process and the product to achieve a more participatory experience in partnership with the community. Traditional research is epitomised by the researcher having full control and the subject having no control and often very little idea of the purpose: a model that can be invasive, exploitative and harmful. An emancipatory approach expects subjects to share control appropriately at every stage of the process, and for researchers to be participants in the research. Of course, there are many intermediate points where participants may be more involved in some stages of the research process than others. True endogenous research is that which is generated and conducted from within the culture by people who are of that culture according to their own knowledge and values (Maruyama, 1981, p 230). This, in its strict sense, is free from cultural invasion and hegemonic exploitation and is culturally 'pure' – a challenge to received academic wisdom.

The new paradigm researchers of the 1980s were profoundly influenced by Freirean pedagogy. An overt example is that of Randall and Southgate's approach to dialogical research using a *problematising* approach with community groups in a community centre (Randall and Southgate, 1981, p 349). The situation is a familiar one in community development: conflict was raging between groups who disagreed on the purpose of the centre, and they were, in turn, blaming the community workers. Using cartoons as codifications, they identified major contradictions that emerged in dialogue, depersonalising the anger and diverting the energy into forming new alliances. Emancipatory approaches to action research often start from a position of *problematising* or problem-posing – the Freirean approach to identifying an issue, which also questions the underlying causes. In developing a critical understanding of social problems and their structural causes, the possibilities for overcoming them become part of the whole. It calls for *dialogue*: a horizontal interaction between researchers and those with whom the research is conducted, embracing both action and reflection. In other words, it is committed not to abstract external knowledge, but to active, democratic participation in the process of change.

In these ways, the work of Reason, Rowan, Heron, Kemmis and others incorporated Freire's thought into a new paradigm for research. This is vital for community development inasmuch as: (i) it makes a clear break with alienating methods based on scientific research; (ii) it offers a method that moves us towards the wholeness that is necessary to heal alienating experience in everyday life; (iii) it offers a holism within which to contain the fragmentation of postmodern thought; (iv) it supports a critical pedagogy that is founded in collective action;

and (v) it offers a language and structure of research that 'yield a deeper and more extensive truth' (Rowan, 1981, p 105).

Reason defines three important, interrelated aspects of this paradigmatic shift: 'the move to participatory and holistic knowing; to critical subjectivity; and to knowledge in action' (Reason, 1988, p 10).

(i)   *Participatory and holistic knowing* is achieved through a critical engagement in and with the world.

(ii) *Critical subjectivity* is the synthesis of naive inquiry (a knowing based on feelings, emotions and experience) and scientific inquiry, bridging the subjective/objective divide to provide an approach to human inquiry that is objectively subjective. This offers a range of possible styles, from heuristic research, 'a process of internal search through which one discovers the nature and meaning of experience and develops methods and procedures for further investigation and analysis' (Moustakas, 1990, p 9) to Heron's form of cooperative inquiry, which is based on different kinds of knowledge: *experiential* (direct encounter with people, places or things); *practical* (how to do something); *propositional* (theoretical knowledge about something); and *presentational* (symbolising the knowing that we cannot put into words in movement, sound, colour, shape, line, poetry, drama and story) (Reason, 1994d, p 42).

(iii) Finally, *knowledge in action* is used by Reason as the term to denote a transcending of the chasm between intellect and experience in which western consciousness has placed value on 'thinkers' at the expense of 'doers', dividing theory from practice. Knowledge in action is, therefore, engaged in the world rather than alienated from it.

> I have been much persuaded over recent months by the image that the purpose of human inquiry is not so much the search for truth but to heal, and above all to heal the alienation, the split that characterizes modern experience....
>
> To heal means to make whole: we can only understand our world as a whole if we are part of it; as soon as we attempt to stand outside, we divide and separate. In contrast, making whole necessarily implies participation: one characteristic of a participative world-view is that the individual person is restored to the circle of community and the human community to the context of the wider natural world. To make whole also means to make holy; another characteristic of a participatory world-view is that meaning and mystery are restored to human experience, so that the world is once again experienced as a sacred place. (Reason, 1994d, p 10)

Schuler's core values of the new community

In practice, I found my adaptation of Rowan's cycle model useful in the way that it focused my mind on important stages of the community development process, and helped me to see the complementary connections between different projects. I am introducing Schuler's core values model because it helped me to understand the need to pay attention to the balance of needs in the process of community development. The core values model (Schuler, 1996) does not come from a Freirean perspective, but complements the cycle model by reminding us that projects in the process of change should not be fragmented from an organic whole. Schuler sees a community as a system that he likens to a human body, each part dependent on the rest for a healthy, fully functioning whole. If one aspect is developed without attention to the rest, the whole will not flourish. If these ideas are applied to regeneration projects that focus on economic developments in community without paying attention to well-being or culture or education, it becomes apparent that the overall process will be weakened. This is similar to understanding that life on earth is an ecosystem, which can be related to human diversity and biodiversity. In other words, if the human world and the natural

Figure 4.2: Core values of the new community

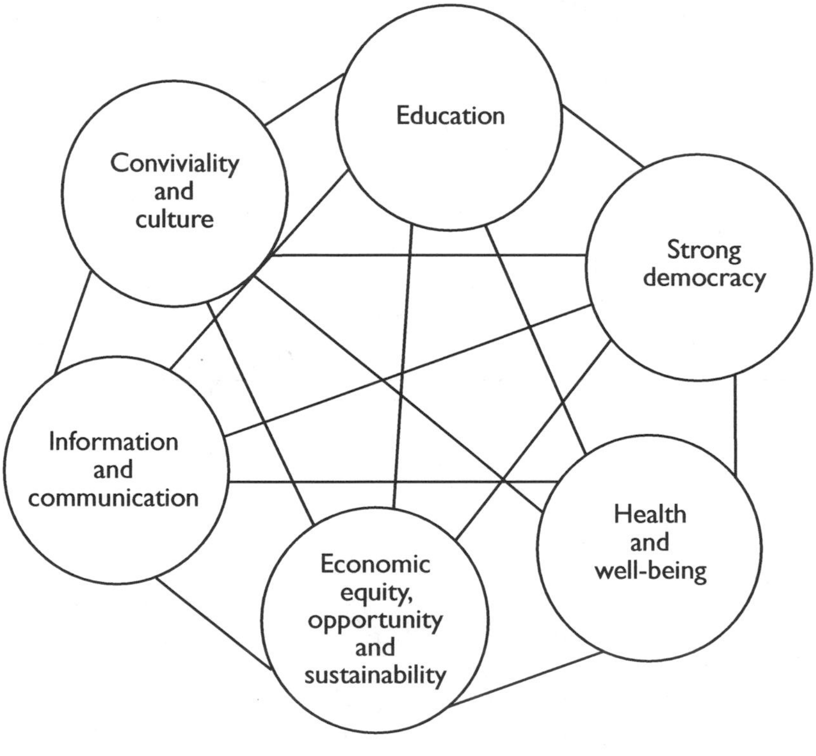

Source: Schuler (1996)

world are to co-exist as a healthy functioning system, we need to pay attention to all its component parts.

The model captures the interrelatedness of the system, and makes it easy to see how under-functioning in one area impacts on the whole. It moves us nearer to a model that demonstrates the interlinked nature of human needs for healthy, thriving communities. I think it is still useful as a systemic representation of the interrelatedness of community needs, but models are essentially outline representations of complex forces and we need to critique them in order to make sure we are not missing anything. For instance, does this model come from a dominant White, male perspective? Does it sufficiently encompass analyses of difference and diversity? Does it pay sufficient attention to environmental sustainability? In focusing on an asset-based approach, does it obscure structural inequalities, in much the same way as we can critique asset-based community development as a movement built on denying discrimination? We need to constantly critique what we use and develop it according to our experience and understanding.

Achieving better community development (ABCD)

The Scottish Community Development Centre (SCDC), with support from government departments across the UK and Ireland, was commissioned to

Figure 4.3: The ABCD model

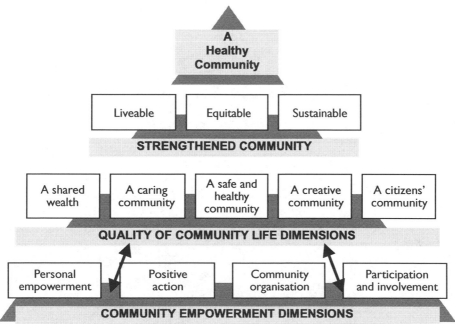

Source: Barr and Hashagen (2000)

develop a core set of indicators for the evaluation of community development. The result is the ABCD framework shown in Figure 4.3 (Barr and Hashagen, 2000) based on the notion that communities should be healthy, thriving places where people flourish in a more satisfying, equitable and sustainable way. The general aim is to encourage local people as well as funders, policy makers, managers and practitioners to be clear about what they are trying to do, how to achieve it and how to embed evaluation into the process as change is effected at policy, programme and project levels. Barr and Hashagen (2000, p 17) argue that 'evaluation is the key to effective practice, and that it should be conducted in accordance with the values and principles of community development'.

This model, a pyramid of outcomes, is a core idea in ABCD. It is founded on community empowerment with its four dimensions:

(i)   *personal empowerment:* individual learning, knowledge, confidence and skills;
(ii) *positive action:* work related to poverty, health, 'race', gender, 'dis'ability and other aspects of discrimination that challenge dominant power structures;
(iii) *community organisation:* the range, quality and effectiveness of community groups, their relations with each other and the wider world;
(iv) *participation and involvement:* by which changes in community life are achieved.

The outcomes from these are related to: (i) learning; (ii) justice; (iii) action and organisation; and (iv) power.

The empowerment dimensions interact with quality of life dimensions, as indicated by the arrows on the model. Quality of life dimensions are the context for change that involves central and local government agencies, and others responsible for policy, management and service delivery in social, economic and environmental areas. The outcomes from this stage of the process are linked to:

(i)   shared wealth
(ii) a caring community
(iii) a safe and healthy community
(iv) a creative community
(v) a citizens' community

and build towards a stronger and healthy community with liveability, sustainability and equitability outcomes. This model has made a significant impact on planning and evaluation in community development, but without critique it can be used in limiting ways to contain community development by failing to analyse wider structural forces of discrimination. Models such as ABCD have an important contribution to make so long as we remember to set them vigilantly and uncompromisingly within the dimensions of critical consciousness, social justice and environmental sustainability, local/global collective action and theoretical analyses of power.

Similarly, the Learning Evaluation and Planning (LEAP) framework, developed by the SCDC, is designed to improve quality of community life. It uses a five-step planning and evaluation cycle that focuses on outcomes rather than outputs, with outcome indicators agreed in advance for use with a wide range of participants, highlighting learning that comes from working together for change at project, programme and policy level.

The trigger questions demand reflection and dialogue from the outset:

- What is the problem/issue?
- Who is this a problem for? (the community? local agencies? policy makers?)
- Who has a stake in the problem?
- Who cares if it is resolved or not?
- What do we know about the problem?
- What experience do we have?
- What does existing research and experience say?

My critique, once again, is that when many stakeholders with competing interests are involved, more than ever an analysis of need includes an analysis of power in relation to social justice and sustainability from a bigger picture perspective. Without this, I fail to see how our practice can be anything more than ameliorative.

Organising within community

In the radical community development of the 1970s and 1980s, Freirean pedagogy influenced those who sought a critical approach that located local community action within a wider social and economic analysis (Lovett, 1982; Lovett et al, 1983). Feminism's insight into the personal as political had brought new perspectives to work with women and children in community (Taylor, 1995). The CDP's challenge to ideologies of poverty as pathology reinforced these views, calling for alliances that were capable of taking on the might of the state. As a response, alliances began to stretch outwards across community and regional boundaries. This process was supported by radical left-wing local governments in the 1980s, who developed policies of participation and empowerment, investing large budgets in both establishing community work teams, and establishing neighbourhood centres where local service provision could be located in the heart of communities. Added to this was the way in which metropolitan counties, formed in the major conurbations, strengthened participatory democracy. Out of this context came the community forum movement, connecting communities in their struggle against poverty. For many, inspiration had come from Saul Alinsky's model of People's Organizations, although the Alinsky model was independently funded, whereas the community forum movement was largely supported by socialist local governments.

The roots of community associations lie in educational settlements such as Toynbee Hall, Oxford House, Friends' House and the Working Men's College, which were based on principles of democracy and participation in relation to the needs of local people. The community forum movement gained strength in the 1980s when it was adopted as a strategy for decentralisation by most left-wing local governments in the struggle against Thatcherism. It strengthened the position that local government was beginning to hold as the 'main focus of opposition to the Conservative government after 1979' (Khan, 1989a). Khan's research into the functioning of forums in Sheffield and Islington led him to form three major conclusions for the limited success that this strategy achieved: (i) lack of political will; (ii) inflexibility in the operation of forums; and (iii) inaccessibility for representatives from those groups that are most marginalised. Interestingly, Khan observed that, whereas the Islington policy on forums heralded a new type of local socialism that was both 'bold and radical, the actual powers that were to be devolved to forums were minimal' (Khan, 1989a, p 1).

The community forum's function is:

- to bring individuals from the community together
- to provide an umbrella organisation for community activism
- to provide a platform for debate and action
- to provide critical education for democratic practice
- to act as a pressure group for improved service delivery
- to organise leisure and cultural activities
- to manage the community centre
- to provide a collective voice for the community.

In this way, the forum becomes the fulcrum of change in community. It offers a structure for organisation, where groups and projects become cross-germinating and more collective, and where networks and alliances are formed. It is a place where the conflicting interests of the community are expressed, and where the interests of the people are protected by participatory, democratic decision making. This is a public space with the potential for critical reflection and collective action, and for the deepening of consciousness.

In the early days, Hattersley Forum often erupted into conflict between those seeking personal power, while those who dared to challenge were personally and vindictively attacked. The rest were silenced, uncomfortable and embarrassed. Freire and Gramsci gave me a political analysis of what would have otherwise felt like a damaging personal experience at times.

The forum meeting was held once a month, and every resident had a democratic voting right. Working together with Hattersley Forum Executive during the early period, our aim was to develop greater democratic participation. We:

- changed the physical layout of the meeting, abandoning the top table and sitting 'in the round';
- welcomed people with refreshments and made the atmosphere more congenial;

- minimised the business side of the agenda and devoted more time to relevant issues and critical debate, often using a problem–posing approach with photographs, video, story and sometimes inviting people from outside communities, agencies or local government departments;
- held collaborative training and analysis days;
- made effective use of the local authority community development policy document as a focus for action;
- adopted a clause that community centre user group conditions require that representatives attended monthly forum meetings;
- developed a community newsletter giving information about community projects, issues and events to encourage wider participation;
- set up a community notice board, which posed local/global issues.

Gradually, the tension of the meetings transformed and the partnership between workers and the forum executive, meeting informally on a daily basis and formally on a weekly basis, went through a political metamorphosis.

The process of *conscientisation* at forum meetings continued as an inner process at the same time as networks were formed outwardly. We became part of wider anti–poverty campaigns and protests. In these ways, the forum provided a vital link between organising in community, collective consciousness and reaching beyond the boundaries of the community in collective action.

The community forum became a focal point in decentralisation policies adopted by many left–wing councils. Khan discusses this shift of power from the parliamentary party to local government as an attempt to relocate a political nexus, harnessing the left of the party with the combined energies of other disenfranchised pressure groups, such as women, minority ethnic groups, left–wing trade unionist and gay and lesbian groups (Khan, 1989b). It was received as a radical move and attracted attention because local government was seen as a site of resistance, with the community forum as the locus of struggle. It failed as a transformative, historical moment because the 'collective will' in which 'inner reasoning is worked out in the popular consciousness' (Gramsci, 1986, p 127) had not been achieved.

Saul Alinsky: People's Organizations

> It should always be remembered that a real organization of the people, one in which they completely believe and which they feel is definitely their own, must be rooted in the experiences of the people themselves. This is essential if the organization is to be built upon and founded upon the people. (Alinsky, 1969, p 78)

The Chicago of the 1930s, in the grips of the Depression and controlled by the Mafia, housed the Back-of-the-Yards neighbourhood, a concentration of extreme poverty set in a vast area of old stockyards. In 1938, Saul Alinsky was assigned to research the causes of 'juvenile delinquency' as a postgraduate student. As a participant observer, he entered the world of Al Capone, an experience that led him to believe that criminal behaviour was a symptom of poverty and powerlessness. He found he could not remain a detached observer. Growing up in Chicago's Jewish ghetto, together with his mother's maxim on not walking away from what is clearly wrong, led to a passionate belief that social justice could be achieved through democracy. His methods were not theoretically founded, but based on the premise that restoring dignity to poor communities by showing them how to organise would give them a power that could strategically outmanoeuvre the powerful. These were the methods he used to create a 'backyard revolution' that spread across cities in the USA (http://archive.itvs.org/democraticpromise/). His vision was an 'organisation of organisations' that embraced all groups: youth committees, small businesses, trades unions and the Catholic Church. On 14 July 1939, Alinsky, Joe Meegan (an organiser with links to the Catholic Church) and Bishop Sheil convened the first Back-of-the-Yards Council meeting, which was to prove a revolutionary step in democratic participation, organising and action.

Alinsky's People's Organizations were based on the use of power, action and justice to fight racism, poverty and isolation. Jacques Maritain saw him as an authentic revolutionary of modern times, describing him as 'an indomitable and dreaded organizer of "People's Organizations" and an anti-racist leader whose methods are as efficacious as they are unorthodox' (Maritain, quoted in Doering, 1994, p xiv). Alinsky's aim was the political education of powerless people to bring about their active participation in local politics. His strategy was based on inventive, creative, non-violent conflict and disruption as a way of identifying the collective power that poor people have to force corporations and authorities to change. His belief was that grassroots political activism should bring about the reform of powerful institutions. On 13 June 1972, Saul Alinsky collapsed and died following a heart attack. He was 63 years old. His colourful character had an impact on everyone who came into contact with him, and Doering described him as:

> ... a gruff, rough-hewn, agnostic Jew for whom religion of any kind held very little importance and just as little relation to the focus of his life's work: the struggle for economic and social justice. He loved crowds, the more unruly the better. His gestures and language were muscular and he used the vernacular of a tough street fighter. His habitual stance seemed one of calculated, aggressive and imaginative irreverence. Alinsky's primary tactic was to stir up nonviolent conflict. (Doering, 1994, p xv)

In his own words, Alinsky's tactic for overcoming apathy was 'to rub raw the resentment of the people of the community; fan the latent hostilities ... to the point of overt expression' (Alinsky, 1972, pp 116-17).

Alinsky and his organisers developed community activism in many cities across the USA. Bailey tells of some of the extreme reactions he evoked: banned from

Oakland, California by the city council; jailed in Kansas; a large corporation hired detectives to watch him; and the former editor of *The Christian Century* described him as developing a 'power structure dictatorship based on slum dwellers' (Bailey, 1974, p 1). He also had many admirers, one of whom was the Governor of Illinois, who said, 'If I were asked to choose a single agency which most admirably represented all that our democracy stands for, I would select the Back-of-the-Yards Council. All that you have done for the health, the social welfare, the economic advancement, and the happiness of the people in your community is to me one of the most heartening accomplishments of our time' (quoted in Bailey, 1974, p 1).

Saul Alinsky's impact has inspired community activism in the UK since the 1970s. Although he did not claim any strong theoretical base, his ideas are consonant with Freire: 'People only understand things in terms of their experience, which means you must get within their experience. Further, communication is a two-way process. If you try to get your ideas across to others without paying attention to what they have to say to you, you can forget about the whole thing' (Alinsky, 1972, p 81). So, let us take a closer look at what he had to say that may be of relevance to organising in community today.

According to Alinsky:

> A People's Organization is not a philanthropic plaything or a social service's ameliorative gesture. It is a deep, hard-driving force, striking and cutting at the very roots of all the evils which beset the people. It recognizes the existence of the vicious circle in which most human beings are caught, and strives viciously to break this circle. It thinks in terms of social surgery and not cosmetic cover-ups. This is one of the reasons why a People's Organization will find that it has to fight its way along every foot of the road toward its destination – a people's world. (Alinsky, 1969, p 133)

We can detect in Alinsky's words an analysis: transformative change needs to target causes not symptoms, and be not ameliorative but radical in its intention. Despite his military terminology, his model for change was based on non-violence, and his recipe for success was based in equal proportions on a formula of *agitate, antagonise, educate* and *organise*.

People's Organizations were carefully structured. One large community organisation comprised representatives from other groups in the community. In this sense, membership was not open to individuals, but to the representatives of community groups – any officially organised group or business that had a minimum of 10 members or employees. Smaller groups could become cooperating agencies with most of the rights of member groups. The fundamental democratic principle was that the community organisation must be open to any community group which wanted to join. The member groups sent delegates to an annual community congress, usually a one-day event, at which officers for the coming year were elected and resolutions passed. The senate, comprising delegates from each member group and elected officers, met monthly and appointed chairs for the standing committees, each of which tackled a different community issue throughout the year.

Bailey's (1974) research suggested that People's Organizations were more likely to be effective where (i) the local churches were involved and had the resources to support action and (ii) residents had the resources for effective participation. There are four key features that Bailey identifies as prerequisites to the success of these organisations: (i) independent funds; (ii) the hire of professional outside organisers with experience and knowledge of protest tactics and organisation building; (iii) grassroots networks for immediate mobilisation; and (iv) the use of protest with the emphasis on disruption. As with Freirean pedagogy, Alinsky's ideas are based on personal empowerment leading to collective change. Confidence, self-esteem and personal power provide community activists with a sense of autonomy and a cause, giving them a greater stake in the community and society at large. This thinking was at the heart of Alinsky's methods of organising in community.

Horwitt (1997) considers Alinsky's ideas more important now than ever:

> In the 1940s, Alinsky organized the basic model in 'the Jungle', the old Chicago stockyards neighborhood made famous in Upton Sinclair's classic muckraking work. There, he recruited and guided indigenous leaders who identified common interests that brought together previously hostile ethnic groups of Serbs and Croatians, Czechs and Slovaks, Poles and Lithuanians into a large organization, the Back-of-the-Yards Neighborhood Council. The Council, like the handful of other large-scale organizations Alinsky organized in predominately black communities in the late 50s and 60s, was in part a pressure group, demanding and negotiating with public and private sector institutions on bread and butter issues like better schools and more jobs, and in part a self-help operation that established credit unions, built or rehabbed housing and provided social services. As important as these functions were, the greater significance of Alinsky's voluntary community organizations is that they provided a connection between the individual and the larger society. This was what made Alinsky's experiment important, Daniel Bell wrote in 1945, in his review of Alinsky's book, *Reveille for Radicals*, because it 'attempts to give people a sense of participation and belonging [and] becomes important as a weapon against cynicism and despair'.

Today, Alinsky's impact is still evident. 'Citizen activists' still use the same strategies for change in urban neighbourhoods across the USA.

Alinsky, known as the father of democratic radicalism, founded the Industrial Areas Foundation in 1940, and it is still effective today, with 60 organisations in over 50 cities moving towards the vision Alinsky had of a large network of People's Organizations that would provide ordinary people with the power to shape their lives and communities ('The democratic promise: Saul Alinsky and his legacy', available at http://archive.itvs.org/democraticpromise/).

This chapter has considered the importance of a highly rigorous approach to community development where EAR plays a key role in praxis binding theory and practice into a unity, and where models are developed to structure stages of the process. Community development reaches from the individual to the group, and from the group to a more coherent structure that embraces a collective consciousness and action across the wider community. A community organisation that facilitates this collective process plays a key role within communities. The next stage of the process is reaching beyond community, from local to global.

FIVE

Collective action for change

> When we turn from reflection to action, what happens is not that our minds become blank while our bodies exercise themselves. It is simply that the conscious intention which characterises us as human beings is shifted to the outside world. Whereas in reflection we are engaged quite literally in changing our minds, *in action we are engaged in changing the world*. (Macmurray, 1996, p 76; emphasis added)

It is a vital aspect of the community development process that we are eternally conscious of the centrality of action and reflection, and the continuum between the personal and political, between the individual and the collective, at levels from local to global:

> Any group committed to radical social change must always take into account, and keep in balance, four different levels of need in their work:
>
> 1 the individual person
> 2 the small face-to-face group
> 3 the institution (or the structures of society)
> 4 the wider society
>
> Without concern for all four of these levels, it is impossible to build a strong movement and if any one of them is neglected the whole movement will weaken and die. (Hope and Timmel, 1984, p 21)

Each stage must include an analysis of power and disempowerment, of difference and diversity.

I like the way that Hope and Timmel weave skills into the levels of development. It keeps our minds concentrated on the process as an integrated whole. The individual level is the foundation of our work. It is the level at which we anchor what we do in the lived realities of the people with whom we work, giving relevance to our work in their lives. Individual stories become collective narratives that express the hopes and fears, needs and strengths that are the basis of theory and practice. Personal empowerment through a process of *conscientisation* is the beginning stage of collective action for transformative change. Practice needs to be informed by concepts such as *identity* and *autonomy* (see my discussion of Doyal and Gough on pp 66-7), and to include such skills as listening and dialogue, which are related to an understanding of interpersonal power.

Community groups form the initial collective stage of the process where trust and cooperation create the context for reflection. It is a stage at which personal prejudice needs to be explored in order to reach a collective purpose. It is a place where *problematising* teaches people to question their reality, to open their minds to altered perspectives on life. This is the bedrock of collective, critical action. At this stage, a worker needs to understand group dynamics and group facilitation. Specific skills include communication, team building, conflict resolution, planning and evaluation, set within an ideology of equality.

The dominant ideology of the powerful in society gives rise to discrimination that becomes structurally embedded in its institutions. Any change that aims to be transformative has to target the root causes of injustice not just the symptoms, and this involves structural change. Marcuse (cited in Hope and Timmel, 1984, p 21) described the revolutionary task as 'the long march through the institutions' – schools, the family, trades unions, religious organisations, mass media and so on – and for this we need an analysis of the role these structures play in the process of domination/subordination, for which an understanding of Gramsci's concept of *hegemony* is vital (this can be found in Chapter Six). Theories and concepts that help to make sense of the cultural, economic, political and social forces that impact on community life are necessary tools for the community worker. These analyses are the basis of collective action that extends beyond community to reach from local to global, and it is this level of organising that is my focus here.

This chapter moves into a consideration of structural sources of oppression and discrimination, demonstrating the need for collective action that reaches beyond the boundaries of community into the wider political context in a more strategic form.

Critical pedagogy

> Critical pedagogy has failed to articulate a vision for self-empowerment and social transformation; consequently, the term 'critical pedagogy' needs to have its meaning specified in more precise terms. (McLaren, 1995, p 34)

Critical pedagogy involves questioning, naming, reflecting, analysing and collectively acting in the world. It is a form of education that liberates rather than controls, in which relations are reciprocal rather than dominant, and where the humility of the educator enables a co-teacher/co-learner relationship to flourish. Critical pedagogy is a democratic process of education that takes place in community groups and forms the basis of transformation. It is founded on *conscientisation*, the process of becoming critically aware of the structural forces of power that shape our lives, and leads to action for change. *Dialogue* focuses on the stories of the people, and in *problematising* personal/local issues, exposes socially constructed identities that have been silenced: 'in this respect, a postcolonial narratology encourages the oppressed to contest the stories fabricated for them by "outsiders" and to construct counterstories that give shape and direction to the practice of hope and the struggle for an emancipatory politics of everyday life. It is a pedagogy that attempts to exorcise from the social body the invading pathologies of racism, sexism, and class privilege' (McLaren, 1995, p 105).

In other words, the community worker is a popular educator who, in the process of dealing with everyday issues, poses questions that encourage people to see their world from a critical perspective, and in turn to pose their own questions. In so doing we:

> ... free ourselves from the dead weight of dominant corporate consumer narratives. We can do this by crossing cultural boundaries and negotiating new, hybrid identities. (McLaren, 1995, p 104)

In rediscovering our histories, we reconstruct our cultural identities and, in doing so, we create narratives of possibility for social transformation. In these ways, critical pedagogy, locating itself both within community and within larger contexts of global capitalism, enables people to identify other possibilities that are based on a more just, participatory democracy 'that promotes sustainable, people-centred development, equal opportunities and social justice' (Craig and Mayo, 1995, p 1). But for this to be effective, we need theoretical analyses that are capable of evolving in relation to specific contexts. Let us take a closer look at key Freirean concepts in this respect.

Key Freirean concepts

> The insistence that the oppressed engage in reflection on their concrete situation is not a call to armchair revolution. On the contrary, reflection – true reflection – leads to action. On the other hand, when the situation calls for action, that action will constitute an authentic praxis only if its consequences become the object of critical reflection.... Otherwise, action is pure activism. (Freire, 1972, p 41)

Freire achieves theoretical coherence because his work unites a philosophy of hope with a pedagogy of liberation. The basic belief underpinning this is that human beings are subjects, able to think and reflect for themselves, and in doing so transcend and recreate their world. This is set in juxtaposition to the dominant view of people as objects, unthinkingly and unquestioningly bound to their world in systems of power and control. Freire's quest was to identify a process of critical discovery through which oppressed people could free their minds and become aware that they hold the key to transformative change. Freire identified the way in which perceptions of powerlessness erode hope and create a *culture of silence*. In the struggle for freedom and justice, critical pedagogy aims to restore people's full human potential:

> This struggle is only possible because dehumanization, although a concrete historical fact, is *not* a given destiny but the result of an unjust order that engenders violence in the oppressors, which in turn dehumanizes the oppressed.... In order for this struggle to have meaning, the oppressed must not, in seeking to regain their humanity (which is a way to create it), become in turn oppressors of the oppressors, but rather restorers of the humanity of both. (Freire, 1972, p 21)

In order to examine the usefulness of such a vision to community workers, certain key concepts need to be understood. My intention here is to introduce these in a brief and coherent way.

Conscientisation is the process whereby people become aware of the political, socioeconomic and cultural contradictions that interact in a hegemonic way to diminish their lives. This awareness, which is based on critical insight, leads to collective action. The process of becoming critically aware is seen by Freire to have three levels. *Magical consciousness* refers to the level at which people are passive and unquestioning about the injustices in their lives. The harshness of their lives tends to be passively accepted, and explanations are often based on fatalism, such as suffering in the present is paying for past sins. *Naive consciousness* involves a degree of insight into the nature of individual problems, but does not connect these with structural discrimination. At this level of consciousness, people are likely to blame themselves, and say, for example, that they are not clever enough, or they should have worked harder, or studied better at school. This individualisation of problems lends itself to the hegemonic blaming of victims, which is so much part of the market economy ideology. *Critical consciousness* is the stage at which connections are made with the way in which the structures of society discriminate, reaching into people's being, shaping their lives in prejudiced ways. The process is rooted in critical reflection and collective struggle. Its antithesis is the *false consciousness* of fatalism or individualism, the way in which subordinate groups are persuaded to accept inequalities by being passive and pessimistic. 'Conscientization is the deepening of the coming of consciousness.' But Freire warns that 'not all coming to consciousness extends necessarily into conscientization'; without curiosity, critical reflection, rigour and humility it is not possible to reveal the 'truths hidden by ideologies' (Freire, 1993, p 109). The process may remain partial.

Freire stresses the political nature of education. It is not possible for education to be neutral. It is either *domesticating* or *liberating*. In its domesticating form, the *banking* approach is used. The educator is seen as powerful and all-knowing, pouring information into the unquestioning minds of learners, who are perceived as malleable and controllable *objects*. The educator is active and the learners passive. This is the traditional, hierarchical model of education, which transmits knowledge based on dominant interests in society. Knowledge is commodified and the inequalities in society reinforced. It is based on *cultural invasion*: the imposition of the values and beliefs of a dominant culture in a way that marginalises and silences in order to dominate. Educators who are committed to liberating people from oppression provide opportunities for marginalised groups of people to value their experience, history and culture in curious, creative and questioning ways, thereby restoring confidence and giving voice. This can be achieved by using *generative themes* in a *problematising* way. A *generative theme* is a relevant issue or concern about which people will feel passionate. This is captured from people's experience and presented to the group in a form that encourages them to see it critically. Originally Freire used line drawings, but equally photographs, drama, video, story, poetry and music are effective forms of *codification*, depending on their relevance to the group. The term *codification* simply means the medium that is used to capture the essence of everyday issues and to present them to the group. Taking an experience out of its context enables people to see it with fresh eyes, rather than from the taken-for-grantedness of everyday experience. The more relevant the theme, the more likely it is to generate the emotion that motivates action. To be effective, it must be *coded* in the language and culture of the people concerned, drawing on their experience and encouraging them to question. One outstanding example is the way in which the Brazilian colleague of Freire, Augusto Boal, developed Theatre of the Oppressed as a medium for *conscientisation*, influencing radical theatre on an international level (Boal, 1994, 2008; Schutzman and Cohen-Cruz, 1995). In Brazil, until his death on International Workers' Day, 1 May 2009, he was still involved in popular theatre as a vehicle for consciousness and a collective force for influencing national policy decisions. Boal's forum theatre is an interactive theatre form that begins in a specific lived experience of discrimination. This could be racism or violence or anything that has been a diminishing experience. The audience participates by discussing the performance, and this is facilitated by the Joker. When the play is restarted, a member of the audience known as a 'spect–actor' (Boal, 2008) freezes the scene and without dialogue, swaps with the protagonist to change the experience. 'The act of transforming is, in itself, transforming' (Boal, 2008, p xxi). This process of participation continues with other 'spect–actors' until it feels appropriate to debate the learning generated by these changes to the original experience. Geraldine Ling, Arts Director, tells a story about the power of Boal's work in action with The Lawnmowers, Independent Theatre Company, founded in 1986, based in Gateshead, North East England. The Lawnmowers is a 'theatre for change' company run by and for people with learning difficulties (www.thelawnmowers.co.uk).

The Lawnmowers: Boal in Gateshead

"At Lawnmowers we have been privileged to work and train with Augusto Boal using Theatre of the Oppressed (TO) methods. We have worked with other TO practitioners worldwide, and as a 'theatre for change' company we have used Boal's system to explore issues that affect the lives of learning disabled people. Using both Forum and Legislative Theatre since 1986, we have changed attitudes and influenced policies at local, national and international levels in a wide variety of ways. In recent years Lawnmowers' actors have been developing their skills as Jokers.

"As a frequent Joker, I witness the power of sharing harsh stories taken from individual or group experiences of everyday social realities and representing these as Forums. So when Lawnmowers present a story of a woman with learning difficulties really wanting a job which she is clearly able to do, the spect-actors can emphasise her disappointment and profound sadness when she is told, 'No, you haven't got the job'. It is a familiar story for people with learning difficulties. However qualified, there are many barriers in the workplace.

"In the scene, the protagonist is devastated, crushed, so do they want to change her story? Will they try? Of course, it resonates. Is it fair? Clearly not. Should she get the job? Is the unpleasant boss wrong? Why is he like that? Who wants to try and change his mind? Most of the people in the room at that moment want to get up there to use all their persuasive skills to change the story. What can we try? Everyone chats and many want to try out their ideas. Every possible alternative can be tested from challenging rejection with, 'Please let me have a trial' to strategies such as advocacy, phoning Citizens' Advice, legal action and campaigning.

"In changing the story, we open up new possibilities. Drawing from Boal's lifework has helped us develop ways to test out everyone's ideas within an engaging, interactive and utterly democratic theatre style."

A problem–posing approach, or *problematising*, whether using theatre, literacy or any other medium, is based on a horizontal model, that of equality between the *educator–learner* and the *learner–educator*. This co-learner relationship is the basis of *dialogue* and is fundamental to the process of liberation. It 'strives for the *emergence* of consciousness and *critical intervention* in reality' (Freire, 1972, p 54; emphasis in original) by placing educators and students together in a mutual educator–learner relationship. It is more than just a technique; it requires a belief and trust in the potential of people to be wise and thinking, with the capacity for *action and reflection*. It is a process that creates critical, inquiring and responsible citizens who 'carry both the seeds of radical change and the burden of oppression' (Popple, 1995, p 64). The role of the educator in critical pedagogy is to provide the context in which shared problems can be critically questioned and analysed. It is a mutual process founded on reciprocity and humility that gets beyond the power imbalance of the traditional teacher–student relationship. The roles of educator and learner become interchangeable because the educator is open to learning as much as teaching. This is the interface of praxis at which the knowledge and theory of the educator come together with the everyday experience of the people.

Let us be more specific. For instance, a group of people may come together motivated initially by the need for safer play facilities in the community. This community group would be termed a *culture circle* by Freire. A culture circle is a community group that, in dialogue, questions an issue that is important to them.

The community worker may choose to focus the group by providing overhead slides of the play areas that already exist. This would be termed a *codification*. The secret to success lies in using an appropriate form of codification that is capable of engaging the group in a way that expands consciousness. Everyday experience is too familiar to be questioned. Taking the reality and capturing it in another form enables people to begin the process of questioning. As questions are raised, the community worker responds with questions rather than answers, taking the questioning to a more critical level. Why? Where? How? Who? What? In whose interests? Why are those swings rusty and broken? Why are broken bottles lying around? Why is it so dangerous? Why is it open to the road? Successive questions probe deeper towards the source of the problem. It is a process that liberates the thinking of the group members as they become confident, analytic and creative in investigating the issue. They move towards a solution that is likely to be nearer to the root of the problem, and as they are active in the process of reflecting on the issue, they are more likely to engage in the action to tackle it. Of course, this process is not uniform; it develops at many different levels both within the group and within the lives of the individuals of that group. But, once the questioning has begun, it continues; like water flowing through a valve, it is propelled forwards. As Freire says, '*starting* with the "knowledge of experience had" in order to get beyond it is not *staying* in that knowledge' (Freire, 1995, p 70; emphasis in original).

When I was a student of David Alexander's at the University of Edinburgh, I had the great pleasure of meeting Gerri Kirkwood who came to talk about her pioneering work in setting up the Adult Learning Project (ALP), Freire in action in Gorgie-Dalry, Edinburgh, in 1979 (Kirkwood and Kirkwood, 1989). At this time, the political context was about to plunge into dramatic change with the rise of neoliberalism on a global scale, expressed through the Thatcher revolution in the UK. The ALP survived its first decade as the rhetoric of the welfare scrounger paved the way for the dismantling of the welfare state at the same time as unemployment escalated. As we witnessed a massive transference of wealth from the *poor* to the *rich*, and were told to tighten our belts, there would be a 'trickle-down effect', social divisions widened and Scottish feelings ran high. Despite Scotland returning no Conservative MPs to Parliament in 1992, it had nevertheless been governed from London by the Conservative government since 1979. Then, Margaret Thatcher had the audacity to test out her Poll Tax on the people of Scotland in 1989, and the riots that erupted as a consequence contributed to her political decline. The resentment in Scotland fuelled a growing movement to demand a Scottish Parliament, and the ALP was active in identifying a range of generative themes:

- power, control and democracy
- culture and identity
- democratic education
- women in Scotland
- land and environment.

This formed the basis of the 1989 ALP co-investigation which responded to popular protest to build a Freirean pedagogy of hope through cultural action and reflection. The Scottish Parliament was established in 1998. ALP continues its political and cultural relevance today, over 30 years on, run by the democratic body at its heart. It is part of a global network of Freire-based initiatives widening through the Paulo Freire Institutes and organisations that act as hubs for the ongoing development of Freire's work in the world: the UK, Ireland, Brazil, Canada, the USA, South Africa, Kolkata, Finland, Germany, Spain and Portugal, to date.

After being inspired by Gerri Kirkwood's account of the early stages of the ALP all those years ago, it was my great pleasure to meet Stan Reeves in Edinburgh recently and to hear all about the ALP as it is now, 30 years later. Here is an inspiring story that captures Freire in action in Scotland through the ALP from Gerri Kirkwood, Colin Kirkwood and Stan Reeves

Adult Learning Project

"Each group appoints a student co-ordinator who acts as a line of two-way communication between the group and the ALP Association. The Association, since the early 1990s, has hosted project-wide seminars, called *Gaitherins*, every year, which are both convivial social events and spawn new forms of learning such as international study visits and exchanges. The Association hosts huge ceilidh dances to raise funds, which enable the wider public to interact with ALP. Some of the learning programmes of this second phase have included opportunities to learn and practise traditional music, song and dance. By 1995 there were 300 students in 22 such classes, and, by 2002, 600 students were learning and playing the fiddle, accordion, tin whistle, pipes, guitar, mandolin, mouth organ, step and social dancing and singing. This programme of learning has generated as an action outcome, the *ALP Scots Music Group*, which is known throughout Scotland.

"A series of political studies programmes and actions have been developed under the banner of the *Democracy Group*. All of these originated in the study of themes of power, control and democracy, and were accompanied by a sense of new democratic possibilities opening up for the people of Scotland. A day-long *Gorgie-Dalry Constitutional Convention* was held, to workshop the principles of the *Claim of Right for Scotland*. Central to the day was the mass decoding of a national photographic exhibition co-ordinated by the ALP photo workshop drawing on images created by local photography groups across Scotland.

"The *Democracy Group* designed a participative public meeting structure and used it to open new possibilities of contestation to people engaging with issues like water privatisation, criminal justice, local government representation, and learning about struggles for democracy in South Africa and the Philippines. The work of the Democracy Group climaxed on the night of the 1997 General Election, which returned to power at UK level a Labour Government committed to establish a Scottish Parliament. Two years later in 1999, they celebrated the elections to the first Scottish Parliament since 1707.

"A key theme in the contemporary politics of Scotland is land ownership and access. ALP has been at the heart of learning and struggling to put an end to the feudal system of land ownership, through its programme *Learning the Land*. Also, the *History Workshop* has developed a dynamic and participative approach to teaching and learning history, using a structured conversation and thematic approach.

"A central theme of a series of learning programmes of the second phase has been the role of women in ALP, women in Scottish history and women in contemporary Scottish society. Among action outcomes were a series of publications celebrating women's contributions to society. Local women initiated action/learning groups including *Damned Rebel Bitches (Scots women's history)*, a *Women's Planning Group*, *ALP Women's Gaitherins*, the Edinburgh-wide *Women ENACT 2000* (ENACT stands for Education, Networking, Action, Culture and Training), and the first *Hidden Heroines* awards (Elsies, not Oscars!).

"Two other examples of ALP's recent work stand out as worthy of mention. One is the very successful and influential cross-cultural project, still flourishing, called *The Welcoming*. The aim here is to welcome to Dalry, to Edinburgh and to Scotland the many refugees from all over the world who have made their way to our country, offering shared words and shared meals, learning about the culture and political situation in their countries of origin, with translation to and from their native languages, English teaching and performance of music, song, poetry and dance from all the countries involved. The lived experience of all those involved is the starting place for all The Welcoming activities of orientation and dialogue. A highlight has been the recent performance by international pipers, drummers and singers of Hamish Henderson's international song of liberation and reconciliation, *The Freedom Come All Ye*. The other is the innovative literacy project aimed at working-class men linking literacy to the enjoyment and decoding of professional football, called *Glory and Dismay*. This project takes place in the stadium of Heart of Midlothian Football Club, involving such generative themes as the globalisation and gentrification of the game."

In these ways, the ALP continues the ongoing work of more than 30 years with current ALP workers Stan Reeves and John Player. Their work is developed as a partnership between local people and the ALP Association to deliver classes, projects and community development through critical popular education. The ALP is celebrated in Scotland and internationally as a prime example of the transformative potential of Freirean pedagogy when it is approached as an 'indivisible totality', as an 'integral whole' (Allman and Wallis, 1997, p 113; for further discussion of this point, see pp 108-9).

Dialogue and *praxis* lie at the heart of the process of humanisation. 'Only dialogue, which requires critical thinking, is also capable of generating critical thinking. Without dialogue there is no communication, and without communication there can be no true education' (Freire, 1972, p 65). Dialogue embodies the notions of human dignity and respect, encouraging people to relate to each other in ways that are mutual, reciprocal, trusting and cooperative. For Freire, this is an encounter to name the world and, as such, is a precondition for true humanisation.

It involves horizontal communication between equals who are mutually engaged in a process of critical inquiry. By listening to the *narratives* of the people and engaging in *dialogue*, the community worker is able to establish strong relationships based on an understanding of local culture; in turn, local people develop a sense of confidence and trust. The opposite of this is *cultural invasion*, or *anti-dialogue*, which involves the imposition of one's assumptions, values and perceptions of the world on others, silencing and disempowering. This is a form of dominance that permeates within and between cultures. *Banking education* is a vehicle for this oppression. It is education for domination and divides people from each other and from their culture.

Praxis is rooted in dialogue, which in turn is only possible when the humility of the community worker gives rise to trust in the capacity of people to transform the world on their own behalf. It refers to the dynamic between action and reflection, building theory in action; a critical approach to practice. In making sense of experience, theory informs action and action generates theory. Both become increasingly critical in nature because they emerge from the history and culture of the people, and place people in a fundamental role in the process of transformative change. Freire sees this as the only way of truly countering oppression. Dialogical relations are the essence of freedom and provide the critical link between Freire's theory and methods. 'No pedagogy which is truly liberating can remain distant from the oppressed by treating them as unfortunates.... The oppressed must be their own example in the struggle for their redemption. It would be a contradiction in terms if the oppressors not only defended but actually implemented a liberating education' (Freire, 1972, p 30).

It is characteristic of oppression that the oppressed turn against each other in acts of *horizontal violence*. This is the way in which divide and rule politics erode solidarity. Oppressed people themselves the victims of hierarchical power, turn against those who are working alongside them in the struggle for change:

> Almost always, during the initial stage of the struggle, the oppressed, instead of striving for liberation, tend themselves to become oppressors, or 'sub'-oppressors. The very structure of their thought has been conditioned by the contradictions of the concrete, existential situation by which they were shaped. (Freire, 1972, p 27)

In my experience, this is characteristic of community groups. The model of power and status in western society is one of experiencing 'success' on the back of someone else's 'failure'. It is based on arrogance rather than humility and lacks compassion and solidarity. When participation leads to new experiences of power in community, this can often result in a desire to possess it and to abuse it, according to the dominant model. This becomes an illusion of democratic power, because although it is located in community it is not representative of the community, and is destructive rather than liberating. This swing towards counter–oppression gradually stabilises if mutuality, respect, dignity and equality are maintained. The process of *conscientisation* becomes increasingly collective, and the oppressed cease striving to oppress the oppressors, but move towards restoring humanity for both:

> Only power that springs from the weakness of the oppressed will be sufficiently strong to free both. Any attempt to 'soften' the power of the oppressor in deference to the weakness of the oppressed almost always manifests itself in the form of false generosity; indeed, the attempt never goes beyond this. (Freire, 1972, p 21)

Similarly, Freire saw the relevance but also the pitfalls of those from the dominant class who join the oppressed in their struggle – Gramsci's *traditional intellectuals*. Although acting as a catalyst in the process of conscientisation, the status and superiority that come with the role can result in an inherent distrust in the capacity of the people to think and act for themselves. A lack of trust leads to acting *for* rather than *with* the people. 'They talk about the people, but they do not trust them; and trusting the people is the indispensable precondition for revolutionary change' (Freire, 1972, p 36).

Freirean pedagogy is profoundly radical. It is rooted in anti-colonial discourse and offers the basis for pedagogies of *difference*. Giroux argues that 'Freire is a border intellectual, whose allegiance has not been to a specific class and culture as in Gramsci's notion of the intellectual; instead, Freire's writings embody a mode of discursive struggle and opposition that not only challenges the oppressive machinery of the state but is also sympathetic to the formation of new cultural subjects and movements engaged in the struggle over the modernist values of freedom, equality and justice' (Giroux, 1993, pp 179-80). By crossing borders we can transgress cultural, theoretical and ideological boundaries, altering our perspectives and thus breaking our patterns of thought. However, if we cross borders as colonialists then we are likely to overlook the oppressive aspects of our being that we have inherited, and therefore fail to analyse situations of oppression. It is probable that we will be culturally invasive, believing that our way of seeing the world is the right way.

The need to struggle with complex ideas in dialogue is essential in making sense of our rapidly changing world. Theory has evolved in the light of postmodern and postcolonial challenges to thought, and a political context of globalisation has resulted in more complex oppressions within and between nations. In these ways, the issues of the world at large become issues for our communities. McLaren, based on dialogue with Freire, cites how 'Freire maintained that when presented with a difficult theoretical language, students always have the right to ask their teachers to translate their ideas. In responding to such a request, teachers have the obligation to strive to be simple, but never to be simplistic' (McLaren and Leonard, 1993, p 7). Complex ideas, in becoming 'simple but not simplistic', transcend the void between academy and community, to play a key role in developing critical praxis:

To be a critical, empowering educator is a choice to be what Henry Giroux has called a 'transformative intellectual'. Giroux's notion of 'civic courage' and a 'pedagogy of possibility' invite educators to become change-agents in school and society, for critical thought and action, for democracy, equality, ecology and peace, against domination, manipulation, and the waste of human and natural resources. (Shor, 1993, p 34)

Collective action: local to global

Critical pedagogy is a process that begins in personal empowerment and extends to critical, collective action, from local projects to movements for change. We cannot dip in and out of Freire in this process; his pedagogy is an 'indivisible totality based on assumptions and principles which are inter-related and coherent ... we cannot take hints from Freire or use bits of Freire; we must embrace the philosophy as an integral whole and attempt to apply it accordingly' (Allman and Wallis, 1997, p 113).

Collective organising in current times is faced with the resistance of a culture of individualism and a politics of consumerism. At the same time, the escalation of globalisation has complexified structures of exploitation under capitalism. Neoliberal globalisation is that form of western corporate capitalism that not only dominates the world economically, but also reproduces political, cultural, racial, gendered, sexual, ecological and epistemological hierarchies on a global scale. In other words, in the name of a free market economy, the same structures of oppression that exist under western capitalism are being reproduced on a complex global scale. 'Capitalism, imperialism, monoculturalism, patriarchy, white supremacism and the domination of biodiversity have coalesced under the current form of globalisation' to form a major threat to a just, equal and sustainable future (Fisher and Ponniah, 2003, p 11). This is precisely why the practice of community development, rooted as it is in anti-discriminatory analysis, cannot justify an approach to practice that focuses on the local and overlooks global dimensions of oppression. Unregulated markets, a free market economy and globalisation do nothing to protect the natural world and the most vulnerable people from the drive of capitalism to produce at lowest cost to maximise profit:

> As the globalization project unfolds, it exposes its bankruptcy at the philosophical, political, ecological and economic levels. The bankruptcy of the dominant world order is leading to social, ecological, political and economic non-sustainability, with societies, ecosystems, and economies disintegrating and breaking down.
>
> The philosophical and ethical bankruptcy of globalization was based on reducing every aspect of our lives to commodities and reducing our identities to merely that of consumers on the global market place. Our capacities as producers, our identity as members of communities,

our role as custodians of our natural and cultural heritage were all to disappear or be destroyed. Markets and consumerism expanded. Our capacity to give and share was to shrink. But the human spirit refuses to be subjugated by a world view based on the dispensability of our humanity. (Vandana Shiva, quoted in Fisher and Ponniah, 2003, p 1)

The collective action that prevailed from the late 1960s, through the 1980s and even into the early 1990s, gave expression to identity politics and saw the rise of the new social movements. Paradoxically, the poststructuralist critiques of class metanarratives generated at this time, which gave rise to a politics of difference, have conspired to create a difficult context for collective organising. In other words, the Marxist analysis that had been the basis of community development was challenged by feminists and postmodernists because it subsumed any other aspect of difference in the name of class. This challenge to class action as a sole form of collective organising has called for alliances across difference as a strategic alternative. In this respect, Fisher and Ponniah suggest that any counter–hegemony must tread that fine line of embracing a respect for difference at the same time as being able to create a common vision: 'If the global movements are to prosper, they have to produce a vision that allows them to maintain simultaneously both their convergence and their difference' (Fisher and Ponniah, 2003, p 13).

In relation to our developing theoretical analyses in the field of critical pedagogy, Hill et al (1999), Allman (1999, 2001) and McLaren et al (1999) present a unified backlash to postmodernism, arguing that it fragments our thinking and our action, blurring our understanding of the power of capitalism in global times. Paula Allman (1999), for example, draws attention to the complex ways that global capitalism simultaneously cleaves divisions of poverty and wealth within and between countries. Global capitalism uses individualism as a smokescreen for its necessary illusion of progress, giving legitimacy to this juxtaposition of extremes of wealth and poverty. She warns that those 'engaged in local struggle need to understand the global significance of what they do … otherwise victories won are used to defuse and depoliticize the significance of the local effort' (Allman, 1999, pp 5–6). If we fix our gaze on the local, we reinforce this exploitative system by celebrating small–scale successes that give the illusion of change, but fail to challenge the wider structures that perpetuate oppressions. Critical praxis is necessary for social transformation, and Freire and Gramsci in powerful combination offer insight into the role of education in politics, and politics in education: their potential is reduced if they are used partially or fragmented (Allman, 1988, 1999). Our praxis is grounded in local reality, but needs a global connection to the whole if our analysis is to lead to transformative change. Linked to this discussion, further theoretical arguments that centre round analyses of class and difference, and those that locate the interface of social justice and environmental justice, can be found in Chapter Eight.

The challenge for community development in the context of globalisation is to find theory and practice which work at local, regional, national and global levels, where we reject a single economic and social worldview for one which embraces a 'universalism of difference' (Fisher and Ponniah, 2003, p 284). At the same time, we need to build strategies for collective action which support moving beyond the local to wider possibilities for collective strength.

Alliances across difference

Community development faces two major sticking points that reduce its critical potential. One is a resistance to developing theory in practice; the other is reluctance to move beyond community to harness a greater collective force for change. Networks, campaigns and alliances offer structures to harness collective power outside community, but if these are to be successful we need to develop theory and skills that support working across difference. To illustrate my point, I will draw on research on alliances across difference undertaken with my late Black colleague Paula Asgill, which is explored in greater detail in other publications (Ledwith and Asgill, 1998, 2000, 2007).

There are widely held assumptions that women come together 'naturally' in action for social justice. Our experience told a different story. We realised that we could not recollect instances in all our years of practice where alliances between Black and White women were sustained over time, but we had many experiences of where they collapsed in rage or fear. In the course of our research, which engaged us in dialogue on our own practice as well as interviews with Black and White women activists, we concluded that clear strategies are needed for the development of sustainable alliances. *Critical alliance* depends on the personal autonomy of Black and White women to reach out to each other in confidence and respect, and this process begins in separate groups where critical consciousness emerges from reflection on shared experiences. Pride in who we are in the world, in our separate identities, leads to more equal alliances where issues of power have been addressed.

Black rage and White fear are the emotions that characterise the breakdown of alliances. Often White women assume the power to set the agenda and invite Black women to join them. Immediately, this creates a power imbalance in the relationship. Fine et al (1997) identify the importance of understanding Whiteness within an anti-discriminatory analysis, otherwise while we have a greater understanding of the nature of Black oppression, we remain ignorant of the insidious and unconscious ways in which White power works (see pp 178–82 for further discussion on this point). These realisations motivated us to approach Black women and White women across England who had experience of community activism, and 16 (eight Black and eight White) women joined us in this inquiry. In order to structure our thoughts, we developed a model based on stages that span from personal empowerment to collective action. To structure our thinking, we adapted Rowan's cycle model (see Chapter Four), which gave us a greater insight into the flow from the personal to the collective, and helped us to identify the importance of personal autonomy as a prerequisite for collective action.

There are five distinct stages in this process: (i) being, (ii) seeking, (iii) separateness, (iv) autonomy and (v) critical alliance.

Being is the stage at which we begin to question our experience. Our difference becomes apparent. We begin to recognise that our Blackness or Whiteness, or age, or sexuality, or class, or culture all interact in complex ways to shape our identity. Think about this in relation to Gramsci's concept of hegemony (Chapter Six), which helps us to understand the complex ways in which the structures of society filter into our minds and the power that these ideas have to construct our worldview. This awareness causes dissonance. We can no longer carry on with the old way of seeing ourselves; it pushes us into a stage of **seeking** new ways of seeing ourselves in relation to our world. Following this we identified a need for **separateness**, a withdrawal into relationships where we feel at ease with those who are similar so that we can share ideas and make sense of our personal experience: 'Every once in a while there is the need for people to ... bar the doors.... It gets too hard to stay out in society all the time.... You come together to see what you can do about shouldering up all your energies so that you and your kind can survive ... that space should be nurturing space where you sift out what people are saying about you and decide who you are' (Reagon, 1983, pp 357-8).

Autonomy is the stage at which we are able to name who we are, feel confident and proud of who we are, and gain a sense of personal empowerment. Our identity is strong enough not to fear dilution. This involves unlearning internalised oppression and internalised superiority (Pheterson, 1990).

The potential for **critical alliance** emerges from this personal *autonomy*, a clearer sense of who we are in the world. From greater confidence in our own identity, we have the humility and compassion needed to understand difference not as a division, but as a strength. This is the basis for joining together in sustainable alliances across difference in action for a more fair and just society.

The importance of emotion and experience as legitimate knowledge (refer to Weiler, 1994, 2001, discussed in Chapter Eight) is a theoretical link that is crucial to understanding the experience of Black rage and White fear and the way that they hinder alliances. Without this, we react with fight/flight behaviour that limits the sustainability of the collective process.

Our research as a whole supported the evidence that, despite popular beliefs in community development about women uniting across difference, there is little to prove that this is found in practice in any sustainable way. Our model provided useful ways in which to structure experience in community and offered possibilities for shifts in understanding. Sustainable critical alliance as a form of collective action offers an alternative to the unifying aspects of class solidarity, while retaining it as a major structural oppressive force, alongside patriarchy and racism. Clearly, there is a need for work on identity and autonomy in community development, despite the fact that this has largely fallen off the agenda. Our five defined stages – (i) being, (ii) seeking, (iii) separateness, (iv) autonomy and (v) critical alliance – offer a structure to community workers that helps to make sense of the staged development of work that needs to take place at a local level as the basis of collective action. Collective action starts with women organising in their locality around their common issues, and then moving outside neighbourhoods by allying with regional and national movements for change, which in turn have the capacity to connect on a global level. Our concern is that the potential for collective action is getting stuck all too often at group or project level in local contexts. We suggest that identity and autonomy are key to unblocking this potential at a time when globalisation calls for a strongly defined self within a cultural/political analysis that attends to difference and power.

Social movements and participatory democracy

Community development plays a key role in deepening democracy. Yet, over recent years, we have allowed ourselves to be persuaded to work to other agendas. Failing to be vigilant, we left the way open for the entrenchment of neoliberal's marketisation of the world as a way of life. When I say this, I have in mind the way that community development unwittingly colluded with dismantling the welfare state by engaging with policies that named social justice as 'improved service delivery', and so became persuaded to erode the rights of the most marginalised communities, eventually reaching a point where civil society has become colonised and held to ransom (Craig et al, 2011). To remain critical, it is vital to identify public spaces for creating critical dissent dialogue, what Angela Cornwall refers to as 'new democratic spaces' or 'participation spaces' which become 'sites of deliberative democracy' (Cornwall, 2007, p 203). These micro-level spaces are vital in the process of macro-level change, as without them the process remains specific, local and disconnected from the bigger political picture.

For Freire all practical projects engage people in critical dialogue, questioning the circumstances of everyday life. It is a process of conscientisation, of becoming critical. It involves dialogue, critique and dissent and this is vital to the deepening of democracy. In these times of unprecedented change we need to reclaim the right to be collective beings in a world that has become disconnected, and for this to happen the beginning of change is to think dialectically in order to bring about new possibilities for participatory democracy.

A helpful summary of the process of re-engagement with democracy emerged from the Learning for Democracy Group (2008) initiated by Mae Shaw, Ian Martin and Jim Crowther in Edinburgh.

Learning for democracy means:

1. Taking sides
Educational workers are not merely enablers or facilitators. The claim to neutrality can reinforce and legitimise existing power relations. Practitioners need to be clear about what they stand for – and against.

2. Acting in solidarity

Practitioners should proactively seek opportunities to engage in a critical and committed way with communities and social movements for progressive social change.

3. Taking risks

Critical and creative learning is necessarily unpredictable and open-ended. Exploring official problem definitions and challenging taken-for-granted ways of thinking can be a liberating process.

4. Developing political literacy

Politics needs to be made more educational and education made more political. Learning to analyse, argue, cooperate, and take action on issues that matter requires a systematic educational process.

5. Working at the grassroots

Democracy lives through ordinary people's actions; it does not depend on state sanction. Practitioners should be in everyday contact with people on their own ground and on their own terms.

6. Listening to dissenting voices

Activating democracy is a process of creating spaces in which different interests are expressed and voices heard. Dissent should be valued rather than suppressed.

7. Cultivating awkwardness

Democracy is not necessarily best served by the conformist citizen. This means that the educational task is to create situations in which people can confront their circumstances, reflect critically on their experience and take action.

8. Educating for social change

Collective action can bring about progressive change. Learning for democracy can contribute to this process by linking personal experience with wider political explanations and processes.

9. Exploring alternatives

Learning for democracy can provide people with the opportunity to see that the status quo is not inevitable – that 'another world is possible'.

10. Exposing the power of language
The words used to describe the world influence how people think and act. Learning for democracy involves exploring how language frames attitudes, beliefs and values.
(Learning for Democracy, 2008)

As local projects and community action grow in symbiotic relationship with changing understanding, aspirations and possibilities, collective action reaches beyond the boundaries of communities to change structures that discriminate and subordinate. The following example of national action on migrant rights in Ireland is an excellent illustration of community development's capacity to influence policy change.

Migrant Rights Centre: local to national campaign against discrimination against migrant workers

Collective action is vital for social transformation. If we stay local, we are failing to engage with the structures of oppression that create inequalities. One of the most impressive recent examples of moving from local to national levels of action that I have had the pleasure to come across is the Migrant Rights Centre Ireland (MRCI), Dublin, action on work permits for migrant workers. In a process that followed through from person to group, from group to project, from project to alliances, from alliances to campaigns, they successfully campaigned to change national policy on work permits in August 2009. Hilda Regaspi, Filipina activist and Helen Lowry, community worker with MRCI, tell the story of their campaign from two different perspectives.

Campaign for the Right to Change Employer

Helen's reflections as a community work practitioner

Why this campaign?
"In Ireland the current employment permit system binds a worker to one employer and is a leading factor in the exploitation of workers from outside the EU. It means migrant workers feel trapped with exploitative employers, face great difficulties securing a new employer if made redundant, can become undocumented in trying to change employer and for others means limited routes out of low paid work. MRCI's community work is 'consciously, actively and specifically focused on bringing about social change in favour of the most marginalised or excluded in society and enabling them to address the social, political and economic causes of this marginalisation' (Community Workers' Cooperative, 2004, p 8). Given the reality of the situation facing employment permit holders, and our commitment to social change, an effort at changing the employment permit system was inevitable. The 'how' of doing so as an organisation committed to community work meant starting with the critical participation

of those affected by the issues and working together collectively to bring about change that would benefit all migrant workers.

The community work process

Participation was initially enabled through the creation of a campaign core group made up of current or ex-work permit holders. This group of 12 individuals met regularly on Tuesday evenings (outside of daytime working hours to enable participation) throughout the year. Facilitated by community workers, participants shared their stories as permit holders in Ireland. A critical and collective analysis soon emerged out of this process, one which highlighted the way the system made workers feel powerless and oppressed and one which ultimately called for greater power to be bestowed on workers by allowing the right to freely change employer. The process started, to use Freire's words, in the 'lived reality of people' and through a process of empowerment resulted in members developing a critical and collective analysis in which to frame the problem and the skills necessary to campaign for change. As the campaign went national meetings were convened with workers around the country and an avenue for mass participation of migrant workers was created.

Building power and pushing a collective agenda for change

Migrant workers from around the country and campaign core group members engaged in collective actions for change throughout the campaign. Letter-writing campaigns to a targeted government minister, a sustained period of visiting local politicians on the matter, a national demonstration outside of the government department, a night in the Dáil meeting public representatives, and so on. These actions served to build worker power by engaging more migrant workers in the campaign, resulted in the emergence of leaders, the development of campaign skills and ultimately served to put pressure on those with the power to bring about change. However, the change being sought aspired to be transformational and, recognising the limitations of a community work organisation alone, we set about building alliances with employer groups, the trade union movement (which took a strong and supportive position on the campaign), onside political allies and other civil society organisations. The building of alliances was crucial in the movement from local to national and in pushing for change. The media was used to powerful effect by workers in the campaign to put across a message of justice and fairness for migrant workers in Ireland. This in itself was political in the context of a recession in Ireland that resulted in limited sympathy for the situation of non-EU migrant workers on work permits. We were clear throughout the campaign that changing the system for current or future generations of migrant workers was a key task but the process itself brought about change in terms of challenging the dominant discourse about migrant workers in Ireland.

Collective action was critical in this campaign, as a necessary and important engagement with power built upon a process of consciousness raising, in turn aiming to bring about transformational change for communities. Currently we are at the final stage in the campaign, and have options on the tables of our decision makers. An important stand has been taken by migrant workers in this country on the right to be heard, the right to be free from exploitation and access a decent standard of living. For more information on the campaign see www.mrci.ie"

Hilda's reflections as a migrant activist and campaign core group member

"I myself, as a migrant woman and a member of the core campaign group, often ask, why I am here? Reflecting on the campaign I had a role as spokesperson of the Domestic Workers' Action Group (DWAG). Many members of DWAG are victims of exploitation and experience first hand the lack of freedom to change employer as migrant women employed in the private home. Throughout the campaign I reminded myself that the most important thing is that I know the issues and understand what we are asking for. Every activist needs to examine themselves and ask what are the values that we believe in as part of this campaign? What do we believe in? The right to participation, the basic right to be free from exploitation and discrimination and the right to collectively push for change. I was reminded of the time I, too, was a work permit holder and how it affected me as a person. The message is more powerful because it comes from your heart, from your own experience and you are empowered to share it.

"Throughout the campaign, whether engaging with the media or lobbying politicians, employment permit holders came across as empowered, not just victims of the issues, but advocates of change. As a migrant woman living in this country, I found this exciting. This was about migrant workers leading the campaign and taking action. Migrant workers are often the ones blamed if the economy of the host country goes wrong, but during the campaign we met with TDs (members of the Dáil) and decision makers and we asked to be considered as stakeholders in this country.

"The core group of the campaign had done a lot of groundwork; studying the issues and how to get people involved, organising meetings and constantly building up a strong strategy for the campaign. It was important to develop our analysis and have a clear understanding about the ways in which this issue affected thousands of migrant workers in Ireland. The most important part of this campaign is the journey of participation for many migrant workers in Ireland. We targeted events where migrants were engaged and encouraged them to write to the minister in their own words saying how the current work permits affected them, and why they needed to be changed. We asked migrants workers to visit their TDs in their own constituency. We held a demonstration that gave work permit holders the power to let their voices be heard on the street. We did media interviews for the television, the radio, newspapers. We developed media skills, did training. We organised a press conference, and we met face to face with the minister. We have been going for 10 months and still the passion and energy is strong.

"The process of this campaign allows me to be a leader. Choosing such an issue that affects larger numbers brings strong solidarity between migrants, supporters and friends. The campaign for the right to change employer provided a road into collective action for many migrant workers leading them to become more politically active. The campaign calls for a shift in the balance of power between the employer and employee. I believe it contributes to migrant workers accessing their basic human rights and towards creating a more fair and just society for all."

The stories told by Helen and Hilda capture the many dimensions of collective action that moves outside community to tackle policy change on a national level in a strategic, systematic and effective way to target the sources of discrimination. Next, I have chosen a story of women's global action to illustrate the levels of organising that make a global alliance possible.

The Beijing Conference: an example of local/global action

Inspiration can be found in the Beijing Conference 1995 as a model of collective action with a local to global reach. At this United Nations (UN) intergovernmental conference, the NGO (non-governmental organisation) meeting runs in a parallel but independent way. This was the context where over 30,000 women came together in Beijing, most to represent their organisations, some as individuals, but all with a commitment to: (i) raise awareness of the violations of rights that affect women in very similar ways but in different cultural and political contexts, and (ii) form global alliances as forces for change. Many women had suffered persecution and harm trying to attend the conference, and the collective unity of women the world over was expressed in a banner that depicted women's everyday lives and our wish for peace, freedom and non-violence. The panels had been stitched by local and national groups, and were symbolically linked by the hands of the women as they snaked their demonstration for world peace and justice to the conference site (Page, 1997). The Women's Forum played a key role in evidencing women's common concerns across the globe. Women united across age, class, nationality, ethnicity, 'race', ability and sexuality to influence the outcome of the final recommendations of the Global Platform for Action. This document, which defines women's demands for justice, was signed by the governments of the 189 countries represented at the conference in commitment to following it through to implementation at national levels (Ledwith and Asgill, 2007).

The success of a global alliance is founded on grassroots organising. Many women who were involved in Beijing had been part of the NGO Forum of the Nairobi Third World Conference and were determined to bring about practical outcomes and strategies for implementation of the Platform for Action.

First, I want to trace the global developments and then look at the grassroots organisation. In Mexico City in 1975, the UN First World Conference on Women took place, and 1976–85 was declared the UN Decade for Women. In 1979, the UN adopted the Convention on the Elimination of All Forms of Discrimination Against Women (CEDAW). In 1980, the Second World Conference on Women emphasised education, employment and the role of women in development. The Third World Conference on Women in Nairobi in 1985 adopted the Forward-looking Strategies for the Advancement of Women Towards the Year 2000. Then, the World Conference on Human Rights in Vienna 1993 adopted the UN Declaration on the Elimination of Violence Against Women, which was received as a significant turning point in the development of the women's human rights movement.

Preparation for Beijing concentrated on campaigns to develop public awareness of human rights abuses against women. Success was based on strategies that linked grassroots activism through networks and alliances in a 'two or three year preparatory process of negotiation and consensus building to produce a programme of action, a declaration, and recommendations for implementation to demonstrate that "women's concerns" must be placed at the centre of economic, social and political agendas, and can no longer be considered in isolation' (Page, 1997, p vi).

Regional conferences were held in preparation for Beijing throughout 1994: in Indonesia for Asia and the Pacific, in Argentina for Latin America, in Austria for North America and Europe, in Jordan for Western Asia and in Senegal for Africa. Grassroots organisations were the bedrock for the regional organisation, which, in turn, sustained the process through to a global level. In the UK, women were active at local, national and international levels across difference, involving grassroots women in the preparatory process by raising awareness about the relevance of the Conference to campaigning work within the UK (Page, 1997).

The Platform for Action is reviewed on a five-yearly basis, and the first follow-up conference, Five Years on from Beijing, happened in New York in 2000. This strategy for change, supported by national governments, represents the interests of women around the world, identifying the specific ways in which globalisation impacts on women in different cultural contexts. Developments are monitored under: health, education, participation, stereotyping and lack of access to the media, the girl child (including harmful cultural practices), violence against women, trafficking in women and sexual and reproductive health. In addition, armed conflict and a commitment to non-discrimination on the basis of 'race', age, language, ethnicity, culture, religion or 'dis'ability, or due to being indigenous people, are also addressed (www.un.org/womenwatch/daw/beijing). For a more detailed account, see Ledwith and Asgill (2007).

For strategic organisation, effective and sustainable over time and space, community development needs to recognise the centrality of personal empowerment in the collective process. Critical pedagogy involves people coming together to explore their own identities across all aspects of *difference* in order to develop confidence and autonomy. This is an essential component of collective action. Local issues are taken on as group concerns and developed into local projects within communities. The sticking point seems to be the leap that takes our thinking and practice outside our neighbourhood to those levels that link with other communities and other countries. Local action is the basis of global action. But, as Alison Gilchrist (2004) stresses, it takes enormous confidence to join any collective activity, and we need to understand the importance of informal social networks in connecting people in community and sustaining people in collective political activity. By understanding the relevance of personal empowerment in the process of collective action, and by developing theories that challenge our thinking, the autonomy needed to reach out across difference in sustainable alliance is seen as a continuum in community development practice. In relation to action for democracy, I want to draw inspiration from the Bolivian social movement.

The Bolivian Social Movement: an example of participatory democracy in action

In 2003, grassroots social movements working for democratic change in Bolivia demanded the resignation of their neoliberal president, Gonzalo Sanchez de Lozada. He fled the country (Chaplin, 2010). In 2006, Evo Morales Ayma was ordained as Bolivia's first indigenous president. This is increasingly recognised as a historic moment for participatory democracy round the world, not just in Bolivia. As democracy in the West runs aground, we realise that we have much to learn from Latin America where the courage to embrace social action for change is more firmly part of their cultural heritage. Nicaragua, for instance, was an inspiration to social movements in the West during the 1980s, as it demonstrated a capacity to strengthen civil society in relation to the state. So, in current times, what can we learn from Bolivia?

Important to understand is the concept of the common good, a cultural characteristic of Andean societies, as Gonzalo Araoz has discussed with me. The Morales' government has brought the collective process of decision-making to the front of the political agenda in Bolivia. This is a model based on cooperation in which mutuality and reciprocity are central, but Gonzalo emphasises that even within indigenous communities there are tensions and contradictions, illuminated by the story told by Porfirio Garcia Canaviri presented on page 121. The notable development in recent political events, Gonzalo suggests, is that the Evo Morales government has given the most deprived and previously ignored sectors of society a voice.

Let us examine some of the key factors in this process. In 1985, neoliberalism became entrenched in Bolivian policy, fuelled by a world recession, in line with world trends (Thatcherism in the UK, Reaganomics in the US, Pinochet in Chile, for example). Previous Bolivian governments of Right and Left, even in the MIR (Movement of the Revolutionary Left), had not acted in the interests of the poorest in their country, and so the way was open for economic and political reforms that reduced state involvement in the economy and welfare, privatising and deregulating nationalised industries in favour of free market enterprise. Bolivia saw the closure of mines, forcing about 27,000 miners and their families to migrate. Poverty rose, with only 16 per cent of the population having their basic needs met. Sanchez de Lozada introduced 'popular participation' in 1994; a process not dissimilar to the 'Big Society'/small state proposed by the coalition government in the UK today. Decentralisation of the state relocated social responsibility to the local level. However, instead of weakening social organisation, this opened up critical public spaces in which indigenous groups and communities could come together to make decisions over the allocation of resources. From a position of extreme marginalisation, experience in local government led to the confidence for indigenous leadership to develop. Chaplin cites by way of example the story of Rene Joaquino, a tailor who became mayor of Potosi for three terms of office. 'In 2009, he stood as a candidate for the presidency' (Chaplin, 2010, p 350). You should note that the successes of such male indigenous leaders masks the absence of women's participation, but the Morales government now stipulates that 30 per cent of candidates should be women. Gradually, women are emerging as role models for girls in a counter-movement for female empowerment, and for this to happen, community development paves the way.

El Alto became the fulcrum of change in Bolivia. It is a city of almost a million people, mostly of *campesino* origin, with a strong tradition of community, together with mining families with a history of trades union organisation. The 2003 protest was against the government's decision to export the processing of the country's gas reserves, a decision that would benefit the Bolivian wealthy as well as foreign corporate interests. At the same time, micro-governments based on autonomous local democracy began to spring up, leading to the election of Evo Morales, an indigenous *campesino,* and his MAS (Movement for Socialism/*Movimiento al Socialismo*) party, a coalition of social movements: 'this was an unprecedented event which displaced the traditional elites from political power' (Chaplin, 2010, p 353). Policies were quickly implemented to increase taxes paid by petrol, gas and mining companies in a process of redistribution of wealth, particularly benefiting children, the elderly, pregnant women and their babies as well as channelling power to regional/local government and state universities. The Constitution was changed to recognise the rights of indigenous people, when 50 years previously indigenous people had not even been allowed in town squares.

> The government's social policy is based on the concept of 'living well', which is an idea rooted in local indigenous culture which seeks to ensure people have access to the means to life. It gives emphasis to relationships of solidarity with others and how to live in harmony with nature, rather than being better off than your neighbour. It resonates with the notion of 'quality of life'; 'living well' implies the covering of material needs, but also involves personal growth and empowerment. In the current global context where capitalist values and excessive consumption are being questioned, this idea rings true beyond Bolivia's borders, and it provides the basis for Bolivian involvement in international meetings on climate change. (Chaplin, 2010, p 353)

If we focus our gaze on the places where democracy is being made we can detect key themes in the process. For instance, a concept of 'living well' cannot be employed without an underlying current of community, of connection, of a collective good, and that collective good cannot be conceived without the good of the more-than-human world. It is a worldview based on harmony and balance, at variance with the values inherent in neoliberalism, those of competition, exploitation and individual gain that undermines the common good. Here, Gonzalo Araoz translates Porfirio Garcia Canaviri's story from Bolivia.

Discrimination between 'Village Indian' and 'Community Indian', Salinas de Garci Mendoza Municipality, Oruro, Bolivia

Case presented by Porfirio Garcia Canaviri (translated by Gonzalo Araoz)

"This is a story from the Salinas de Garci Mendoza Municipality, in the Department of Oruro in western Bolivia. Geographically the Municipality is divided in two related cultures, those living in the hills (*Serrania*) producing quinoa and regarding themselves as superior, and those living on the flatlands (*Pampa*) producing quinoa and raising llama herds, and seen as inferior.

"The reasons for this seem to date back to the Spanish colonial period, when towards the end of the 16th century mineral riches had an impact on the locals' self-esteem and their feelings of superiority in comparison with other ethnic groups in the region. They had rejected, for example, the creation of an indigenous school in Salinas (1930), arguing that they were not 'Indians' but 'civilised people'. This attitude was continued and reinforced by integration policies that encouraged the 'Indians' to become 'peasants' (1952), rejecting their own cultural values and their agricultural knowledge as synonymous with backwardness.

"Those residing in the hills are known as the 'plaza circle' and have always held local power, while the others were only approached when they needed to sign documents. Current laws that prioritise rights to political participation continued to close spaces of power to the flatlands settlers, calling them '*pampaqawra*' or flatlands llamas, even though they all belong to the same socio-cultural group.

"The first election of a local mayor and municipal council in the rural municipalities took place after the Popular Participation Law (1994), when candidates of the *Pampa* participated for the first time through the political party of the former vice-president of the country Victor Hugo Cardenas, which was 'representing indigenous peoples'. They achieved the election of two councillors, despite discrimination for being 'llama herders' from traditional political parties of Left and Right which expected to be represented by 'civilised' people (from the hills). This heralded an awakening of these communities. They started to be aware of their rights and confronted these discriminatory attitudes. This became part of wider indigenous movements for change that resulted in the victory of Evo Morales Ayma in the general elections. Now, these communities feel they are equal and belong to the rest of the indigenous population.

"This indigenous municipality is currently attempting to write an indigenous autonomic statute, but some surviving traditional leaders still hinder this work. The important issue is that, in contrast with the past, there has to be consensus on all political decisions, within all the socio-cultural groups that comprise the municipality."

Bolivia is an example of how social transformation can give rise to a movement that does not get assimilated into the state, but remains a movement fuelled by grassroots participation. In these ways, not only does dignity and belonging get integrated into community life, but power and control of society also creates a participatory autonomy. Bolivia, in 'politicising the social' has created a new form of politics – the MAS acts as a double feedback loop which constantly balances power by keeping national government connected with the social movement, facilitating ongoing participation (see Ledwith and Springett, 2009). This ensures that indigenous values based on a common good do not get diluted. Democratic power remains with the people rather than handed over to a political party or a leader. Evo Morales, within this model, is the voice of a movement with ongoing accountability (Chaplin, 2010).

In the UK we have dislocated the connection between community development and politics, and in doing so disconnected politics from the everyday lives of people. It is precisely because resources are allocated unjustly that the key to understanding injustice lies in everyday life – and it is the analytical awareness of this injustice that is the process of conscientisation. Therefore at the heart of action for change is the notion of politicisation, that through becoming critical we identify the contradictions: 'power asymmetries become visible which at the level of the state and everyday life, generate the exclusionary logics which doom millions to poverty, inequality and subjugation unless they act on them. Community development is deeply political, because for communities to "develop" they need to grasp these power logics and realize that they can be changed' (Pearce et al, 2010, p 270).

In places where East meets West, there are ideological battles to preserve more traditional cultures in the face of external forces wanting to exploit profit opportunities. One such interface is Easter Island, off the coast of Chile, which has become a popular tourist destination. Carolina Leonardini Aris talks about her first visit to establish a research project on HIV/AIDS and her engagement with other ways of seeing the world, an alternative worldview.

"People asked me if I was mad, planning to go to Easter Island with a 13-month-old toddler. 'What about your little daughter if she gets ill on an island where there is no proper medical treatment? How will you manage to travel and do your research with a breast-feeding baby? Who is going to host you with your little daughter?' Although I had my own concerns about the difficulties I might find, I started to realise how children are seen as a nuisance in many western societies, where they are often left at home with a baby sitter.

"Easter Island, territory of Chile since 1888, is the world's most isolated inhabited piece of land. Located in the South Pacific, where the mysterious huge stone statues called *Moais* stare in silent watch, it has become increasingly attractive to tourists.

"'You have good energy. We believe in your purposes, your aims are fair!' said Petero Edmunds, the Easter Islander mayor at that time, after giving me a welcoming hug. 'Family, our children, is the most important thing. We respect and uphold the clan, our ancestors and descendants, and we like people that understand and share the same values!' Petero indicated that the bottle of *noni* – a natural Tahitian immune system enhancer – that lay on his desk provided him daily energy and health to carry out his duties as indigenous leader. 'Good to know that you have children and they are important for you. I trust you understand how important the well-being of our people is. My responsibility here is to achieve the best for *Rapanui* people, especially for the new generations. The Chilean authorities and policy makers declare their interests are aligned with our local needs, but most of the time they fly in *first class* to eat a nice fresh tuna and have a drink on the beach. I think they get amnesia on the flight back to Chile and forget all that they have promised here!' complained the mayor.

"I understood his words and why Easter Islanders mistrust the external intrusion. While staying on the island I witnessed the sign of a Clean Production Agreement proposed by the Chilean government in order to reverse the environmental degradation. 'You come here and tell us how to be environmentally friendly … which our ancient culture has known for more than 1,500 years….The current contamination threat derives from the foreign arrival, with all their litter! I told the Coca Cola Company: "If you want to sell Coca Cola on Easter Island, you must develop a biodegradable bottle." But they haven't. So now we need this agreement to take the bottles and cans back to the [South American] Continent. It is not because *we* generate the problem, it's because *you* bring it and now we hope you help to resolve it!' said Petero Edmunds during the agreement signing ceremony.

"When I left the town hall, after interviewing the mayor, a car stopped and somebody shouted: 'Hey, I'll give you a lift! You need a pushchair for your baby! You can borrow my daughter's one! I'll leave it for you with my secretary so you can use it as long you are on the island!'

"The woman who was offering me and my daughter this friendly help was Carolina Hotu, Easter Island's governor. I had interviewed her the day before as the main authority of the island. She was happy to receive me in her official meeting room with my babe in arms, far from the notion of power that places 'normal' people so distant from the ones that make decisions."

Carolina's story illuminates the contradictions between two very different worldviews, with contrasting values that lead to opposing realities.

Ideological shift

This concept of 'living well', an indigenous understanding of human flourishing, is yearned for in the West. In this age of centre politics, Gary Craig (Craig et al, 2011) talks about there being no sign yet of an alternative political project to engage the popular imagination, but it seems to me that, after all the ideological buffeting of past decades which have shunted us firmly into an ideology of the market, there is an emergent epistemological turn based on what we might loosely term 'collective human well-being'. Within the project of participatory democracy, this has infinite possibilities. Long have I puzzled over the resistance to change within a capitalist system. This is because its fundamental ideology is rooted in the justification of profit and exploitation to benefit some at the expense of others. It seems to me that we have been trying to reform a system that is essentially corrupt. But, a new movement rooted in an ideology of cooperation, mutuality, reconnection, what I see as a horizontal worldview that embraces difference and diversity as essential dimensions to human flourishing provides an intervention at the level of human kindness to dismantle the top-down competitive ideology of neoliberalism. In 2007, the UNICEF report on childhood well-being in rich countries shockingly ranked the UK bottom of 21 in creating happy childhoods, and raised many questions in the process. Happiness, which I take to mean well-being, has become a preoccupation as more people have become unhappy, unfulfilled and emotionally stressed. Wilkinson and Pickett (2009, p 45) suggest that our quality of life is no longer dependent on further economic growth: it is about community and the way that we relate to each other. This teases out links with participatory democracy as an alternative worldview, one in which we are connected by a commitment to a common good. The UNICEF report of 2007 highlights the importance to children of being loved, valued and included in society. Layard and Dunn (2009) also emphasise this in their work on childhood, arguing that the tilt towards individualism has gone too far and what we require instead is a society based on the law of love.

And from this I detect a new understanding emerging that also finds voice in Richard Layard's work on happiness. He says that a society cannot flourish without some sense of shared purpose, that the self needs to be connected to something larger, a common good in which we pursue the greatest happiness for all (2005, p 234). Richard Layard is founder director of the Centre for Economic Performance at the London School of Economics and Political Science, and I was enchanted when I found myself, together with my son and granddaughter, in a tent at Hay Literary Festival in 2010 listening to his ideas on a happiness movement, a web-based movement that supports people to live different lives. The Movement for Happiness will be launched in 2011, and calls for us to change our culture, to reject competition for cooperation, and to create a mass movement with a global reach. The aim is to create a society in which all people can flourish, a world without the excessive inequalities that create unhappiness.

Freire talked of love as a love for all humanity: 'Love is an act of courage, not fear … a commitment to others … [and] to the cause of liberation' (1972, p 78). His belief was that the process of dialogue, so central to the transformative project, could not exist 'in the absence of a profound love for the world and for people' (1993, p 70). He talks about dialogue as not only the way to question the status quo, but also as an expression of our being: dialogue is nurtured by love, humility, hope, faith and mutual trust – then, and only then, can this result in true communication (Freire, 1972).

Revisiting Freire is useful here: more than a strategy, he offers 'a way of living, loving, and interpreting the world', and when we embrace his pedagogy as a whole we find that we undergo 'a profound transformation of ourselves as human beings in our work with others' (Darder, 2002, pp 205-7).

This notion of humility as a collective compassion linked to wisdom is also expressed by Kabat-Zinn (2005), who claims that growth that does not result in harmony for the greater whole destroys wholeness and balance – and is unsustainable. He calls on us to embody peace and liberty and justice for all by mobilising a collective will to bring about a transformation for wisdom as kindness. This leads my thinking to a recent encounter with Jack Whitehead at the Collaborative Action Research Network (CARN) Conference in 2010. Jack talked about Eden Charles' research into the transformational capacity of the African wisdom of *ubuntu* as a way of being in the world, a way of being fully human in interconnectedness with all humanity so that what each one of us is understood to affect the world. It is the antithesis of individualism. It encourages us to embrace difference rather than fear it. It is characterised by a loving and life-affirming energy which, in its respect for the humanity of the other, seeks to change power relations that are oppressive in the search for a common humanity that celebrates difference and diversity. Living *ubuntu* offers us the possibility to co-create 'a world order in which we can live in a state of wellness together to celebrate and contribute to the movement of humanity towards sustainable peace and justice locally, nationally and globally' (Charles, 2007). This is what Eden Charles calls 'living *ubuntu*'.

The concept of *ubuntu* may resonate with Steve Robson, who tells this story of his practice in Barrow-in-Furness.

Why do they keep coming back?

"I work in a 'one-stop shop' style office in the heart of the town centre which is closely interwoven with densely populated terraced housing, stretching a mile or so either side of the office. This is also in the heart of two electoral wards which are amongst the town, and county's, most disadvantaged areas, and often feature at the wrong end of national league tables in statistics on health, teenage pregnancy, worklessness, and so on.

"We act as a bridge between the community and public services, speaking to dozens of people each day either in person, on the phone or by email dealing with a wide range of issues from a missed bin collection to more serious concerns about drug use, anti-social neighbours and crime.

"During our three years here, we have established a regular group – Mary, Andy, Mrs Thompson, George, Mr Carton, Jane, and many more. Originally they came to ask for our help: now they come back, and keep coming back, sometimes for help but often to say hello, passing the time of day, asking our opinion or advice, or sharing a story or some news from their lives.

"I have increasingly asked myself, 'why do they keep coming back?' And I think I know the answer: they keep coming back because we care. We demonstrate our caring from our first interaction. We are polite, welcoming and warm. We listen, giving the time to hear the full story. We ask for clarification and check we've got it right. We discuss with people what we think we can do to help; we ask if that's what they want. We also let them know the outcome if we can't solve the issue there and then, phoning them to update them on progress.

"This is borne out of a number of things which include:

- our care about what we are doing
- our care for others
- our care for the wider community in which we live and work.

"For me personally this caring comes from my belief that love is a transformative force, and that through caring and acts of kindness as demonstrations of a loving practice, we can transform a world which often seems predicated on self-interest, greed and a lack of time or thought for others.

'Let me say, at the risk of seeming ridiculous, that the true revolutionary is guided by great feelings of love.' (Che Guevara, quoted in Freire, 1993, p 70)

"Beyond the shared benefits of these positive personal interactions, there are possibilities for working together on wider concerns. I believe in developing relationships built on mutual trust and respect, our visitors become interested in wider possibilities. Two good examples of this are the 'Bringing Communities Together', a local network of community groups, and 'Conversations for Change', a project sponsored by the Tutu Foundation; both involve people from around the town getting together to discuss issues/ideas and explore possible solutions/ actions. By building trusting relations, our visitors are more inclined to feel safe in engaging with new experiences. In this way, the loving act of showing care and compassion for visitors to our office becomes the starting point for transformative change through collective action.

"Our practice is a caring one which stems from a loving concern for others and I believe people recognise this and they come back, again and again to share their stories of life because we can be trusted to hear them, value them and in that we share our humanity. We feel the better for it and I believe our regular visitors do too!

'Too often we underestimate the power of a touch, a smile, a kind word, a listening ear, an honest compliment, or the smallest act of caring, all of which have the potential to turn a life around.' (Buscaglia, 2010)"

This emergent interest in living more compassionately by connecting with a common humanity is the basis of participatory democracy; it counters a competitive worldview in favour of the mutual well-being of people and planet. Locating the potential for change on a sustained transformative level in this epistemological turn is where the challenge lies. We have long understood that emotions generate a driving force of energy for change – passion, anger, disillusionment – but not in the apathy born of hopelessness, which results in inertia (Freire, 1972). Our challenge is how to maintain that momentum for change in some sort of structured sustainable way until it becomes transformative. It is, I believe, not possible to engage in the process of community development without a global perspective. As Gary Craig (Craig et al, 2011) says, 'In many ways, globalisation has made the local more important'. The sustainable collective energy for change now lies, I believe, in national and transnational alliances, a connection between local communities and global movements. To make this connection possible and effective, we need to improve social networking skills as part of everyday practice.

One such example came upon me by surprise. I received an invitation from Vincent O'Brien to join a collection of community activists based in Lancaster and Cumbria, UK, electronically dialoguing with Flavio Wittlin, Director-President of Viramundo and coordinator of health education courses at PUC-Rio in Rio de Janeiro, Brazil.

Viramundo

"That's the name of our non-governmental organisation. It is a Brazilian neologism that means we want and encourage everybody to change the world.

"Since 2003, we have been working with the community of Favela da Rocinha, the largest slum in Rio de Janeiro, where more than 100,000 people survive in abject poverty, low garbage disposal, ill health, poor access to health and sanitation services, and extreme violence exerted by drug gangs and truculent and/or corrupt policemen.

"On the other hand, close to this slum, São Conrado, with around 15,000 residents, exhibits all the signs of wealth, with unlimited access to food, regular garbage disposal, access to high-tech health services, as well as the hedonistic consumption of drugs with some of its residents.

"In sum, both are part of the same exquisite landscape, a voluptuous valley on the shores of the Atlantic Ocean, Rocinha and São Conrado are like a mirror of the social apartheid that characterises the inequalities in Brazilian society over five centuries.

"Anyway, Viramundo recognises that in recent years the federal government has adopted social programmes aimed at reducing inequalities in the country, not only economically but also expanding opportunities for increasing access to knowledge for the poorest Brazilians. The efforts have embraced Rocinha. Even the violence in the slum may be substantially contained, since the government, in addition to implementing the planned Police Pacification Unit (UPP), combine this action with other public policies aimed at education, culture, health, environmental sanitation, housing and transportation and the human rights fields.

"Seven years ago, we began a community radio program in Rocinha called 'Talking About Health, with Dr Health'. Abandoning formalities, I played a character, 'Dr Health', who interacted with the community answering questions on everyday health issues. While we adopted a popular media format, we also maintained accurate technical content within our messages.

"In 2006, we founded the NGO Viramundo, bringing together social activists from Rocinha and others from the urban middle-class neighbourhoods. A year later, we began a partnership with Vincent O'Brien, sociologist at University of Cumbria, UK, and the creator of the international

Visible Voices Social Network, exploring digital media (photos and videos) focusing on health and daily life issues identified by youngsters (15–19 years old) who live in Rocinha and have become certified as Health Education Visual Agents. A grassroots NGO, Viramundo endorsed the value of this approach, and gave the residents responsibility for creating pictures and videos about the community's main problems: migration, health and daily life, the growing rat infestation, the spread of tuberculosis, and increasing teenage pregnancy rates. The audience has been the community itself, focusing on what the neighbourhood can do to protect its own health, regardless of government intervention.

"However, Viramundo's work, while focused on improving the community's public health, spreads beyond this immediate local goal. Through music and social events, our creative organisation brings middle- and upper-class residents together with poor urban neighborhoods in order to face prejudice and discrimination and collaborate on shared public health concerns.

"The films and their corresponding photos have been shown not only throughout the community of Rocinha, but also in other similar areas and in different universities across the world, and were exhibited at the 2009 World Social Forum. For us, the *universal, equal and resolutive access to health system* of all socially excluded people in Brazil and on a worldwide scale, as well as their *civil emancipation*, both mean irrefutable human rights.

"Next year, with Viramundo's and the Italian–Brazilian NGO Amigos da Vida's support, we will run the Health Education Course at Pontifícia Universidade Católica do Rio de Janeiro (Pontifical Catholic University of Rio de Janeiro, abbreviated as PUC-Rio). A key orientation of it will be the course participants will take part in community workshops to train or improve the performance of those Health Education Visual Agents: (1) in the management of digital equipment, and (2) in basic health topics epidemiologically linked to their community. *Our purpose is to leave the technical grip of the microscope that reveals the world of germs to the scientist, and entrust the management of photo and video cameras to the residents of communities, who are more capable of revealing the vulnerability of their historical living conditions.*

"Viramundo's engagement came from Rocinha and we want to impact the world and vice versa. With an initial focus on health and daily life issues of local communities and cultures, we dream to connect them around the planet, recognising that beyond our different nationalities we are first of all human beings, all of us!"

The approach adopted by Flavio and his team is analytic, creative and relevant to people's everyday lives. It is an inspiring example of local empowerment driven by a passion for a flourishing world. It is precisely this energy that leads local action to move beyond the boundaries of community to reach out in movement for change. Dialogue is a process of compassionate engagement that begins in community. It arises from a profound love of life and the drive to co-create a better world. As we seek to weave the emotional and intellectual into a more complete way of knowing, using experience as the basis of connection with the whole, so that dialogue becomes the process of mediating reflection and action, and therefore the process for integrating the fragmented self and integrating the fragmented world in a process of co-creation – reaching out in dialogue with others, forming alliances that transcend boundaries to make connections with those who are similarly striving to create new possibilities. For Freire, thinking and feeling are not dichotomised, but within our physical bodies as part of our conscious being. 'It is an absolutely humanly peculiar existence, where, while knowing what we want and feel, we are able to transform the world ... through cultural action propelled by *dreams,* to make viable our *liberating utopia...*' (Freire, Ana Maria Araújo, 2007, p x). In this chapter, I have touched on the idea of an epistemological turn, claiming that disillusionment with the way things are, *dystopia,* can create the desire for a better world, and that those notions of *utopia* can become a driving force for creating that reality. Freire referred to utopia as 'a fundamental necessity for human beings. It is part of [our] historically and socially constituted nature ... there is no tomorrow without a project, without a dream, without utopia, without hope, without creative work, and work toward the development of possibilities which can make the concretization of that tomorrow viable' (2007, pp 25–6).

But, to make that utopia a viable reality, we need to develop strategies that maintain our rigour. Taking community development beyond the boundaries of local communities is a sticking point in practice. A simple framework that identifies the level of collective action and reminds us of the essential need to set our local practice within the wider context is necessary.

Figure 5.1: A framework for local/global action

LEVELS	IDEAS	ACTION	EXAMPLES
Local projects	Personal/local issues	Community-based/local authorities	Community garden
Connecting community groups	Structural awareness	Policy change/national level	Migrant Rights Campaign
Movements for change	Interdependence/mutual responsibility for humanity and the earth	Global governance	Beijing Conference

This is a framework for reflection, setting projects, campaigns and movements within their widest potential, a reminder to follow through from community groups to reach outward in alliance.

SIX

The power of ideas

This chapter demonstrates the power of ideas in the processes of both dominance and liberation, exploring the usefulness of Gramsci's concepts of *hegemony* and the role of *the intellectuals* to radical community development praxis. Linking this to Thompson's (2003, 2006) PCS (personal, cultural, structural) model offers insight into the way that the personal, cultural and structural contexts interact in the interests of power and privilege, in turn locating key sites of intervention for change.

Antonio Gramsci

Antonio Gramsci has much to offer community development. His insight into the complexity of power relations in society provides a profound understanding of politics that certainly helped me, in conceptualising *hegemony*, to understand the notion of *the personal as political*. In addition, his analysis of the role of *the intellectuals* in the process of social change enables us to locate community development as a site of resistance. Paula Allman claims:

> A socially and economically just and an authentically democratic alternative to capitalism is possible, but … it can only be created by people who understand why capitalism invariably leads to crisis and why of necessity it is driven to produce wealth for a minority and either endemic insecurity or perpetual poverty and scarcity for the vast majority, and by people who also understand why its remedies for environmental destruction must be inextricably linked to profit margins. (Allman, 2001, pp 2-3)

It is precisely in Gramsci's emphasis on the centrality of critical education as a mutual process of learning to understand the forces of hegemony, the way that economic, social and political forms of domination weave through our lives and minds, that Allman locates the struggle for reform as preparation for the critical action that leads to authentic transformation (Allman, 2001, p 139). It is in the process of critical education that these struggles take place and lead to altered consciousness. Myles Horton talks about the Highlander Folk School (now the Highlander Research and Education Center) (see Chapter Three) in the early days, concluding that 'reform within the system *reinforced* the system, or was co-opted by the system. Reformers didn't change the system, they made it more palatable and justified it, made it more humane, more intelligent … so I think when Highlander was first recognized to the extent that we were invited to talk about education was after Paulo made this kind of education respectable by being a professor at Harvard' (Horton and Freire, 1990, pp 200-2). Gramsci, from his own experience, felt that the unions offered a corporate stage of consciousness, but that this was based on a limited sector of the economy that could, therefore, achieve nothing more than reformism (Forgacs, 1988). Reforms begin the process of change, but this does not become transformative unless a more collective form of revolutionary change creates an alternative worldview. Gramsci saw critical education as the key to grassroots change.

In order to examine Gramsci's relevance it is important to locate him historically and culturally. Not only does this offer a richer appreciation of his intellectual contribution, but Nairn suggests that lessons from Gramsci can only be understood in the specific light of the Sardinian and Italian historical context (Nairn, 1982, p 159). Gramsci's life was epitomised by loneliness, poverty and struggle. His life was fraught with 'struggle against physical deformity and recurrent illness, the struggle against material hardship and poverty, the struggle against political adversaries and finally the psychological struggle for survival in prison' (Ransome, 1992, p 54).

The life and work of Antonio Gramsci

Gramsci was born on 22 January 1891, in Ales, Sardinia, the fourth of seven children. His father, Francesco Gramsci, was a civil servant from mainland Italy, and his mother, Guiseppina Macias, was from a moderately wealthy family by Sardinian standards. Living conditions were harsh in comparison with mainland Italy, a contrast that was to form the basis of Gramsci's ideas on injustice. He did not have an easy childhood. At the age of four, he developed a back deformity, which, at the time, was attributed to falling down stairs, although this is now refuted. It is now considered likely that his condition was because of tuberculosis of the spine, and that his parents wanted to hide this due to the superstitious beliefs that were so much part of Sardinian culture (Mayo, 1999). It was a culture in which werewolves, ghosts and witches were feared (Davidson, 1977). 'The spinal deformity that subsequently became apparent and produced a hunchback and abnormally short stature has also been attributed to tuberculosis of the spine, a condition known as Pott's Disease, with which he was diagnosed in 1933' (Kenway, 2001, p 48). Gramsci resented the fact that the power of popular superstition, which cast 'dis'abled people as possessed by evil spirits, had prevented his parents from getting the right treatment to overcome it in the early stages (Mayo, 1999). On the advice of a specialist, he was suspended from the ceiling in a leather corset for long periods of time in an attempt to straighten his back. The spinal deformity persisted and he became a solitary child. When he was six, his father was imprisoned for over five years, accused of fraud and embezzlement, but it is more likely that it was an act of political retribution. The family was reduced to a state of bare survival and returned to Ghilarza where his mother's strength and hard work saved the family from destitution. This was a significant turning point in Gramsci's early life. Until then he had been protected from persecution by his parents' relatively privileged position in local society. Due to his poor health and his mother's desire to protect him from discrimination, he started school late, at the age of seven. His 'dis'ability and his family's reduced status caused him to be bullied and rejected by the other children. This was a formative experience and led to his passion and commitment for all who suffer injustice (Davidson, 1977). His schooling became fragmented, he suffered from malnutrition, and by the age of 11 his father returned home and forced him to leave school to help support the family. He worked 10 hours a day for six-and-a-half days a week, carrying heavy ledgers around the Land Registry Office, 'many a night I wept in secret because my whole body was aching' (Gramsci, 1988, p 238).

This marked the start of feelings of great resentment towards his father. His schooling was resumed once his father considered that the family was sufficiently back on its feet, and he was boarded out 11 miles away to receive what he considered an inadequate education based on principles of 'intellectual dishonesty'. His solitary nature led to a great passion for reading. Gennaro, his older brother, away in Turin on military service, started sending him *Avanti!*, the Italian Socialist Party (PSI) paper. At this time, Sardinia began to erupt in the face of the rising discontent of the poor. Fiori (1990) describes Gramsci's cultural and political times – widespread malnutrition and premature death from chronic diseases and work accidents – together with his political reading as having changed Gramsci's political perspective. His dream was of action that would lead to social justice.

His move to the lycée at Cagliari saw the dawn of his active political life. He lived with Gennaro, who introduced him to the socialist movement, and he started reading Marx. Sardinia increasingly rebelled under the weight of the abject oppression of the poor, and Gramsci's identification and involvement with the socialist movement deepened his critical consciousness.

Eventually, he was offered a scholarship to Turin where the combination of a large, industrial, working-class city and the stimulation of critical thinkers was to influence his philosophical thought. However, the transition from Sardism to socialism was lengthy and protracted. The image is one of extreme unhappiness, a man who was 'too appallingly miserable for people even to want to approach him' (Davidson, 1977, p 70). The liberal intellectual Piero Gobetti saw him as 'seething with resentment' and described his socialism as 'first of all a reply to the offences of society against a lonely Sard emigrant' (Nairn, 1982, p 161). His compensation was, once again, found in excessive study, which, combined with poverty, increasingly damaged his health.

A turning point came in 1916. He abandoned his degree in linguistics, and his long-term ambition to become a good teacher, to work full time on the political paper *Avanti!*. Turning his back on academic life, Gramsci the revolutionary political activist emerged. A simultaneous change in his personality took place. He became more happy and sociable. 'He was in the process of remaking himself in what Marxists call praxis. By engaging in a practical and active rather than a contemplative life, he was purging himself of the emotional and ideological incrustation of [his] past' (Davidson, 1977, p 72). As a political journalist, he put into practice his belief in bringing theory to the workers. He saw this as the route to self-knowledge for the industrial proletariat, liberation of the mind. In a process of reflection on history, he saw the beginnings of emancipation of the masses.

By early 1917, the time of the Russian Revolution, his ideology expressed through his journalism synthesised with a vision of practice located in the factory councils to offer a critical praxis with transformative potential. He was central to the development of the factory council movement in Turin and became increasingly involved in political journalism, helping to found the socialist paper *L'Ordine Nuovo* in 1919, as a tool of consciousness. Its motto spoke clearly: 'Pessimism of the intellect, optimism of the will'. The factory council, for Gramsci, was the initial context of praxis, the point of contact with the workers: workers' democracy organised through workers' and peasants' councils, which he saw as an educational force that would put ordinary people in touch with their own potential political leadership.

The factory council movement spread rapidly between 1919 and 1920. The moment of crisis came when 600,000 workers from the Italian industrial cities occupied their factories. Gramsci and his friends closed the offices of *L'Ordine Nuovo* and went to live in the factories with the workers. However, as a revolution it was doomed to failure. Gramsci believed that the moment of conflict had been determined by capitalism, and that the workers were unprepared. The result was that the whole movement was premature and uncoordinated. He blamed himself for failing to understand the need for parallel growth in both theory and practice in order to achieve a *unity of praxis*. It was his belief that, had the process been critical and the timing right, it would have enabled the workers to run the new society and the party to play its key role in taking over the bourgeois state.

After the collapse of the factory council movement, Gramsci became actively involved in the formation of the Communist Party of Italy (PCI). These years saw, once again, his emotional withdrawal into a life governed by the intellect. In May 1922, he was a Communist Party delegate on the Executive Committee of the Communist Third International in Moscow. His health deteriorated while he was there and he was sent to a sanatorium near the Black Sea where he met Giulia Schucht. She was of Russian Jewish ethnicity, and a music teacher who had studied violin in Rome (Kenway, 2001, p 48). They married in 1923.

It was only over time that Gramsci realised the significance of the growth of fascism. His analysis was founded on the idea that fascism was a rural phenomenon that released suppressed passions and hatred in the masses. Politically, he saw fascism as separate from the bourgeois state because of its decadence: an uncontrollable cross-class movement dominated by the petit bourgeoisie and characterised by legitimate violence. In 1922, Mussolini took power with his March on Rome, which marked the final death throes of the Italian proletariat drive for a Soviet-style revolution. By early 1923, communist leaders were being arrested and Gramsci sought to unite the working classes against this wave of fascism.

The volatile political climate made it unsafe for Gramsci to return to Rome until 1924, and he did so without Giulia. In the general election of April 1924, he was elected to parliament and subsequently became the general secretary of the PCI. He was travelled the country, addressing meetings and organising the party on the basis of workplace cells. May 1924 saw Gramsci's inaugural speech in parliament. His fearlessness was a constant threat to the fascists who determined to circumvent his parliamentary immunity and silence him. He was constantly followed around the country and eventually arrested on charges of conspiracy, agitation, inciting class war, insurrection and alteration of the Constitution and the form of the state through violence. Davidson considers his chief threat to the fascists to have been his awareness 'that the main battle to overthrow fascism lay among the peasantry' (Davidson, 1977, p 118).

Gramsci returned to Moscow briefly following the birth of Delio, his first son. Between October 1925 and July 1926, Giulia joined him in Rome with Delio. She left because of the deteriorating political climate in Italy, just two months before Gramsci was arrested. Their second son, Guiliano, was born in Moscow in August 1926. Gramsci never saw him. Giulia remained the romantic love of Gramsci's life, but she suffered badly from depression, and eventually had a breakdown, never to return to Italy.

From 1926, the international political climate deteriorated and the situation 'demanded a new analysis of the political and ideological resources of capitalist societies, the sources of their extraordinary resilience' (Forgacs, 1988, p 189). It was this analysis that occupied Gramsci's thoughts throughout his prison years. In November 1926, he was arrested, along with other communist members of parliament. He was moved from Rome to exile on the island of Ustica, and then to Milan to await trial. His first plan for the *Prison notebooks* was formed in this period. Tatiana Schucht, Giulia's elder sister, devoted her life to supporting Gramsci in the difficult years of his imprisonment, and Gramsci became dependent on her for emotional sustenance. It is Tatiana who is responsible for ensuring that the Gramscian legacy was preserved by smuggling his letters and prison notebooks past the prison censor into the public domain. She passed a letter on to his old student friend, Piero Sraffa, who was now a Marxist economist at Cambridge, outlining the subject of his notebooks. It was Sraffa who brought Gramsci's plight to public attention in an article in the *Guardian* on 21 October 1927, but to no avail. Gramsci was transferred to Rome in May 1928. On 4 June, the prosecuting attorney, Michele Isgro, echoed Mussolini's personal instructions in declaring a need to stop Gramsci's brain from functioning for 20 years, such is the threat of powerful ideas to the status quo (Milne, undated; Davidson, 1977). Mussolini's enforcement of the 'long Calvary of Antonio Gramsci' had begun (Fiori, 1990). 'His active political practice had finished. He now had four and a half thousand days to think on its theoretical implications for Marxism and revolutionary socialism' (Davidson, 1977, p 231).

In July 1928, he was transferred to a special prison in Turi, in the South, because of his ill health. Not until early 1929 was he given permission to write, and he started work on the first prison notebook in a school exercise book. As part of the amnesty programme for the 10th anniversary of the fascist 'revolution', his sentence was commuted to 12 years and four months. By this time his health was deteriorating rapidly. After he collapsed in his cell in March 1933, his doctor recommended that he be transferred to a clinic. This was supported by Sraffa who, as well as paying for Gramsci's supply of books, worked endlessly to help him over the years by putting moral pressure on the fascist regime. Gramsci's writing continued from the clinic at Formia until 1935, when illness forced him to stop. There were by then 2,848 tightly packed pages of his writing in 33 prison notebooks, an achievement that signifies what Henderson calls 'a prodigy of will, intellect and indomitable staying power' (H. Henderson, quoted in Gramsci, 1988, p 10). He saw this period of his life as 'a time of waiting, a pause and preparation' (Lawner, 1979, p 39).

Not prepared to compromise his political position, Gramsci suffered an arduous 10-year confinement under the fascist regime in Italy, while his health slowly disintegrated. A cerebral haemorrhage killed him on 27 April 1937, six days after his freedom had been granted. Tatiana, in a letter to Sraffa on 12 May 1937, describes how, on the very day she brought him news of his freedom, he collapsed. She stayed with him the two days it took for him to die. 'I kept watch over him doing whatever I thought best, wetting his lips, trying to help him get his breath back artificially when it seemed to stop. But then he took a last deep breath and sunk [sic] into a silence that could never change' (quoted in Lawner, 1979, p 280).

Tatiana saw that all his work was safely deposited at the Banca Commerciale in Rome, from where it was transferred to Moscow, and then to his friend, Togliatti. Since then, his writing continues to be analysed and published, challenging the thought and the practice of those who read it.

Gramsci's contribution to critical pedagogy

> ... the relationship between teacher and pupil is active and reciprocal
> so that every teacher is always a pupil and every pupil a teacher.
> (Gramsci, 1971, p 350)

Gramsci recognised the inadequacy of Marxist economic determinism to offer sufficient analysis for the increasing complexity of social forces in the 20th century. He reconceptualised the moral, cultural and political influences in society to offer profound insight into the pervasive nature of these forces in everyday life. Of particular relevance to critical pedagogy are his concepts of the nature of *hegemony* and the role of the *intellectuals*. Education and culture were two themes that were of constant relevance to Gramsci. Much of his early thinking was preoccupied with the problem of achieving working–class intellectual autonomy. His belief was that everyone is innately cultured and capable of intellectual thought, but that this is undisciplined and incoherent without critical education. By placing emphasis on the learner, not the teacher, a learning process can be stimulated that moves through self-knowledge to liberation (Forgacs, 1988). His influence on Freire can be seen in these ideas. Ideology, according to Marx and Engels, assumes that the class with the power to control the material forces of society also controls the dominant ideas in society, which are passively absorbed into working-class minds as the *false consciousness* of *common sense*. So, 'not only does the ruling class produce the ruling ideas, in view of its control over the means of intellectual production, but the dominated classes produce ideas that do not necessarily serve their interests' (Mayo, 2004, p 41). Although Marx and Engels introduced the role of ideology as an instrument of class struggle, their emphasis was on the role of the party in developing consciousness. Gramsci developed a revolutionary ideology, 'a theory of popular, as well as working-class, ideology of protest' to a much more sophisticated degree (Rude, 1980, p 22).

Fundamental to Gramsci's thinking is the notion of revolution as process. He rejects cataclysmic change in favour of progressive revolution through critical education. His belief was that society could only be transformed by the systematic construction and consolidation of new social relationships. The capacity of the people to play key roles in their own destiny is central to this process. Intellectual and moral reform is Gramsci's term for what Freire would call *conscientisation*: the process whereby people critically reconceptualise their roles in society from their *false consciousness*. 'The philosophy of praxis is the crowning point of this entire movement of intellectual and moral reformation, made dialectical in the contrast between popular culture and high culture' (Forgacs, 1988, p 351). Gramsci's writings offer an originality of thought and a practical base, a praxis that reflects his experience as an activist.

According to Gramsci, Lenin's belief that there can be no revolutionary movement without a revolutionary theory is of fundamental importance to understanding the function of critical education. Examining traditional working-class organisation and leadership, which had proved so ineffective in conquering capitalism while at the same time existing within it, he developed insight into the dynamics of social, political and economic relations that had never been achieved before. His vision of progressive revolutionary change was based on the role of critical education in achieving mass political consciousness with a democratic, grassroots base rather than an elite leadership.

'Classical Marxism, by emphasising the coercive nature of politics, has been correspondingly weak in analysing the problem of consent' (Hoffman, 1984, p 1). Gramsci's substantial contribution is found in his analysis of consent in relation to *hegemony*.

The concept of hegemony

Gramsci's analysis of the concept of *hegemony* is profound. Hegemony is the means by which one class assumes dominance over the masses in society. Traditional Marxism emphasised that this was achieved through coercion, the way in which the state exercised control through the law, the police and the armed forces.

Gramsci extended this understanding by identifying the way in which dominant ideology, as a form of ideological persuasion, permeates our lives through the institutions of civil society. By these means, dominant attitudes are internalised and accepted as *common sense*, and thereby legitimised in the minds of people. Not only did he develop the notion of *consent* within a Marxist framework, but he analysed *hegemony* as 'the entire complex of practical and theoretical activities with which the ruling class not only justifies and maintains its dominance, but manages to win the active consent of those over whom it rules' (Gramsci, 1986, p 244). This development of the cultural and moral aspects of hegemony challenges the entire Marxist conceptual analysis of the state as an instrument of coercion (Hoffman, 1984). His notion of the *historical bloc*, a term that encompasses the interrelationships of the economic, cultural and political alliances in society, is bound together by the cohesion of hegemony. Hegemonic dominance established through an intellectual and moral bloc is likely to be much more stable than power achieved through coercion. 'Gramsci is very specific about this object, which is not successfully fulfilled by all parties – the establishment of an integral State, a State which has a fully developed hegemony in civil society encompassing the mass of the population and thereby cementing together a strong historical bloc' (Showstack Sassoon, 1987a, p 150). But hegemony is not a system, it is a process of constant struggle to maintain dominance over subordinate classes, which is actively maintained and modified by agents of the state – in itself a form of praxis (Ransome, 1992). So, having achieved dominance, a ruling class has a continuing need to maintain hegemonic control. The complexity of the concept of hegemony is that its structure is open to constant analysis, challenge and modification (Entwistle, 1979). It is not likely that hegemonic dominance can be maintained effectively without the collective will of the people – therefore the development of a counter-hegemony plays an essential part in the process of change. This is where Gramcsi saw the importance of critical education. He also transcended the dichotomous class divide of previous Marxist thinkers by identifying potential alliances between many social groups in the process of collective action. Hegemony is 'characterised by its non-static nature (it is constantly open to negotiation and re-negotiation, therefore being renewed and recreated) ... there exist moments in which cracks can be detected' (Mayo, 2010, 24). Mayo points to the fact that in current times there are many excluded areas of social life that offer critical democratic spaces for counter-hegemonic activities.

Gramsci saw the embodiment of social equilibrium in the interrelationship of coercion and consent. Also of central importance in this respect is the flexibility of hegemony, the way in which peripheral criticisms can be absorbed as acts of compromise. In this way, reformist measures can be negated before they threaten the bedrock of the dominant ideology. By offering such palliatives, the status quo can be maintained without resorting to the use of coercion, which is both expensive and difficult to maintain. In a similar vein, Freire refers to *false generosity*, or tokenism.

One extreme example of the use of ideological persuasion to cement cracks in a crumbling status quo could be seen in Margaret Thatcher's use of the Falklands War to unite the UK in the face of the threat from an outside enemy, namely Argentina. On the other hand, state reversion to coercion during the 1984–85 Miners' Strike, as well as ideological persuasion, aimed at the rest of civil society, that the miners were the 'enemy within' (Milne, 1994), demonstrates the might of the state when the full force of coercion and consent are used in combination. *False generosity* is used within the process of *hegemony* to create an illusion of democracy and justice. Just one example is the tokenistic way that the hegemonic education system allows individuals from some oppressed groups to flourish, while the groups as a whole remain disadvantaged. This individualises educational failure and success, creating a smokescreen for the hegemonic function of schools.

Gramsci provides community workers with insights into the way in which community groups can begin the process of transforming society for the common good. His analysis offers critical insight into the power of ideas to infiltrate the inner recesses of our being to persuade us to accept the dominant order of things unquestioningly as *common sense*. Whereas coercion is exercised overtly through the armed forces, the police, the courts and prisons, consent is subtly woven through the institutions of civil society – the family, schools, the media, political parties, unions, religious organisations, cultural, charitable and community groups – in a way that permeates our social being and asserts hegemonic control by influencing our ideas. The struggles against oppression around issues of *difference* and *diversity* are located in civil society. This places the community worker at the heart of the process. The values, attitudes, morality and beliefs that are internalised as *common sense* by the masses but serve the interests of dominant groups have to be challenged at a local as well as a structural level. In order for this to happen in a critical way, Gramsci believed that the *false consciousness* of the subordinated classes needed to be transformed to release full potential for participation in the process of social action. This is why both Freire and Gramsci locate critical education at the heart of the process of transformative change.

Based on his political activism, Gramsci recognised that *hegemony* is a resilient and flexible force. He believed that the critical consciousness of ordinary people is vital in any effective intervention, but that this will not erupt spontaneously. External agents need to act as catalysts in this process, and he conceptualised these as *traditional intellectuals*.

The role of the intellectuals

Central to Gramsci's thought was how to raise the consciousness of oppressed people without simultaneously destroying their innate energy. He believed that without emphasis on intellectual understanding, the consciousness of oppressed people is likely to be fragmented, manifesting itself in a simple form of anti-authoritarianism – a generic hatred of the state rather than a critical analysis of power and domination. Gramsci recognised that critical consciousness could only come about through a political understanding of the illegitimate foundations of class domination. *False consciousness* is powerful and the questioning needed to reach a more critical awareness does not usually happen without external intervention.

Gramsci saw every person as having intellectual capacities for thinking and reasoning. He used the term *intellectual* to refer to people who occupy a wide range of organisational or ideological/cultural roles in society. Within this concept, *organic intellectuals* are those who emerge from their culture of origin. Every social group produces individuals who possess 'the capacity to be an organiser of society in general, including all its complex organism of services, right up to the state organism, because of the need to create the conditions most favourable to the expansion of their own class' (Forgacs, 1988, p 301). *Traditional intellectuals* he saw as the product of a previous historical period, whose role has continued to exist in the present, and who are not deeply committed to a class. He particularly had in mind the Catholic Church, which at that time in Italian history had a monopoly not only of religious ideology but of education, morality and justice. *Traditional intellectuals* have an important preliminary role in challenging hegemony by acting as a catalyst in the process of transformation, unlocking mass consciousness (Boggs, 1980). They bridge the divide between theory and practice by becoming committed to social justice, and begin the process of liberation by creating the context for questioning the legitimacy of everyday experience.

Gramsci felt it ultimately essential that intellectuals should be generated from the very heart of the working class, but he saw the role of the *traditional intellectual* as one of sympathetic allegiance to justice, and vital in setting the wheels of change in motion. He was sceptical that their allegiance would be sustained; converts who do not emerge from the people, according to historical analysis, are prone to defect in the face of persecution. But, having cut the ties to their own class, *traditional intellectuals* could perform a useful role as catalysts for change. The most important function falls to the working class *organic intellectual*, a person of ideas, a person with a passion for the people that transcends the dichotomy between *knowing* and *feeling*. Without this holistic element, the struggle will remain peripheral. (The knowing–feeling divide is addressed in Chapters Seven and Eight in relation to feminism.)

Organic intellectuals remain committed to their cultural roots. They articulate new values, pose critical questions and invite new ways of thinking about the world. The role, in its commitment to its class of origin, shares the inherent dilemmas of that class, and plays an integral part in the process of change. When *organic intellectuals* emerge from everyday life into that role, their specific purpose is raising the critical consciousness of the people; they remain central to the creation of a just society.

> The organic intellectual of the working class is a builder, an organiser, a permanent persuader so that he [sic] is able to engage in all aspects of the struggle.... These attributes, developed before the revolution, will serve after the revolution as the tasks of the organic intellectual

continue in all these areas, from the organisation of socialist production to the building of a new culture … the creation of a new intellectual begins in the heart of the old society. (Showstack Sassoon, 1987a, pp 149-50)

This reminds me of Cathy McCormack, an inspirational community activist from Easterhouse, Glasgow, who is a true *organic intellectual*, in every sense of the concept. She learnt about popular education in Nicaragua after becoming political in a housing campaign in Easterhouse in the 1980s. 'It was only through my experience in Nicaragua that I started to understand the truth. Now I was getting to the roots of my own poverty. That's when I really became involved in the international struggle for justice…. I wanted the people in both communities to learn and benefit from each other's experience. So I established the Greater Easterhouse Nicaragua Solidarity Link Group' (McCormack with Pallister, 2009, p 116). 'Whether you live in a village in Central America or in a Glasgow scheme, the people's experience is still the same and they want their voices heard. When I started on this journey, I was politically ignorant but I was able to make sense of things and start making connections. I was experiencing an education no university could have given me, but it was a shattering education because I was realising how badly human beings could treat each other' (2009, p 104). She brought popular education to Easterhouse from her encounter with Freire in action in Nicaragua. At this time, after an intensive Training for Transformation programme in Ireland, she set up, with others, the Popular Democracy Education Resource Centre (PODER) in Easterhouse, which led to her involvement in the Scottish Popular Education Forum, aiming to bring popular educators together from all over Scotland to constitute a movement for change. I had the great pleasure of meeting Cathy in Edinburgh in 1999, when she came to talk about her experience at the International Association for Community Development (IACD) Conference in Edinburgh. Her book, *The wee yellow butterfly* (2009), is a vital resource for community development workers who want to understand the work of organic intellectuals.

Organic intellectuals become leaders in the process of change, but they are not an elite. Gramsci distinguished the role by its function rather than its status. In this sense, he moves beyond a revolutionary leadership model to one where these key roles function within an overall unity that is inspired by critical consciousness. This unity can be seen in the type of socialism discussed by Fromm (1962), by which people become the conscious subjects of history, experiencing themselves as powerful, not powerless, and by such intellectual emancipation are able to free themselves from the chains of *false consciousness*. 'Through a constant process of theoretical preparation and political education, members of the rank and file could develop their political capacities and eventually become leaders. In this way the necessary division between leader and led was no longer arbitrary and formal, but merely functional' (Showstack Sassoon, 1987a, p 85).

According to Gramsci, *common sense* is a collection of myths and superstitions that is resilient to spontaneous critical thought. The *traditional intellectual* unlocks popular critical consciousness by offering a coherent understanding of oppressive forces in history and society. In contrast to this initial function, the *organic intellectual* integrates this critical consciousness into everyday culture. Everyday thought and action are questioned, transformed and, in turn, collectively transform society. The organic intellectual stratum grows both qualitatively and quantitatively, for every person is innately an intellectual, and by this process *false consciousness* transforms into *critical consciousness*.

Gramsci's insight into the complex nature of *hegemony* changed the very essence of the concept by recognising that people are not only controlled by coercion, but consent to their own oppression as a result of the subtle forces of ideological persuasion. As a powerful form of control, dominant attitudes and values permeate people's lives through civil institutions – the media, the family, schools and all other social groups that we experience. The result is *cultural invasion* (Freire, 1972): our minds become colonised with how we should think, feel and act. We are robbed of the confidence to be critical because the interests of power and privilege invade our thinking, influencing our perceptions of the world and our place in it.

Gramsci's emphasis was on praxis in the process of change. The term he frequently used in his notebooks, *philosophy of praxis*, is the concept of a unity of theory and practice. 'For Gramsci the philosophy of praxis is both the theory of the contradictions in society and at the same time people's practical awareness of those contradictions' (Forgacs, 1988, p 429). bell hooks (1993, p 151) talks about making a commitment to work from a 'lived understanding' of people's lives rather than accepting as authentic the distortion of a 'bourgeois lens'. She cites Freire's words from *Pedagogy in process*: 'authentic help means that all who are involved help each other mutually, growing together in the common effort to understand the reality which they seek to transform. Only through such praxis – in which those who help and those who are being helped help each other simultaneously – can the act of helping become free from the distortion in which the helper dominates the helped'.

If we work with greater understanding of power embedded in the structures of society, in civil society, and in everyday encounters, we begin to see much more clearly that action for change needs to target each of these levels in order to make a difference. How then do we begin to operationalise these ideas in practice?

Locating and dislocating oppression

An analysis of power and the structures of discrimination is needed in order to develop practical strategies for change. This analysis needs to incorporate not only 'race', class and gender, but the whole range of patterns of power and subordination that exist. A simplistic, dichotomous analysis of power of oppressor/oppressed is no longer adequate for our emerging understandings of the complexity of overlapping, interlinking patterns of discrimination. This overarching emphasis on class discrimination subsumed the complexity of difference within class relations, and it was the development of feminism and early, progressive postmodernism that led to the refinement of our analysis.

Discrimination as formalised oppression

An understanding of Gramsci's concept of *hegemony* is essential to this analysis. Maintaining power by persuading people that dominant attitudes are *common sense* works in a much more subtle way than a dominant group overtly coercing others into subordination. Power is located within a multidimensional system of oppressions in which we are all simultaneously oppressors and oppressed. It is essential that we see this as a complex whole that interlinks and reinforces at every level.

Ideology, the ideas that are formed around values and beliefs in society and inform the way society is organised, reinforces and justifies the divisions and power imbalances between groups in order to maintain the status quo. These ideas are difficult to change because they have been sold as *common sense* – a term that Gramsci defined as fragmented, disjointed, contradictory thinking that justifies reality for the mass of the people (Hall, 1996c). In these ways, the ideas of the most powerful in society sustain their own interests. This can be seen in relation to 'normality'. Take *the family*, which has fundamentally changed in role and structure over recent decades. A 'normal' family, despite an understanding of difference and changing structures, is still perceived in a White, western, heterosexual, fully able, middle-class way as a man and a woman living together with their two perfectly formed children. Anything different is 'other', deviant and undesirable, and therefore undermining of the moral base of society. This thinking, in turn, justifies policy decisions that target groups that do not conform to this norm – and, ironically, this constitutes the majority of people in society. But, due to the power of dominant thinking, it is perceived as a statistical norm rather than an ideological norm (Thompson, 2006), with the result that the *deviant* label is perceived as *common sense*.

Ideology not only defines what is *normal*, but also what is *natural*. Discriminatory ideas become embedded in the structures of society and accepted as *common sense*, so are not questioned (Thompson, 2003). The way in which biological or medical determinism is used to justify *normal* stereotypical roles in society (women as natural carers; Black people as less intelligent; old people as feeble; 'dis'abled people as dependent) presents a false logic, what Thompson (2006) terms the *logic of discrimination*. These are powerful ideas, appealing to a *common sense* of what is normal and natural, which, in serving the interests of the status quo, not only subordinate, but diminish life chances by creating poverty, poor health and reduced opportunities. This terrain of ideological struggle is where prejudice, discrimination and oppression interact to weave power relationships into everyday lives. By locating the sites of prejudice and discrimination, we are also locating the most powerful points of intervention and transformation.

The first step in locating power and control is to understand the ways in which the legitimising of power is achieved. By this, I mean that prejudiced social attitudes reflect social divisions in society and help to reinforce them. *Prejudice* is an irrational thinking that primarily operates at a personal level, but reflects structural discrimination. It is often based on *stereotypes*, and works in a way that limits people's potential (as in the case of 'dis'abled or older people being treated as dependent), and at worst is life-threatening (as in domestic violence and racist attacks). *Discrimination* defines the way in which *prejudice* is structured in society by powerful and privileged dominant groups exploiting and subordinating groups who are less powerful, and therefore less able to act in their own interests. *Oppression* refers to the subordination, marginalisation and exclusion from society of these groups, thereby denying them social justice, citizenship and full democratic rights to participate in society. *Empowerment* is a term that is applied simplistically. As Barr states (1995, pp 121-2), 'we need to be clear about the framework of reference within which we use the term because different agencies, and within them different actors, appear to have different expectations of empowerment and there is often a credibility gap between aspirations of communities and actual achievements'. In radical community development, this concept links to the process of *conscientisation*, that of critical questioning and analysis as the basis of social change. Empowerment is therefore the ability to make critical connections in relation to power and control in society in order to identify discrimination and determine collective action for change. In this sense, it embraces identity and autonomy.

An excellent model, which is widely used in community development practice, is Thompson's (2003, 2006) PCS model (Figure 6.1). Three concentric rings indicate the three levels of interaction that we have considered in our exploration of Gramsci, the personal, cultural and structural. The model is particularly helpful

Figure 6.1: The PCS model

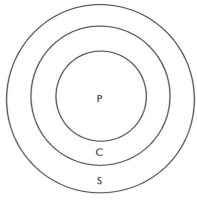

Source: Thompson (2001, 2003)

because it symbolises the ways in which these different levels mutually reinforce each other. Too often, analysis stops at the P-level – that of individual, personal prejudice. Challenging sexist comments, or even tackling the behaviour of racist groups in community, will never be enough to redress the problems of inequality in society. It will not even be enough to stem the tide of discrimination that constantly reinforces attitudes by permeating our thoughts and actions in the most subtle of ways.

Thompson, in a simple but effective way, embeds the P-level (the personal or psychological – a level of thoughts, feelings, attitudes, action and prejudice) at the centre of his model. Empowerment at this level involves believing in people in order to foster self-belief, trust in people in order to develop confidence and self-esteem, creating the opportunity for people to explore their stories, their histories, their experience in dialogue, deepening a sense of identity and personal autonomy. This is set within within the C-level (that of the cultural, shared ways of seeing, thinking and doing – a level of commonalities, consensus and conformity). Foucault's contribution has been to give us insight into power as discourse, as threaded through everyday conversations to convey meaning, assumptions and behaviour through the dynamics between language and social relationships. It is vital to know how this works if we are going to challenge and change the way that these assumptions reproduce dominant power relations, not only related to class, but to 'race' and patriarchy. They become so embedded in our cultural attitudes that they construct our reality, defining what is normal and acceptable and frame our identities (Thompson, 2007). Working in culture circles/community groups, people engage in dialogue that explores common experiences and builds a sense of connectedness and belonging. This, in turn, is set within the S-level (the structural level where social divisions are sewn into the fabric of society and oppression and discrimination become institutionalised – the socio-political power base) (Thompson, 2006). Structurally embedded in society is a hierarchy of power relations based on 'race', class and gender as central dimensions of power, but within this we also have to understand a complexity of other oppressions that intersect to greater or lesser degrees – age, 'dis'ability, sexual identity, religion, language, body, education... Concientisation is the form of empowerment that is needed for action at a structural level. People, through a process of problematising, begin to identify the complex nature of power that has created poverty and privilege, a living contradiction in a democracy, and become embedded in the structures of society and legitimised as common sense.

Each level indicated on the PCS model interacts with the others in ways that mutually reinforce prejudice and discrimination. This understanding is essential. It indicates why it is impossible to counter oppression by targeting one level at the exclusion of the others. This dynamic is so powerful that it negates any action that fails to address the whole. In this way, individual prejudice can only be understood within the cultural context, which in turn needs to be made sense of in relation to the structural context. These levels can never be seen in isolation from one another simply because they form an interactive dynamic that constantly maintains social divisions and serves the power relations in society. The PCS model offers an analysis that helps us to see the need for action to extend beyond community to address change at all levels, in order to bring about transformative social change.

In addition to the PCS levels of power, Thompson (2007) offers an analysis of four types of power:

1. power to
2. power over
3. power with
4. power within.

The relevance of these to the community worker is that they give us an insight into the nature of power on which to build theory in action, making interventions on all levels within all dimensions in order to work effectively with the concept of empowerment.

1. 'Power to' can be understood as personal power to achieve our potential in life, and so is important for community development in understanding that self-esteem and self-belief are fundamental to the process of change. It links to Doyal and Gough's emphasis on personal autonomy as the foundation of collective action (see pp 66-7). It helps us to understand how domination leads to a 'culture of silence' by diminishing self-esteem and pathologising poverty, that is, convincing people that their social status is due to their own failings. In this sense, 'power to' is vital to releasing the energy for change.
2. 'Power over', on the other hand, is related to relations of dominance and subordination that get acted out at structural, cultural and personal levels. These levels do not operate exclusively: they interact and reinforce, and that is why change has to take place at all levels before empowerment and equality will be cultural norms that replace disempowerment and inequality. The dominant ideas that are embedded in structural relations feed interpersonal attitudes and vice versa.
3. 'Power with' is particularly important to the process of change. It implies not only solidarity among groups of people who identify with each other, but also alliances across difference in mutual commitment to change for the greater good for everyone. 'Power with' is central to collective action as a collective power that brings about more equality than any disconnected projects can achieve. It links us from local community projects to movements for change.
4. 'Power within' is a personal resilience that connects the individual to the collective. It is an inner dimension that is the basis of self-worth, dignity and self-respect, the very foundation of integrity, of mutual respect and equality, a dislocating of 'better than' or 'worse than' in order to create a world that is fair, just and equal. It embraces the confidence to act and take risks.

Power is reproduced on all these levels and in all these ways to legitimise knowledge that maintains domination and subordination. In the very language we use, dominant knowledge that reinforces power differentials is implicit in every encounter, in every spoken or written word, even in body language that is speechless. However, these sites also provide the key to interventions that create counternarratives that challenge dominant narratives. Foucault (1980) directs our attention to the way that power produces knowledge in discourses themselves, and the beginning of the process of empowerment for the community worker is to shift power from object to subject, from the known to the knower, from the pathologiser to the pathologised, as the basis for transformation.

A critical approach to community development calls for anti-discriminatory practice to be set within the social and political context. The first step to this is an openness to exploring attitudes, values and beliefs in ways that are both critical and self-critical. Out of this comes the courage to experience challenge and a willingness to understand different ways of engaging with the world. We have to become 'border-crossers', that is, we have to let go of the cultural, theoretical and ideological parameters that enclose us and offer us the security of 'home', the familiar and the known. 'To move away from "home" is to question in historical, semiotic and structural terms how the boundaries and meanings of "home" are constructed in self-evident ways often outside of criticism' (Giroux, 1993, p 179). Becoming 'homeless' in this sense is to shift to a space where life can be seen more critically, and possibilities for change can be explored. This is why creating contexts for critical debate in democratic public spaces is a vital concept for the community worker; by decontextualising the taken-for-grantedness of everyday life we see things from another perspective. From here we can focus on the individual in relation to the cultural and political context. And this is exactly what the PCS model, in all its simplicity, helps to locate: it is a structure that represents the embeddedness of discrimination at every level of society.

Making even more critical connections

The strength of the PCS model is that it takes community workers beyond a simplistic notion that we can change the world by challenging oppressive behaviour on a personal or even community level. It emphasises the importance of collective action beyond the boundaries of community. The limitations of this model are that it does not offer critical connections with the complex interweavings and intertwinings of oppressions in a multidimensional structure needed to move Gramscian/Freirean thinking from dichotomy into complexity. In relation to classroom teaching, Magda Lewis captures this complexity as follows:

> Pedagogical moments arise in specific context: the social location of the teacher and students; the geographic and historical location of the institutions in which they come together; the political climate within which they work; the personalities and personal profiles of the

individuals in the classroom; the readings selected for the course; and the academic backgrounds of the students all come together in ways that create the specifics of the moment. (Lewis, 2000, p 104)

Gramsci's contribution to action can be seen in the way that he refocuses our attention from the state to civil society, and the way in which it serves the interests of the state. Community, in this analysis, becomes not only a site for critical education, but also a site for critical action. Gramsci's use of military terminology is unfortunate, but this should not detract from the conceptual insight it offers. He warned against a *war of manoeuvre*, a targeting of the state apparatus, in the first instance at least. Instead, he saw revolution as a process of consciousness rooted in popular adult education in the context of civil society. Gramsci's *war of position* involves linking all manner of social organisations in alliance, and, importantly, identifies a space for the role of social movements in this process (Mayo, 1999). Community work has always paid attention to networking and alliances, but we now need more complex levels of action. In globalised times, the dynamic between the local and the global challenges reflection and action that is preoccupied with neighbourhood as the definitive site of community work.

Gramscian and Freirean thought remain as relevant as ever if we re-vision the insights they offer within an analysis of difference and diversity. 'Gramsci's specters are whispering to us, reminding us that the struggle ahead is a politics of passionate remembrance, of re-visiting anti-fascist struggles of the past, of recognizing the lessons embedded in history's dreams and nightmares, of moving forward into the new millennium with renewed hope and an optimism of the will' (McLaren et al, 1998, p 30).

Finally, let us move on to explore some practical possibilities for working in these ways in community.

Practical feminist approaches to dislocating oppression

Hustedde and King (2002) cite Dillard's feminist spirituality approach to individual and collective inner journeys to the soul, which help to dislocate prejudice that is held deep inside us. The move is an inner rather than outer spirituality, one in which the concrete realities of our lives remain the focus of our attention: 'when individuals and communities go within they meet the violence and terror within themselves that they project on to others. We hate others because we can't face the enemy within; so we project that enemy onto people of other races and classes or other institutions and communities' (Hustedde and King, 2002, p 341).

The tools that they offer community development for undertaking this approach are based on story as a route to engaging community in self-inquiry and self-knowledge: 'the telling of a story slows the mind down and lets the story sink underneath the skin to reveal something of the spirit' (2002, p 342). They also emphasise the importance of rituals to community as 'part of the search for who we are and the search for meaning as a community ... community rituals can provide stability and continuity and can promote a sense of solidarity and cohesion' (2002, p 343). The process takes communities forward as the creators of their own futures. This has clear links to the use of story discussed in Chapter Three.

They identify the following rituals as practice tools:

1. *Rituals of transition* create order out of the chaos of change. The Native American tradition of acknowledging seven generations of community takes the past–present–future dimension from solid historic connections through to marking change and planning directions for the future. This could be a valuable approach where family, community and tradition have gone through massive transition at the hands of unregulated economic forces. Another example they use is the Samoan Circle (developed by Lorenz Aggens in Chicago in 1970) where everyone is allowed to speak in turn in a safe, democratic listening environment, not led or chaired. This has been found to be effective if there are controversial issues to be tackled by a large group of people, as everyone has a stake in the success of the meeting. Conflict is more likely to be resolved because people are giving others their full attention.

2. *Rituals of healing* are based on empathy, compassion, forgiveness and justice. Community healing rituals can be used for reconciliation and dialogue. The authors give an example of the way that a unity candle was used in a public meeting in a community torn apart by land disputes and coal mining. The meeting opened with community leaders and coal mine operators symbolically lighting candles to indicate their willingness to talk, and then lighting one unity candle together to symbolise their desire to find a common resolution to their differences. This set the tone for cooperation as a value for healing divisions. Other examples include the Vietnam War Memorial in Washington and the AIDS quilt.

3. *Rituals of celebration* build on common solidarity and cohesion by expressing gratitude, joy and a sense of belonging. They focus on abundance rather than poverty, on strengths rather than weaknesses. Festivals celebrate the roots of a community, generating a sense of pride, confidence and belonging. They can also bring people from all walks of life together to learn and to negotiate differences. Two examples that come to mind for me are (i) the Bristol Festival Against Racism (Gilchrist, 2004, p 64) and (ii) the annual world Credit Union Day celebrations in Hattersley.

Gramsci's concept of *hegemony* is powerful in its simplicity, helping us to understand the power of ideas and the ways in which our minds are colonised unquestioningly by dominant attitudes. It provides the basis for developing more complex anti-discriminatory analyses based on a plurality of oppressions, set within the wider political context of globalisation. The next chapter explores critiques of Freire and Gramsci in order to arrive at a critical perspective from which to re-vision a pedagogy for our times.

SEVEN

Critiques of Freire and Gramsci

Critique and dissent are vital processes in deepening democracy. This chapter takes thinking from the class-based dichotomous analysis of Freire and Gramsci into the critiques that are vital in developing the relevance of their thinking for current times. I demonstrate the ways that making sense of the world through a dichotomous analysis reduces life experience to an either/or, 'this' or 'that', binary simplicity, which is only capable of defining something in relation to its 'Other' (for example, male/female, Black/White, young/old), thus denying the complexity and plurality of oppressions. It was the predominant emphasis on a class analysis that subsumed women's experience within the working-class struggle. In turn, the same dichotomous thought blinkered White women to see women's experience from a male/female analysis, overlooking the centrality of racism in interlinking, multiple oppressions in a politics of difference. Today, we are much more aware of the complex nature of oppressions, and the ways in which these engage social justice with environmental justice. So, this is a good point at which to explore the interface of social justice and environmental justice in terms of current challenges for community development theory and action:

> Freire's original work emphasized class while ignoring gender ... [he] did conceive his pedagogy in singular "class terms" growing out of his experiences among peasants and workers in impoverished Brazil. Therefore, as feminist educators have proposed, his foundational work from forty years ago needs correction for a theme like gender, among others. Freire himself acknowledged this missing dimension; he also urged educators to avoid copying him and to develop pedagogy suitable for their local situation. (Shor, 2000, p 6)

I begin my inquiry by relating it to my own community development practice. The period from the 1970s to the early 1990s was an inspiring time for community workers, which emerged from the optimism of the 1960s. 'Freirean and feminist pedagogies emerged at about the same time ... just after the activist 1960s, when dissent and participation were ideas whose time had come ... that legendary age of civil rights actions, student protests, anti-war campaigns ...' (Shor, 2000, p 2). This was the birthing ground for new social movements and the time when Freire made a massive impact on emancipatory practice – including liberation theology, radical community development and human rights activism. Second-wave feminism, and other new social movements, emerged from grassroots dialogue and changed our understanding of the world – anti-racist, Black women, green, lesbian and gay, 'dis'ability, 'grey power' – and we began to stretch our minds from the limitations of either/or dichotomous thought, framed by Enlightenment's search for a single truth, into the complexities of difference and diversity.

Freirean pedagogy has been the biggest single influence on radical community development theory and practice in the UK from the early 1970s. Emphasising *dialogue* as a critical encounter between people, and the centrality of *praxis* in that process, he located theory in everyday experience. More than this, he helped community workers to understand that the practice of social justice is rooted in its ideology of equality. In this way, democratic values create a frame for the way we see the world, analyse experience of the world and challenge the world. Beginning with every encounter, we learnt that true reflection leads to action: that personal consciousness is the basis of collective action for change, but that 'action is human only when it is not merely an occupation but also a preoccupation, that is, when it is not dichotomized from reflection' (Freire, 1996, p 35). This period saw community development redefine itself as a radical emancipatory practice based on critical consciousness.

There was an immediate feminist backlash against Freirean pedagogy, initially because of his use of dominant male language in *Pedagogy of the oppressed*. Since then the feminist critique has developed a wider analytic perspective, which offers insight into the limitations of Freire and the benefits of a feminist re-visioning of his work. Freirean pedagogy and feminist pedagogy have had a rocky ride in relation to each other, but they have much in common. Beneath the surface of commonalities lies a tangled web of what Shor terms 'conflict and convergence' (2000, p 3), and it is that web that I want to explore here.

Critiques of Freire and feminism

> The desire for transformation and the critique of inequality are ... common ground shared by Freire-based critical pedagogy and feminist pedagogy, two dissident schools of thought with a close and troubled relationship in recent years. (Shor, 2000, p 2)

I have been profoundly influenced and inspired, in theory and practice, by Paulo Freire, and I witness the ways in which he continues to have that same impact on practitioners in community development today. I want to begin this critique by exploring why a Brazilian man should continue to attract feminist attention.

Feminist pedagogy, like Freirean pedagogy, is founded on grassroots education for critical consciousness as a tool for understanding the nature of structural oppression. Crucial to this understanding is an awareness that emancipatory potential lies in collective action for change for a just and sustainable world. Feminist and Freirean pedagogies converge in their fundamental assumption that dominant ways of knowing need challenging, and that all people have a basic human right to be valued and active in their world. Freire, in offering a praxis of liberation that involves an understanding of the nature of oppression, the process of *conscientisation*, and the importance of culture and history in the struggle for transformative change, complements feminism. Feminist pedagogy diverges from Freire, however, in its challenge to patriarchy as a fundamental oppressive structure that echoes through women's lives everywhere, complexified by difference.

Feminism has had a powerful influence on community development. The ways in which women at grassroots level have demonstrated that *the personal is political* have been transformative for both theory and practice. Prior to this, women's experience, in the home and community, was seen as 'soft' and apolitical. These altered perspectives led to an analysis of the way in which the public/private divide has oppressed women for generations by creating the myth that politics stops at the parameters of our communities, and certainly at the thresholds of our homes. Let us apply this thinking to a practical issue. This way of seeing things was so deeply entrenched in the public psyche that such injustices as the police refusing to intervene in incidents of domestic violence led to women being denied the protection that was their human right. The women's refuge movement, pioneered by Erin Pizzey in the 1970s, shunted domestic violence into public awareness. Yet, domestic violence remains a worldwide violation of human rights, transcending all aspects of cultural diversity. In 1990, in my practice in Hattersley, Janice came to see me. "My ex-husband came round the house and started knocking me around. I managed to get him out and lock the door, but I was terrified for my life, so I called the police. They took me seriously until I gave them my Hattersley address: 'If you live there you must be an old slag, and you're getting no more than you deserve!' and they put the phone down on me." These are the types of experience that feminists challenge as hidden from view by a class analysis.

In these ways, we begin to understand why, despite Freire's compatibility with second-wave feminism's emphasis on the personal as political, he received harsh criticism from feminists. His pedagogy is based on a universal analysis (oppressor/ oppressed) that denies the complexity of different experiences of oppression. His sexist language, evident in his early work, was also seized on as evidencing an unconsciously gendered approach to his pedagogy. His response was that *Pedagogy of the oppressed* needs to be set in its historical and cultural context. It cannot be read as if it were written yesterday and retrospectively criticised, with the benefit of hindsight, using conceptual tools that were not available at the time it was written (Freire and Macedo, 1993). The influences of postmodernism and an increased understanding of *difference* have challenged the assumptions of metanarratives that are based on a universal, collective experience as reducing the nature of lived experience to a naively simplistic unity. A theory of liberation that glosses over divisions in society, attempting to universalise experience shaped by gender, 'race', ethnicity, age, sexuality, 'dis'ability and so on, entrenches those divisions still further.

bell hooks poses an interesting contradiction. She states that Freire offered her a structure within which she could define her own experience of racism on a global level, when 'the radical struggle of Black women to theorize our subjectivity' was not welcomed by early, White, bourgeois feminist thinkers (hooks, 1993, p 151). hooks refers to Freire's 'blind spot' to questions of gender, and his failure to acknowledge the specific gendered nature of oppression. Nevertheless, she honours the way that his pedagogy gave her the conceptual tools with which to analyse her own oppression as a Black American woman, helping her to see herself as a subject in resistance.

Freire emphasises that we all have a right and a duty to participate in the transformation of society because the struggle belongs to us all, wherever its specific location. He emphasises that his pedagogy is not universal, that it emerged from his own experience, and needs to be adapted for other contexts. Engaging in different cultural contexts, in a climate of political change, calls for critical questioning as the basis of an ongoing analysis. Freire was clear that giving answers, rather than asking questions, is 'the castration of curiosity' (Freire and Faundez, 1992, p 35). hooks challenges feminist thinkers who separate feminist pedagogy from Freirean pedagogy: 'For me these two experiences converge.... I have taken threads of Paulo's work and woven it into that version of feminist pedagogy I believe my work as a writer and teacher embodies' (hooks, 1993, p 150).

Feminist pedagogy, like Freirean pedagogy, places everyday stories at the heart of the process of critical consciousness. The notion that the deeply personal is profoundly political leads to a critical understanding of the nature of structural oppression, and the way that we are shaped in all our difference by structures of power that permeate our lives. By exploring the political nature of everyday encounters, we move towards the critical consciousness necessary to demystify the dominant hegemony and to change oppressive structures.

In much the same way as feminists challenged the universality of Freire's theory, Black feminists challenged White feminist analysis on grounds of difference. In other words, White feminists stood accused of defining 'woman' from a generic male/female perspective, which overlooked racism as a major structural oppression. This is typical of the limited binary thinking that epitomises western ideological thought. Stereotypes, or controlling images, mystify the nature of social relations and confound the ways in which 'race', class and gender intersect with each other. These images are 'key in maintaining interlocking systems of race, class and gender oppression' (Hill Collins, 1990, p 68).

Western consciousness, in its 'despiritualisation of the universe' (Richards, 1980, cited by Hill Collins, 1990, p 70), required the separation of the 'knowing self' from the 'known object' in preparation for a materialised world based on profit and exploitation. Inevitably, in a subject/object analysis, those who are seen as 'Other' are subordinated to 'object' because their reality is named by those who have the power to locate themselves as 'subject'. This power relationship dehumanises people as objects rather than subjects in control of their own lives (Freire, 1972). In our unravelling of the nature of oppressions, it is easy to see how readily we fall into the trap of this dichotomy at successive stages of our understanding. Criticising the universality of Freire, second-wave feminism failed itself by overlooking the different experience of Black women. Our current challenge is to focus our analysis on the insidious nature of White power, rather than continuing our preoccupation with what it is to be Black and subordinated

(Fine et al, 1997). This represents a subtle shift of gaze that takes us firmly into the need for *problematising* power, not only powerlessness, in the struggle for liberation (see Chapter Eight).

In order to get to grips with justice and sustainability, there is a need for a sudden and dramatic shift in western epistemology, a way of seeing the world from a dominant perspective that denies indigenous and subordinated worldviews:

> This interdependent world system is based on the exploitation of oppressed groups, but the system at the same time calls forth oppositional cultural forms that give voice to the conditions of these groups. White male bourgeois dominance is being challenged by Black people, women and other oppressed groups, who assert the validity of their own knowledge and demand social justice and equality in numerous political and cultural struggles. In the intellectual sphere, this shifting world system has led to a shattering of Western metanarratives and to the variety of stances of postmodernist and cultural–identity theory. A major theoretical challenge to traditional Western knowledge systems is emerging from feminist theory ... [which] like other contemporary approaches, validates difference, challenges universal claims to truth, and seeks to create social transformation in a world of shifting and uncertain meanings. (Weiler, 1995, p 23)

Dichotomous thought, based on oppositional difference, is a simplistic analysis for complex social hierarchies, hiding as much as it reveals. Domination based on difference results in a hierarchy of fragmentation: an incompleteness held together by relationships of superiority/inferiority. Within this concept, 'as the "Others" of society who can never really belong, strangers threaten the moral and social order. But they are simultaneously essential for its survival because those individuals who stand at the margins of society clarify its boundaries' (Hill Collins, 1990, p 68). Hill Collins suggests that African–American women stand at the convergence of a series of the inferior halves of these dichotomies and that this is central to the understanding of their subordination (Hill Collins, 1990).

Angela Davis vividly captured the dangers of dichotomous thought in relation to the way that class can fragment Black women's activism:

> Black women scholars and professionals cannot afford to ignore the straits of our sisters who are acquainted with the immediacy of oppression in a way many of us are not. The process of empowerment cannot be simplistically defined in accordance with our own particular class interests. We must learn to lift as we climb. (Davis, 1989, p 9)

In these ways, we are able to see that feminism, as a political movement, powerfully placed patriarchy as an oppressive force alongside that of class. However, because its analysis was dichotomous, it focused on 'woman' as a unitary category in relation to its 'Other', 'man', as if all women had the same experience in relation to ethnicity, class and culture. This is not a simple oversight. It represents a struggle of consciousness that, in focusing on this essentialist analysis of patriarchy, fails to offer an adequate explanation of the complex oppressions that construct female identities, including historical and cultural dimensions of gender relations. Gender inequality is not a singular experience, but the complex interplay of any number of political, cultural and historic dimensions. The social construction of gender is immensely complex, but our limited consciousness often traps us into dichotomous explanations rooted in the assumptions of a White unitary experience (Amos and Parmar, 1984). The endemic racism of White feminism not only failed to recognise the anti-racist struggle as central to feminism, but also overlooked the way it pathologises Black people in relation to sexuality and family relations (Anthias and Yuval-Davis, 1992).

So, while Freire is criticised for not dealing with the specific nature of the subordination of women within a class analysis, White feminists stand accused of failing to engage with racism within a feminist analysis. The assumption of a universal sisterhood rendered Black women invisible. This ethnocentric approach overlooked cultural and historic relations, and in its preoccupation with the male/female dichotomy became oblivious of the hegemonic White, female, often middle-class focus (Anthias and Yuval-Davis, 1992). Critique is essential to unpacking the complex interactions of 'race', class and gender and other aspects of difference, otherwise we move from one form of fragmented consciousness to another. Struggles cannot be based on one major identity, just as 'Black' and 'White' women cannot be understood as essentially fixed oppositional categories (Anthias and Yuval-Davis, 1992).

Reflecting on the process of my own consciousness, I am aware that I owe my altered perceptions of social reality to Freire. His pedagogy equipped me with the conceptual tools necessary for my own struggle, and in turn this gave me the confidence to grapple with understandings that were outside my own specific experience. In this respect, bell hooks (1993, p 148) says that while Freire adopted a 'phallocentric paradigm of liberation – wherein freedom and the experience of patriarchal manhood are always linked as though they are one and the same', his profound insight cannot be rejected. Without his help in deepening my own understanding of *praxis* in the process of change, it is likely that I would have remained ignorant of just how necessary it is that 'our lives must be a living example of our politics' (hooks, 1993, p 148).

From a feminist perspective, the problem with Freire is that he fails to include women's experience by subsuming gender within class, and does not recognise the patriarchal assumptions of the European intellectual tradition from which his own thought emerged. His early use of dominant masculine pronouns could be dismissed as a sign of the times, but feminists feel it reflects deeper assumptions about men and women. For instance, he refers to 'feminists' as though they are one voice or a single movement. Many feminists see Freire as offering a generalised and abstract analysis of dichotomous struggle where he presents himself as the heroic teacher. His sense of the revolutionary hero, imagined as male and solely existing in the public world, is problematic to the woman educator who is working with the *authority* of the teacher role and the subordination of 'woman' at one and the same time (Weiler, 2001). His later work became more inclusive and made fewer claims to revolutionary transformation, but he never critiqued the revolutionary leader and so his male assumptions failed to locate the teacher as positioned, in respect of 'race' and gender, at intersections of the private/public divide, in a matrix of interlocking oppressions.

Similarly, his assumption that liberation takes place in the public world led him to overlook the importance of the personal domestic world, thus reinforcing the public/private divide that creates the dichotomy between rationality and emotion. The contradiction here, as with Gramsci, is that he consistently recognised the influence of women in his life. Elza, his first wife, he always acknowledged in terms of intellectual debt. He was a man for whom personal relationships were central to his flourishing and whose work was driven by passion and a love for people. He had qualities that inspired:

> Words seem not [to] be good enough to evoke all that I have learned from Paulo. Our meeting had that quality of sweetness that lingers, that lasts for a lifetime, even if you never speak to the person again, see their face, you can always return in your heart to that moment when you were together and be renewed − that is a profound solidarity. (hooks, 1993, p 154)

He identifies love for humanity as the foundation of critical education, yet fails to elaborate fully on these dimensions in his theoretical analysis. Yet, the contradiction remains that it is precisely because his work is so decontextualised and his claims so sweeping that so many can identify with his pedagogy.

Despite the range of criticism that Freire generates among feminists, we continue to be moved by his visionary humanity, humans as subjects making our own history. But, in global times, it is more apparent than ever that a pedagogy of liberation founded on class power and privilege is incomplete without an analysis of 'race', ethnicity, gender and all other aspects of difference that construct vastly diverse life experiences and life chances. The essence of feminist critiques of Freire is that he did not understand the complex nature of patriarchal, White privilege or the complexities of overlapping oppressions (Weiler, 2001).

Critiques of Freire from a class perspective

Postmodernism and an analysis of difference engendered a backlash from those critical pedagogues who believe that 'postmodernism is an obstacle to the formation of open and radical perspectives which challenge inequalities and the deepening of the rule of capital in all areas of social life' (Rikowski and McLaren, 1999, p 1). Their concern is that 'for postmodernists, all concepts are decentred (fragmented, splattered) and all dualisms (such as the Marxist notion of two major social classes) deconstructed' (Rikowski and McLaren, 1999, p 2). Their driving preoccupation is that postmodernism, in attempting to negate the Enlightenment project's emphasis on reason, rationality and a single truth, results in the search for meaning becoming so hopelessly fragmented that it offers a smokescreen for the Radical Right and its continuing path as the 'Third Way' (Hill, 2000).

Jenny Bourne expresses the dangers of relocating 'race' and 'gender' analyses from their sometimes violent and crushing everyday realities, where grassroots feminism emerged, to an elite position in the academy, not only removed from real life but relocating power in the hands of the already powerful (Bourne, 1999). She identifies the way in which 'the "personal is political" concurrently shifted the centre of gravity of struggle from the community and society to the individual', thus replacing action ('What has to be done?') with the reflection ('Who am I?') of identity politics. Her claim is that *identity* and *difference* have created a fragmentation, a view of society that cut through the 'horizontal divisions of class [with] vertical divisions of gender, sexuality, ethnicity, religion, etc' (Bourne, 1999, p 137). This, of course, is problematic for community development when its process rests on collective action. Conversely, Spretnak (1997) suggests that while modernity sees the world as a collection of objects, and deconstructionist postmodernism dissipates this into an aggregate of fragments, ecological postmodernism offers a community of subjects, which are community-based, but structured politically in a model that embraces a community of communities. The pendulum swings back in this way to offer us insight into the relationship between difference and collective action. The position of the class backlash is that 'unless feminism and identity politics cultivated in the soil of poststructuralism ally themselves more squarely with a politics of class struggle, their contributions will not nourish the revolutionary praxis necessary in the struggle ahead' (McLaren et al, 1999, p 213). We are in a context of globalisation where more than half of the largest economies in the world are multinational corporations, not countries, which exploit the most vulnerable people and resources around the world in the name of capital. While critical pedagogy must engage with a politics of difference, we must at the same time situate this in a larger collective movement for liberation that focuses on the new oppressions created by globalisation:

> My activism can never become dissociated from my theoretical work; on the contrary, the former has its tactics and strategies formulated on the latter. The moment we recognize that food production around the world could be sufficient to feed twice its population, it is desolating to realize the numbers of those who come into the world but do not stay, or those who do but are forced into early departure by hunger. My struggle against capitalism is founded on that – its intrinsic perversity, its antisolidarity nature. (Freire, 1972, p 88)

Lockhart (1999, p 92) claims that there is no evidence that Freirean pedagogy is capable of transformative social change, that he was 'always more important in terms of educational method than "revolutionary futurity"'. This is a position hotly contested by Paula Allman, who attributes the dilution of Freire's potential to the way he is often reduced to a technique by pedagogues; we cannot be partially Freirean, she warns (Allman, 1999). Peter McLaren also warns of the dilution of Freire:

> Contemporary critical pedagogy needs to rescue Freire's work from the reformists who wish to limit his legacy to its contribution to consciousness-raising. Reformists are often victims of a subjectivism that occurs when people verbally denounce social injustice but leave intact the existing structures of society. (McLaren, 2000, pp 192-3)

Allman (1999, 2001, 2009) and McLaren (2000) both challenge the potential of a critical pedagogy that is based on reformism, within rather than against the existing structures of society, and emphasise that Freirean concepts disjointed from the whole pedagogy simply give the illusion of addressing capitalist social relations, 'a limited praxis ... that simply reproduces the given social relations' (Allman, 2009, p 419). However, 'reform, and struggling for it, is crucial both because we must attempt to make life more palatable for those suffering the harshest consequences of capitalism and because we must try to forestall environmental collapse. But it is also important as well as essential because it is through and within the struggles for reform – the shop floor, the community, the environment or any other site where the ramifications of capitalism are experienced – that critical revolutionary praxis develops' (Allman, 2001, p 139). McLaren warns of setting class relations against cultural insights, and advocates a re-reading of Marx with the insights of identity politics if we are to attain any coherent theoretical challenge to globalisation. Knowledge, he says, is transformed through an epistemological critique, which not only examines the content of knowledge, but also the way in which we produce and reproduce that knowledge. He calls for greater collective links between critical educators and students, community activists and the people, to come together in a dialogical relationship in the process of collective action for social change, in praxis.

Paula Allman (2001) poses some crucial questions for our time. How does capitalism seduce us into accepting massive contradictions of suffering and excess as natural and inevitable? How has it managed to win widespread consent at the same time as creating a culture of constant discontent? Her thesis is that a Marxist analysis provides the most complete interpretation of the nature of capitalism, and that the greatest barriers to our understanding remain a misinterpretation of his work. Praxis, for her, embraces all thought and action, not merely the application of theory to practice. Uncritical praxis has the potential for reproducing the conditions for capital to flourish; critical praxis has the infinite possibility to transform our engagement with the world. By exposing the ways in which global capitalism has been internalised and integrated into everyday subjective awareness, we thus begin a process that becomes ever critical and self-critical.

Both McLaren's and Allman's arguments are based on the premise that we remain uncritical as long as our practice relocates us within the same social relations. Praxis only assumes its critical potential when we become aware that ideological statements are partial truths that, in turn, partially distort the truth they are based on, thus reducing our understanding at the same time as convincing us that the version of reality they portray is the real truth. Capitalism, Allman stresses, cannot be reformed; the only way forward is a new worldview founded on justice, both within humanity and between humanity and the natural world. The fundamental role of critical education in this process is in *problematising* reality, constantly probing into how we know and feel. While acknowledging the contribution of the 'new antagonists' – environmentalists, feminists, human rights organisations and other new social movements – she claims that these can do no more than shake capitalism. Her criticism is that some of our finest minds remain trapped within the parameters of capitalism and liberal democracy.

According to Allman, critical pedagogy that has transformative potential needs to be informed by Marx's theory of consciousness, in which principled ethics of compassion and social justice reach out in a form of social interdependence based on a re-reading of class relations. She envisages collective action for change in the form of an international alliance. This strategy is based on an analysis of the way that capitalism cleaves social divisions based on racism, homophobia, environmental destruction, gender disparity and so forth, and so recognises that capitalism is the common enemy, that oppression has a common core. From grassroots organisations, she sees this alliance gradually growing into a global movement (Allman, 2001).

Freire was always very clear that his pedagogy needed to be adapted to, not superimposed on, different political and cultural contexts, yet Blackburn (2000) sees weaknesses in Freirean pedagogy around its potential for ideological manipulation. Any pedagogy can only be as effective as the integrity and vigilance of its practitioners. While we need to be critical in re-visioning Freire in relation to our rapidly changing world and our equally rapidly changing understanding, maybe we also need to get better at practising Freire. Arguably, we are all inextricably trapped in our experience of the world, struggling for an uncluttered, unambiguous clarity. While the criticisms levelled at Freirean thought should be taken seriously, they also give it increased strength. As we push beyond the parameters of the dichotomous thinking that formed Freire's worldview, we are beginning to grapple at the edges of complexity, and develop his pedagogy in accordance with these new awarenesses. Although Freire is hailed for his pedagogy as opposed to his theory, many criticise his lack of guidance on how to become a critical practitioner. McLaren counters this, stating that:

It is precisely his refusal to spell out in a 'bag of tricks' fashion alternative solutions that enables his work to be re-invented in the contexts in which his readers find themselves, thereby enjoining a contextually specific translation across geographic, geopolitical, and cultural borders. It also grants to Freire's corpus of works a universal character, as they are able to retain their heuristic potency (much like the works of Marx) such that they can be conscripted by educators to criticize and to counterpoint pedagogical practices worldwide. In fact, Freire urged his readers to reinvent him in the context of their local struggles. (McLaren, 2000, p 164)

Gramsci and Foucault

Foucault, even though he is associated with post-stucturalism and postmodernism, adds to rather than detracts from Gramsci's analysis by suggesting that power is everywhere, not only on a mega-level of state and the local level of civil society, but permeating the micro relationships of everyday life. As with Gramsci, he sees knowledge and power as inseparable, and this adds to community development's emphasis on critical consciousness as a liberating process, placing critical education at the heart of transformative change. He, like Gramsci, is preoccupied with how people become the conscious subjects of history by intellectual emancipation, and by this I mean that by questioning our lived experience we expose the contradictions we live by, and by seeing the world through a different lens, we claim back our power as subjects in the world. Once again, it reminds us that the key to unlocking grassroots action for change lies in freeing the mind from the chains of *false consciousness* that persuade us to be passive objects in the world to 'self-determining agents that resist and challenge power structures' (Danaher et al, 2000, p 150). Foucault has been embraced into the evolving body of literature that searches for an analysis of power for critical praxis to help us to understand the ways in which a social hierarchy is constructed through power/knowledge relations and reinforced in everyday encounters. Some have the privilege to assert a truth as a statement of power; others accept its truth and transmit it. This is a cumulative process, reinforcing power structures at street level (Giroux, 2009).'For Foucault, power comes from everywhere, from above and from below; it is "always already there" and is inextricably implicated in micro-relations of domination and resistance' (McLaren, 2009, p 72). This calls on us to identify the ways in which power embedded in racialised and gendered relations becomes reinforced in the practices and discourses of everyday life.

> Power must be analyzed as something which circulates, or rather as something which only functions in the form of a chain. It is never localized here or there.... Power is employed and exercised through a net-like organization. (Foucault, 1980, p 98)

In these ways, power is 'an active process constantly at work on our bodies, our relationships, our sexuality, as well as on the ways we construct knowledge and meaning in the world' (Darder et al, 2009, p 7). Power is embodied in the self, as well as embedded in society, not only out there in structures of domination, but also in sites of resistance interacting within the relationships of those who claim to be on the same side. Importantly, Foucault identifies the dangers of a society that 'neither questions itself nor can imagine any alternative to itself ... [feeding] ... the growing ineptitude, if not irrelevance, of (in)organic and traditional intellectuals whose cynicism often translates into complicity with the forms of power they condemn' (Giroux, 2009, p 177).

Thinking of power in this way, rather than only a polarity between the state and civil society, we are more able to see how dominant ideology reaches into the processes of life permeating people's relationships in every interaction, influencing attitudes, identities and perceptions (Foucault, 1980). For instance, when my younger son Duncan's Black British friend Owen came to stay with us after our move from culturally diverse Manchester to predominantly White Lancaster, he told me, "The gaze lingers for just a little bit too long as I walk by". It lingers, of course, just long enough to make a statement of Other. Power relations, according to Foucault, are acted out in all our practices – educational, scientific, religious, legal – that embed dominant discourse in their processes.

'Critical educators argue that *praxis* (informed actions) must be guided by *phronesis* (the disposition to act truly and rightly). This means, in critical terms, that actions and knowledge must be directed at eliminating pain, oppression, and inequality, and at promoting justice and freedom' (McLaren, 2009, p 74). As McLaren points out, *empowerment* means not only setting the learning context for participants to understand the world around them, but also to find the courage to speak truth to power, as Quakers would say. This is what Freire meant by denunciation. We need to be able to understand power in order to denounce it, and by denouncing it we create an interruption in *what is*, a space in which to build new possibilities for *what could be*. In these ways, much as Gramsci redefined *hegemony* to include power as ideological persuasion, not only coercion, so Foucault argues that we must direct our attention from a concentration on the role of the state and the institutions of civil society to include the micro-levels of social interaction.

> Hegemonic or global forms of power rely in the first instance on those 'infinitesimal' practices, composed of their own particular techniques and tactics, which exist in those institutions on the fringes or at the micro-level of society. (Foucault, 1980, p 99)

These analyses give us a better idea of what form power takes in different contexts and at different levels, and how community development needs to engage with each appropriately.

Kothari (2001), Craig et al (2008) and Darder et al (2009) warn of the dangers to any liberatory practice of simplifying the nature of power. Kothari says that while we fail to see knowledge as an accumulation of norms, rituals and practices that are embedded in power relations, we fall back on simplistic dichotomies of power, and change nothing. Gary Craig (2008) warns that an inability to analyse power at policy and personal levels has led to an inability to understand racism or multicultural societies, so that issues of social justice, culture and identity constantly get swept under the carpet. Darder et al (2009) note that there was a point at which postmodernism threatened to fragment understanding of major structures of power by reducing critical theory to a disconnected whole while 'advanced capitalism whipped wildly around the globe, [consolidating] neoliberal effort to perpetuate structures of economic domination and exploitation' (Darder et al, 2009, pp 16-17). As I address in other parts of this book, within a multiplicity of power relations that get acted out on all levels, 'race', class and gender remain crucial overarching sources of oppression and exploitation. Without getting to grips with analyses of power, we not only reduce the social justice intention of our practice, but, much worse, we also unwittingly reinforce the status quo.

Gramsci and feminism

The relationship between capitalism and patriarchy are separate but interrelated systems of oppression, and the view that feminism is less important than class or even divisive of class has been a contentious issue. Here, I will explore the invisibility of male power to Gramsci in an exploration of the contradictions between his intellectual and personal/emotional understanding of power relations.

Paradoxically, yet unsurprisingly, the personal sustenance of Gramsci during his prison years and the survival of his contribution to thought in the form of his prison notebooks were due to his sister-in-law, Tatiana Schucht, yet any political analysis of her 11 years of commitment to him was overlooked by Gramsci. Holub (1992, p 195) reminds us that we should not 'assiduously polish the tainted mirrors of theoretical heroes'. By the same token, it is equally important not to dismiss significant contributions to the development of our own thought, as women, out of hand. We need to engage with this paradox. As with Freire, Gramsci's thinking was historically and culturally specific, and it is therefore hardly surprising that it fell foul of the public/private divide. His thinking did not benefit from the coherent feminist awareness that has developed over the last few decades. The deep affection and admiration he felt for his mother, his sister Teresina, his wife Giulia and his sister-in-law Tatiana are well-documented and undisputed (Kenway, 2001). Paradoxically, Gramsci accepted as 'natural' the roles of the women in his personal life without recognising their political implications. However, there is a glimpse that he was aware at some deeper level of the complex subordination of women. In 1916, Gramsci's first public address was on the emancipation of women 'taking as his cue Ibsen's play "The Doll's House"' (Hoare and Smith, in Introduction to Gramsci, 1971, p xxxi). In his discussion of Americanism and

Fordism he not only acknowledges women's exploitation in the public domain, but also recognises our vital function in the reproduction of the workforce, thereby identifying sexuality as a locus of oppression (Gramsci, 1986). However, 'although Gramsci supported women's rights and saw sexuality as a basic aspect of emancipation, women's issues were not central to his thought' (Kenway, 2001, p 56). Holub, too, points to an inherent contradiction in his thinking from a feminist perspective: 'Gramsci insists on the centrality of sexuality, a woman's rights over her body, when it comes to the emancipation not only of women, but of society as a whole', but this is contradicted by the way his analysis is limited to 'the need to discipline women's sexuality for economic and political purposes' (Holub, 1992, pp 197-8).

By gaining insight into the subtle ways in which power transcends the divide from public to private through the institutions of civil society – religion, education, the family and other forms of daily life – Gramsci offers understanding of the ways in which domination permeates the most intimate aspects of our being, transcending the public/private divide. This is the basis for Gramsci's acknowledged contribution to feminist thought through his concept of hegemony, which has provided a tool of analysis for understanding the sites of gendered oppression in society. Feminists have found the concept of hegemony to be a powerful conceptual tool. For instance, Arnot in the early 1980s argued that male hegemony consists of a multiplicity of moments that have persuaded women to accept a male-dominated culture and their subordination within it. The result is a constructed reality that is qualitatively different from that of men (Kenway, 2001). In understanding the nature of consent, we come to see that hegemony is always in process, in continuous struggle, and we begin to see that feminist consciousness has grown through questioning the nature of consent in relation to women's lives.

Holub's (1992, p 197) interpretation of Gramscian feminism is that he saw economic independence as only part of the story; true emancipation involves freedom of choice in relation to sexual relationships. What he referred to as a 'new ethic' (Gramsci, 1986, p 296) is the transformative moment gained from a war of position that frees women in a truly liberatory way. Gramsci's feminist consciousness therefore connects women's sexual rights not only with women's liberation, but with the total transformation of society. Gramsci in this sense gives us a model of the way in which the *personal* is fundamentally *political*. Disappointingly, he loses credibility by calling for a sexual discipline that serves the economy:

> So the promising concessions Gramsci makes to the liberation of feminine sexuality are severely curtailed by his deterministic view of progress, his belief in the liberatory potential of industrialisation and above all his uncritical deployment, indeed, his 'forgetting', of one of his own powerful analytical tools in the demystification of power: the ubiquitous operations of hegemony, of certain ways of seeing and

validating relations in multiple sites of political and social relations, in the public, but above all in the private sphere, in political, but above all in civil society, in the social, in the cultural, in the micro-spaces of everyday life. (Holub, 1992, p 198)

So, while Gramsci helps us to understand that without consent the whole nature of domination is weakened, it has taken Foucault to illuminate the ways in which power permeates the nooks and crannies of everyday existence. This understanding of power extending from state to civil society to the micro-spaces of life helps us frame our analyses for action.

Patti Lather in her work in the mid-1980s drew on Gramsci's notion of the *war of position* and the role of the *intellectuals* in relation to feminist political action. She chooses to substitute 'counter-hegemony' for 'struggle', inasmuch as it shifts the emphasis onto ideological alternatives. Lather takes Gramsci's belief in everyone's innate capacity to be philosophers and considers this in relation to the way that women have documented experience-based knowledge and acted to become prominent in all social institutions, claiming that this constitutes a *war of position*: 'many small revolutions ... many small changes in relationships, behaviors, attitudes and experiences' (Kenway, 2001, p 59). She places particular emphasis on the role of the intellectuals in the tide of developing critical consciousness, but raises a note of warning about the need to stay critical, vigilant and self-questioning. Jane Kenway (2001) calls for a renewed Gramscian perspective from which we could engage with the big issues of our times, but Peter Mayo points out that 'one has to go beyond Gramsci to avoid Eurocentrism and beyond both Gramsci and Freire to avoid patriarchal bias' (Mayo, 1999, p 146). However, together Gramsci and Freire present a profundity of thought that offers us the basis for a critical approach to community development. 'And where they relate most clearly is in Freire's consideration of the political nature of education and in Gramsci's consideration of the educational nature of politics' (Allman, 1988, p 92). Our responsibility is to wrestle with these ideas with the privilege of our new understandings.

We must hold this vision in a past–present–future dynamic, 'moving between present and past with a view to contributing towards a transformed future' (Mayo, 1999, p 147). Throughout their radical past, Freire and Gramsci have inspired community development and popular education. Peter Mayo explores the complementarity of Gramsci and Freire coherently and confidently from Malta (1999), making a massive contribution to the Gramsci–Freire project. This, linked particularly to the work of the British and the North American critical pedagogues, provides a body of thought that offers a new possibility for radical community development theory. (For a fuller discussion of Gramsci and feminism, see Ledwith, 2010.)

Social justice, environmental justice and sustainability

> Unless development leads to greater equality, environmentally sound
> outcomes, and improved opportunities for human growth it cannot
> meet the goals of sustainable development. (Gamble and Weil, 1997,
> p 220)

From an environmental justice perspective, Freire and the Freirean movement
stand accused of neglecting both globalisation and the environmental crisis
(Bowers and Apffel-Marglin, 2004). The argument is that Freire's emphasis on
critical consciousness in relation to class liberation, most particularly through
literacy, is founded on western assumptions that prioritise humanity, freedom
and empowerment through dialogue over subordinate indigenous belief systems
that are founded on biodiversity, claiming that critical pedagogy 'fractures
knowledge and supports the further alienation of human beings from nature'
(Darder et al, 2009, p 17). These critiques have sharpened our understanding of
the inextricable relationship between social justice and environmental justice.
Community development has embraced the understanding and now overtly
claims to be predicated on principles of social and environmental justice. The
Paulo Freire Institute for Ecopedagogy is committed to 'the construction of a
planetary citizenship, so that all, with no exception or exclusion, may have healthy
conditions, in a planet able to offer life because its own life is being preserved'
(Darder et al, 2009, p 18). In this way, ecopedagogy embraces all forms of life on
earth in diversity and biodiversity as a love for all life. Paulo Freire was working
on ecopedagogy when he died, and some of these ideas are included in his
posthumous *Pedagogy of indignation* (2005). Other examples of Freire's ongoing
influence on action for social and environmental justice and the connectedness
between community, empowerment and sustainability includes Blewitt's (2008)
work under the banner of 'The Converging World', a charity which links people
to address education, poverty and environment developed by local, community-
led sustainability groups in a process of action and reflection towards a movement
for change. This all started off in 2004 with the Coffeehouse Challenges which
gained inspiration from the coffee shops of 18th-century London which were
the context for dialogue on big issues as the basis of action. A series of meetings
in Starbucks in Bristol led to the village of Chew Magna, nearby, looking at how
they wanted their community to develop. Just one person who was a common
denominator in both processes gathered support and organised a series of
coffeehouse conversations in the village on moving towards a zero-waste society,
and each time numbers grew:

> The first response was surprising – something had tapped deeply into
> the consciousness of the local population and had released energy. Not
> only were people concerned, even anxious, but it was apparent that
> they were keen to make something happen. When, one evening, more

than forty people turned up, it was too late to stop the momentum and soon four groups formed to take action. (Roderick with Jones, 2008, pp 18-19)

Freire has been accused of failing to understand the ecological crisis the world faces because he emphasises poverty in relation to capitalism and its economic domination in the process of globalisation. Ecological thought emphasises that diverse indigenous cultures live in harmony with their natural environments. Cultural diversity thus becomes essential for biological diversity, and histories based on local economic development offer alternatives for the future that reflect values other than consumer lifestyles: a harmonious co-existence between social justice and environmental justice.

Gamble and Weil spell out the necessity of understanding the interconnection between community development and environmental justice because 'the concept of sustainable development now functions as a unifying concept in several ways. It connects local and global perspectives; it provides a focus on protection of both the physical environment and human populations; it imposes a long-term view of the consequences of present-day activities; it can serve the goals of gender equity; and it provides a way effectively to integrate social and economic development' (Gamble and Weil, 1997, p 211).

They cite Estes' seven fundamental concepts as a frame for analysis and action:

(i)   the unity of humanity and life on earth
(ii) the minimisation of violence
(iii) the maintenance of environmental quality
(iv) the satisfaction of minimum world welfare standards
(v)   the primacy of human dignity
(vi) the retention of diversity and pluralism
(vii) universal participation.

Riordan, in her essay on adapting to climate change in Africa, warns that the absence of a gender analysis 'can obscure the gap between having a stake in environmental protection and the capacity to act on it. Some essential differences in the way in which men and women typically organise environmental action (usually formal among men, informal among women) can be missed ... [leading] to a failure to identify the constraints that women face and need to overcome for their effective involvement in the formal institutions of local resource management' (Riordan, 2008, p 47). Research constantly reaches similar conclusions:

- women in poverty are most at risk from dangers associated with climate change
- women are largely ignored in climate research, policy and development

- women are key actors in developing local coping strategies for climate change
- women are critical agents of change in communities
- women's skills and leadership are crucial for survival and recovery of all
- women's empowerment is needed for sound management of environmental resources
- women possess initiative, creativity and capacity to find grassroots solutions for climate change.

Lack of a gender analysis not only places a disproportionate burden on poor women the world over in relation to action on climate change, but it also limits the effectiveness of initiatives. (Riordan, 2008, p 49)

Ecofeminism's embrace of the environment and sustainability arises from a critical connection between the 'death of nature' and the rise of patriarchy, and can be explored through the work of such people as Charlene Spretnak, Carolyn Merchant, Arundhati Roy and Vandana Shiva. The central argument from ecofeminism is that 'a historical, symbolic and political relationship exists between the denigration of nature and the female in Western cultures' (Spretnak, 1993, p 181). Ecofeminism is rooted in principles of 'harmony, co-operation and interconnection' that challenge the perceived male principles of competition, 'discrimination, extremism and conflict' (Young, A., 1990, p 33). This competitive worldview elevates men over both women and the natural world in a system of ranked order importance, deifying a male God, and downplaying the femininity of God, illustrating how organised religion plays a key hegemonic role in legitimising the common sense of subordination (McIntosh, 2001). Women continue to be active in organising and theorising an alternative worldview based on harmony and cooperation, non-violence and dignity, a view that embraces both public and private, local and global, humanity and the natural world in equal measure. It reflects women's concerns for preserving life on earth over time and space. Our western worldview, founded on a complex system of domination and subordination, creates physical and spiritual alienation. This calls for a new way of seeing the world:

We need, I believe, a way of knowing which helps us to heal this split, this separation, this alienation. We need a way of knowing which integrates truth with love, beauty and wholeness, a way of knowing which acknowledges the essential physical qualities of knowing. We need a new story about our place in the scheme of things. (Reason, 1994b, p 14)

In relation to the interface of social justice and environmental justice, Crescy Cannan made an immense impact on community development thought when she stated that the environmental crisis is a crisis for us all, but it disproportionately affects both the poor and the South and so 'intensifies forms of inequality and threatens collective goods – thus it is a human crisis as well as a threat to the entire planet' (2000, p 365). Her argument is linked to the impact of globalisation and the way that massive increases in economic growth have simultaneously been accompanied by massive poverty gaps, both between nations and within nations. Current standards of consumption are not only creating global ecological degradation but massive inequalities. The problem lies in the individualist/consumerist ideology that is central to western capitalism justifying the disproportionate access to the earth's resources of the rich. Our challenge is to change the unsustainable living habits of the West while reducing the disparity between rich and poor, both in and between countries. Sustainability and social justice involve the wealthy examining the destructive nature of consumer lifestyles, in much the same way as anti-discriminatory practice involves Whites understanding the nature of White power and privilege.

An alternative ideology, based on the principle of a common good rather than individual greed, raises questions about a drive for profit that holds no accountability for human or environmental well-being.

Eurig Scandrett of Queen Margaret University, Edinburgh, tells the story of community direct action against environmental degradation in Scotland.

Community action against environmental injustice

"Greengairs is a former mining town of 1,500 people in North Lanarkshire with high levels of unemployment. The deep mines in this area closed well before Margaret Thatcher's onslaught on the National Union of Mineworkers, but the coal seams have continued to be extracted by open cast. As open cast mines have been exhausted, the resulting holes in the ground have been transformed into landfill sites and 'rehabilitated' by receiving municipal and commercial waste, primarily from Glasgow. This leaves Greengairs surrounded by opencast coal mines and landfill sites, including one of the largest landfills in Europe, which dominates the skyline of the village and is the source of smells, pests and constant heavy vehicle traffic. Members of the community regularly contacted Friends of the Earth Scotland in Edinburgh for advice, and periodically complained to the Scottish Environment Protection Agency with little satisfaction. The community was therefore known to Friends of the Earth that was starting to develop an approach to environmental justice that was later to become a community action team.

"In 1996, Friends of the Earth staff were routinely scrutinising the latest issue of the *ENDS Report*, a technical journal of environmental management, and spotted a notice telling that soil contaminated with polychlorinated biphenyls (PCBs) was being dumped in the Greengairs landfill site. PCBs are known carcinogens and the handling of contaminated materials by waste facilities is governed by licensing by the Scottish Environment Protection Agency. Greengairs was one of the few landfill sites in the UK whose license had not been upgraded to take into account stricter regulations on the handling of PCBs. The operator was exploiting this loophole – legally – by transporting the contaminated soil from Hertfordshire to Lanarkshire.

"Having identified the problem, a small group of staff and volunteers visited some people they knew in the community. Word had travelled and a small crowd of concerned local residents gathered to hear what the Friends of the Earth folk had to say. Although they were well used to bad treatment from the various operators of mines and waste facilities in the area, the cynical exploitation of a legal loophole to risk the health of the community was a step too far. Moreover, since the company was technically acting within the law, it seemed as though there was little they could do about it. Despite having no experience of militancy, the feeling of the community was such that they decided to take direct action. The town was mobilised and blockaded the entrance to the site with local men, women and children, with some organisational and technical support from Friends of the Earth. Careful to avoid conflict with the lorry drivers and the police, the community devised a scheme whereby lorries coming into the landfill site would be allowed to enter the quarter mile driveway to the gate, but stopped from going into the site by a group of local families barricading the gate. Whenever sufficient lorries were backed up to fill the driveway, a few lorries were permitted through. In this way, the operations of the company were slowed down without danger.

"Following days of standoff, the company's Chief Executive travelled to Scotland to meet with the community, who were being advised by Friends of the Earth. Eventually, he conceded to a few demands and agreed to abide by the recommendations of an independent consultancy commissioned to find alternatives to the dumping of the contaminated soil. Significantly, the management of the landfill site was also changed, bringing in a regime with greater openness and accountability to the community. A local environment group was formed which spearheaded a number of other local environmental campaigns – maintaining vigilance over the landfill and other local operations, constructing environmental improvements and fighting new unwanted developments. Activists politicised by these events went on to study courses on environmental justice, lobbied ministers on waste policy and linked up to share their learned expertise with others throughout Scotland in similar struggles (Coleman, 2003; Dunion, 2003). Greengairs became the iconic community in Scotland which mobilised against environmental injustice."

Eurig captures the ways in which community action can be strengthened in partnership with a campaigning body, such as Friends of the Earth, experienced in non-violent action and strategic tactics, to great effect. This action, in turn, inspires other communities.

The problems that we face today around health, poverty, inequality, education and the environment, have become perceived as inevitable rather than as a consequence of capitalism. Community development practice needs to develop strategies that challenge this consciousness and balance the needs of business against the needs of local communities.

One of the ways in which this understanding can be incorporated into our practice is by developing a system of community accounting that checks a wide range of environmental and social justice issues. 'The enterprise paradigm has established an accounting system that measures revenue, costs and incomes for enterprise owners. A new community paradigm must do the same for communities

... if there is to be a shift in viewpoint, a system will have to be set up that looks at matters that usually escape individual enterprise accounts. This assumes a moral and not a mechanical universe' (Roxas, quoted in Douthwaite, 1996, p 336). The thinking implicit in this idea is that of a new worldview, one in which the economy is not elevated over other aspects of life, but where the emphasis is on harmony, sustainability and justice. Any model of development that fails to see community needs as a balanced system will overlook human well-being and environmental justice.

Competition driven by profit is increasing as a result of globalisation, therefore the power of communities to argue for the common good is vital; business continues to be 'subsidized on a massive scale by taxpayers, society and the environment' and thus has a social and environmental obligation (Douthwaite, 1996, p 341). We have to come up with new possibilities, and one of these is illustrated by the story of Dorrit Seemann. She struggled for five years to make her shop viable based on competitive economic principles. Eventually she developed the idea of inviting her customers to take out a monthly subscription to give her an income and cover her overheads, which in turn meant she was able to offer them goods at cost price. 'Enough people took up the idea to make it work; this radically altered her relationship with those she supplied because instead of setting her prices at the highest level she felt her customers would tolerate, the challenge was now to buy as well as she could on her subscribers' behalf and to make the shop and its services as attractive and convenient for them as possible' (Douthwaite, 1996, p 343). Douthwaite is optimistic that if we can get enough communities to develop independent, parallel economies and to become mutually supportive in the process, the swing from global to local will increase our chances of a sustainable future.

Community development has taken more interest in the environment over recent years, particularly with the development of Local Agenda 21 programmes. The challenge for community development praxis is that our analysis of social justice should not compromise the life chances of future generations or the lives of those in the developing world. Social justice and environmental justice come together in community development in places where we offer alternatives to the values of capitalism. Fair Trade, LETS (Local Economic Trading Systems) and credit unions are examples of how an alternative local economy can place cooperation rather than competition at the heart of new approaches to community, changing fundamental core values (see www.neweconomics.org). The community gardens movement is an example of how economic factors can be linked to other aspects of well-being. When I visited a community near Wigan in North West England, I was taken with pride to their community garden. One day, a row of terraced houses disappeared down a mine shaft when the ground subsided. This became a derelict space for dumping, drug dealing and other depressing activities. It has now been transformed into an oasis in the midst of all the tightly-packed, gardenless miners' cottages, providing a central social space surrounded by a range of different planted areas, including a market garden. It is a sanctuary for reflection, nurturing people when they feel they cannot face the hardship of their lives. It has provided a place for the community to gather together for barbecues, carol services and other community events. People get to know each other, and it cheers them up. Vegetables are harvested and sold locally. In these ways, we see how a simple idea contributes to the health and well-being of the community (see Figure 5.1, p 129, 'A framework for local/global action').

Burningham and Thrush (2001), investigating environmental concerns of marginalised groups in the UK, importantly for community development emphasise that 'many small problems are symptoms of deeper and more complex social and economic issues. Sustainable solutions to local environmental problems require these wider issues to be addressed' (Burningham and Thrush, 2001, p 44). In these ways, we tease out the links between environmental and social justice, and local to global action.

Critiques of Freire and Gramsci from coherently argued perspectives provide us with the basis for extending community development theory into more adequate analyses of *difference and diversity* in relation to social justice and *sustainability* in relation to environmental justice. Within this, it is important to take into account critiques of capitalism as a system capable of reform (Allman, 1999, 2001; McLaren, 2000), and the call for a new worldview, one that is based on an ideology of cooperation rather than competition (I.M. Young, 1990; Spretnak, 1993; Reason and Bradbury, 2001; Reason, 2002). *Praxis* is the bedrock of this process: theory in action, building a body of knowledge based on experience. The collective struggle for social justice and environmental justice is the basis for alliances between community activists and environmental activists in global times. In fact, many community workers are seeing this as a natural extension of their traditional work. However, Hillman (2002) raises concerns that the naive belief that sustainability can be achieved within the current economic system de-radicalises the environmental movement. The local/global dynamic is vital here: local people experience the impact of environmental degradation most immediately, and action is more relevant when it begins in people's communities as part of the process of critical consciousness and grassroots action (Burningham and Thrush, 2001). From local participation, this reaches out beyond community to engage with collective action that takes on global issues of justice and sustainability.

The environmental justice movement was formed as a response to the disproportionate environmental problems experienced by already disadvantaged communities and poorer nations. This has created a tension between what are perceived as top–down issues (for example, climate change, endangered animal and plant species, pollution and degradation of land and water resources) and grassroots action, a tension between strategy and participation. Cannan (2000) suggests that by identifying links between environmental justice and social justice, we can move into new areas of action and development. She includes vertical and horizontal links between grassroots participation and social movements that concentrate on alliances as the basis of organising for a sustainable and just future. Polly Higgins, ex-barrister turned environmental campaigner, takes this a stage further calling for ecocide, the extensive destruction of ecosystems, to be recognised as a crime to be tried in the International Criminal Court, denouncing crimes against the environment as we do crimes against humanity (Higgins, 2010b).

The Sustainable Seattle project, set up in 1980, developed indicators based on a range of measures that affect the quality and sustainability of human life. This approach was adopted by the Earth Summit in Rio de Janeiro, Brazil in 1992 establishing a blueprint for sustainability in the 21st century and Agenda 21 became a commitment to sustainable development agreed by many of the world's governments. The detailed action plan for regional and local sustainable development is Local Agenda 21 which focuses on grassroots action at community level as the most effective intervention for change. The UK government guidelines for sustainability indicators can be found at www.defra.gov.uk/sustainable/government. Issues of poverty, hunger, over-consumption, health and education are set within guidelines for everyone, from governments to businesses to local people. Similarly, Social Return on Investment (SROI) is a tool for measuring social, environmental and economic costs and benefits by assigning a monetary figure to social and environmental value to reduce inequality, prevent environmental degradation and improve well-being (available at www.neweconomics.org). 'We're all interconnected, interdependent. Lose the planet and we lose our habitat and means of survival' (Higgins, 2010b, p 24).

Grassroots action includes changes in the way we live our lives. This is why initiatives such as Transition Towns, inspired by bigger picture concerns of peak oil, climate change and economic stagnation, focuses on community environmental justice, low energy lifestyles that situate us within our responsible place in the ecosystem of life on earth. Plant ecologist Naomi van der Velden, of the University of Cumbria, captures the empowering and creative dimensions of collectively exploring different approaches to life in her story about forest gardening in Cumbria.

Forest gardening

"It started a year ago. We had begun work in our forest garden and it started to rain.

"'We need a shelter,' someone said. We all nodded thoughtfully in reply.

"The next forest gardening day, I'd sourced some willow saplings to cut and use to build a shelter. I'd once helped make a small semi-circular 'bender' using sticks bent around to form a frame then thatched with branches to make a rough shelter. I showed the others where the willow was and a few pictures of the sort of thing I had in mind. When I looked back an hour or so later, an impressive willow-weave roundhouse was under construction! It was over two metres high and large enough for everyone to sit in to enjoy a well-deserved cup of tea. Much more than that, it was an inspiration.

"It showed me how great the combined ideas and efforts of others can be. They had worked together to conceive and build something far more practical and elegant than I ever would have imagined. I am a teacher, a university lecturer. This moment taught me that empowering people to make their own decisions and use their combined creativity is far more rewarding than students simply learning what they are told to; that it is this independence of thought and cooperative action which truly dictates the future.

"Our forest garden was started by the shared vision of a few inspired people. We know a forest is the most productive of land ecosystems. The aim of a forest garden is to integrate our understanding of woodland ecosystems and of plant ecology with a touch of human ingenuity to create a highly productive way of growing food. Complementary plants are selected to maximise the use of space. For example, an apple tree gives shelter and support to climbing beans, and the beans fix nitrogen so increasing the soil fertility for other plants. It is about creating a diverse community of interacting plants. It follows permaculture principles to maximise production with minimal inputs. It's about creating a sustainable, productive system.

"We are not alone in our approach. We have become part of a group of similar projects. The Cumbria Forest Food Network seeks to link up forest food projects in our region to help us learn from one another, to share ideas, skills, knowledge, successes, and failures. Permaculture is coming into the national consciousness through such community projects in woodlands and gardens. In a time of soaring food prices, increasing demands on land for biofuel and wood, massive cuts in government spending, and tightening legislation on carbon emissions, the interest in locally produced, low-carbon, low-cost food is growing. People are being inspired and empowered. Local action is receiving national attention. We are joining with other projects across the country to research the tools, methods, plant communities, and benefits to wildlife and to human health and well-being of forest gardens. We are creating a diverse, interactive community of people, maximising the use of our shared spaces, and developing a sustainable and productive system.

"Another university year has started. Yesterday, old students and new worked together on the roundhouse. It has evolved. New ideas have influenced its shape and design. I watched them discussing and building. Building the roundhouse, building relationships, and building our future. It's nice to be part of it."

Naomi captures the essence of collective action for change; the way a bigger picture idea, explored from a local perspective, inspires an interactive process of thought and action, building practical projects based on new consciousness, where local projects link together, extending outwards to form networks. In this case, Naomi illustrates how the Forest Food Network is part of a wider change in consciousness; rising from grassroots action, local projects engage with the bigger issues of our times, social justice and sustainability, in a groundswell movement for change. In a similar way, Lancaster Cohousing (www.lancastercohousing.org.uk) was the vision of a few local people concerned about the future of the planet in relation to environmental degradation. The issue became a project, and the project is reaching fruition as an ecologically sustainable community: Forge Bank on the banks of the River Lune at Halton in North West England. The twin aims of building houses based on ecological values in a community based on collective, cooperative values, with a common house at its heart as the connecting point, leads the way in demonstrating that other choices based on responsibilities to humanity and the planet are possible.

Any effective action calls for altered consciousness. Fisher and Ponniah (2003) emphasise the need for challenging the supremacy of the market economy in western consciousness:

> Sustainability requires putting the environment and society above the market. To make progress towards sustainable societies requires policies based on the inclusion of all races and cultures, equity and solidarity among societies, and cooperation among governments. The first step in meeting this challenge is repairing the environment and society. (Fisher and Ponniah, 2003, pp 127-8)

And one way of moving into such an alternative worldview is to develop a Freirean-feminist-anti-racist pedagogy fundamentally rooted in an ideology of cooperation, where a desire for peace and non-violence forms the basis of the will to develop new possibilities. This is the subject of the next chapter.

EIGHT

Towards a Freirean-feminist-anti-racist pedagogy

The basis of community development's transformative potential lies in its analysis of power in relation to changing political times. We have considered the contribution of Gramsci in extending our understanding of hegemony beyond state coercion to include ideological persuasion, a process that reaches through civil society to influence the way people think and behave in the interests of dominant ideology, as well as the role of traditional and organic intellectuals in the process of change. Influenced by Gramsci, we have explored in some detail the analysis and action of Freire who directs our attention to the stories of everyday life as the key to unlocking unequal power relations that are lived out as everyday contradictions. We have extended this to include Foucault's analysis of power as present and reinforced in everyday encounters in a myriad of power relations at the micro-level of society. These levels of power demand our attention in the process of radical social transformation. Power, in these ways, becomes a mutually reinforcing process operating from the bottom up as well as top down. This places consciousness at the heart of change, suggesting that the beginning of this process lies firmly in the stories of everyday life as the beginning of a process of progressive social change.

From the mid-1980s, postmodernism led us from metanarratives towards mini-narratives, multiple identities rather than political identities, obscuring the need for collective action (Kenway, 2001, p 60). Retrieving our position from analytic fragmentation, bell hooks reminded us that Freire had 'offered her insight into the nature of her own oppression as a Black American woman, helping her to see herself as a subject in resistance, thus locating a contradiction between White women and a third-world man' (hooks, 1993, p 150). In these ways, Freire has spoken with more integrity to people from a non-White, non-European, developing world perspective. Our current challenge is to keep apace with globalisation's marketisation of life on earth which operates on a multiplicity of hegemonies, reproducing racial, patriarchal and class divisions. Gary Craig (2011) reiterate the need for a strong theoretical base for community development if we are to preserve our distinctive identity, that our poverty of literature has weakened our capacity to develop sufficiently strong 'race' and gender analyses. Problematising power shifts us from a preoccupation with powerlessness to *powerfulness* in the struggle for liberation with anti-racism at its heart (Fine et al, 1997).

At this point I want to re-engage with the seminal essay of Peggy McIntosh in 'White privilege: unpacking the invisible knapsack' (2004). More than ever our reflections on everyday experience, the stories we tell, hold the answer to the change we want to live.

The dangers of overlooking Whiteness mean that multicultural reforms are routinely 'sucked back into the system' and the 'multicultural paradigm is mired in liberal ideology that offers no radical change in the current order' (Ladson-Billings and Tate, 2006, p 579). This radical critique can, I believe, come from ground level by confronting some painful truths in a process of self-reflection and dialogue.

Problematising Whiteness

Whiteness is an issue. The assumed privilege of Whiteness still remains largely unexposed and understood in relation to anti-racist practice. Dyer (1997) argues that the particular way in which White superiority gets expressed is through its invisibility to the point of non-existence. It is an assumed superiority in which the colour of skin becomes symbolic of an intellectual ideal that gets acted out as moral superiority. By assumed, I mean that its subtlety is not understood by White people. This makes it elusive and hard to challenge, as it is so fully embedded in the practices of everyday life.

As community development practitioners we are also action researchers engaged in theorising everyday lives in dynamic with changing political times. In our theorising, we have failed to understand Whiteness as a key source of power, and in overlooking it, we leave it invisible. Critical whiteness, a move to explore the tenacity of White privilege in the face of civil rights, emerged from the USA in the late 1980s (hooks, 1989; Fine et al, 1997; Frankenberg, 1997), but has still not been embraced into the theoretical base of community development. Yet, Frankenberg (1997) argues that White communities are racialised by the very act of accumulating 'unearned privileges', and that we need to name Whiteness in order to expose it. In the following story, Diane Warner talks about ways in which Whiteness is reproduced, and her work in creating learning contexts that make it more visible.

Seeds of resistance

"As a black university teacher in a nearly all-white university, I sometimes find this a curious and sometimes exciting situation to be in. When it troubles me, I wonder what I am doing here and think a lot about the whiteness of most of my students – they both study in a white university and come from white home backgrounds. I am worried about unwittingly being part of extending this monoculture and reinforcing their existing ways of thinking and acting. As they are training to be teachers, the terrifying question is what will this racist effect have on future generations of children?

"In answering this question I recall bell hooks' (1991) desire to open our eyes to the casual and almost porous nature of racism; an entity which infiltrates our existence and to which most people are party. In talking to my students I found doorways into their worlds which defied me making simplistic views about their outlook. I admit to being dismayed about their view that teachers should not notice a child's colour or ethnicity because this betrayed an adamant blindness to the reality of being black in a white society. I was cautiously optimistic when they started telling me vignettes which revealed other dimensions about them. I call these 'seeds of resistance', resistance against adopting a negative mindset.

"There was Lou's story of growing up in a white, working-class area of a racially divided northern town, further compounded by attending a white, church school. Yet on placement, at a white primary school she described as narrow and inward-looking, she was confronted by an unpleasant situation.

> '... they had an Asian child join the school, the parents were very against it and they complained. It was white, working-class ... really old-fashioned, values like that, but they were coming from the parents, rather than the school. Maybe they [school] were concerned about upsetting people, that's why they didn't challenge it.'

"Jessica related her feelings of being hampered by the monocultural nature of the university campus and the views of other white students, who have told her that they are disappointed to be in schools with little or no white children.

> 'I think it's important ... it's the different experience. I know some people would say "teaching's teaching", but from what I know [about multiculturalism], this is very different from the way I'm teaching at the minute.'

"Will, white in colour and culture, came from Ukrainian grandparents which he realised, as an adult, did affect his outlook. He said:

> 'My grandparents were Ukrainian, my granddad was dark skinned and my mother was a single teenage mum, so although I did not know it at the time, I grew up understanding what it meant to be different.'

"After growing up in a white Lancashire village, Will recognised how his background had undergirded some of his feelings towards racial issues. He firmly stated that teachers should 'reflect what's life', not hide facts about the reality of multiracial Britain and racism.

"These students are beginning to comprehend the essence and immorality of racial injustice and inequality. They are unformed and small insights, but they make it possible for me to move forward with hope."

Diane captures the resistance of White superiority to questioning its own privilege, at the same time as demonstrating the capacity of a skilled Black educator to work across difference in supporting student teachers to reflect on the ways in which White privilege reproduces itself. She is nurturing 'seeds of resistance', as a Black woman in a dominant White context. However, considering Frantz Fanon published *Black skin, White masks* in French in 1952 (Fanon, 2008) based on Black experience of western domination, it is high time, as White people, that we seize the baton and take responsibility for exploring the injustice of White privilege more systematically if we are seriously committed to a just world.

The cultural reproduction of Whiteness as privileged and superior plays a central role in the embeddedness of 'race' and racism. McIntosh (2004), in her compelling self-definitions of moments in everyday life that contain the unconscious privilege of Whiteness, reveals the insights into the insidious nature of power that are revealed when we focus on power not powerlessness. A change of emphasis from understanding racism to concentrate on the invisible systems of privilege that reinforce dominance challenges White people to examine our assumptions of 'normality'. McIntosh's metaphor of an 'invisible knapsack' containing a plethora of unearned privileges that can be unpacked and examined contains the key to dismantling the way that those privileges have remained invisible, assumed, equating normality with White culture. Mekada Graham (2007) reminds us that by concentrating on giving voice to silenced voices we have encouraged the long silence on Whiteness as a social construct: 'Whiteness carries a positive identity and without racial others it could not exist' (Graham, 2007, p 61). Bhavani et al (2005, p 50) outline the key areas as:

- White is seen as the majority, the norm, therefore tied to power;
- Whiteness lacks racial/ethnic features, making it invisible;
- Whiteness is naturalised so has no need to define its cultural traits, as with minority groups;
- Whiteness is confused with nationality, therefore central to power;
- White is not expressed as ethnicity, and so avoids a label.

But, Peggy McIntosh, in unpacking her knapsack, finds the embeddedness of Whiteness in ordinary, everyday encounters of power, a web-like reinforcement at ground level, just as Foucault identified. Instead of us looking out there at the structures that reinforce these attitudes and values, we find the beginning of the process right here, under our noses, in everyday life. McIntosh, in self-reflection, discovered and named 46 daily privileges that she took for granted as normal and available to anyone. She tried to eliminate class, religion, ethnicity or geographical location from the experience in an attempt to isolate and understand the elusive nature of these 'unearned assets' and these are some of her insightful reflections:

- I can if I wish arrange to be in the company of people of my race most of the time.
- I can be pretty sure that my neighbours will be neutral or pleasant to me.
- I can go shopping alone most of the time, pretty well assured that I will not be followed or harassed.

- I can turn on the television or open the front page of the paper and see people of my race widely and positively represented.
- Whether I use checks, credit cards or cash I can count on my skin colour not to work against the appearance of financial reliability.
- I can remain oblivious of the language and customs of persons of color who constitute the world's majority without feeling in my culture any penalty for such oblivion.
- I can go home from most meetings of organisations I belong to feeling somewhat tied in, rather than isolated, out–of–place, outnumbered, unheard, held at a distance or feared.

These statements trigger a myriad of experiences in my mind. As a woman, I find I am able to relate some of these experiences to patriarchy. But most of all, I find the story of my shared moments with Paula Asgill coming to life, and I honour the insight into Whiteness that she brought to me.

Paula and Margaret: the interface of Black and White

"In Lancaster, a predominantly White community, whenever I saw Paula from a distance I noticed her proud and beautiful stature slumped, and her eyes cast down at the pavement. One day, at work, she greeted me with a big smile, and told me the story of Duncan, my 17-year-old younger son:

'I was walking up from town, deep in my own thoughts, feeling that I don't belong here as I did in Manchester. "Yo Paula!", echoed across the street. I looked up and there was Duncan driving his pizza delivery van, waving out of the window with a big grin on his face, so pleased to see me. It made me feel part of the place.'

"I laughed when I heard this, knowing that Duncan would indeed be so happy to see Paula out and about. We moved to Lancaster from Manchester at the same time as Paula, and Duncan had grown up in a multicultural community with many close Black friends in his life.

"In the years that we were both friends and colleagues, Paula and I used to travel to the USA on work trips. I walked through passport control and customs confidently assuming that I would not be searched. Gradually, I came to realise that inevitably Paula was the one chosen from the line of White visitors to the country to have her bag checked, these were not random acts. I used to walk over and demand to know whether there was a problem, but was always told it was 'routine'. Paula had learnt to accept it as part of her life. Despite our mutual research into the problematic relations of alliances between Black and White women, we only partially addressed the very painful ways in which this got acted out in our friendship – and there were many! When we were on work trips to the USA, she was often furious that I had more privileges and was less challenged. But, when she took me into one of the most volatile Black areas of Chicago she was at home, she belonged and I received the

> gaze as outsider, I was dislocated from my assumed comfort and acutely aware of the danger of being different, of being a White women in a Black community. Over the years until she died, my deep friendship with Paula bounced through these challenging and painful experiences that educated me into racism as a lived experience.
>
> "When Paula was taken ill, and rushed to hospital, I followed the ambulance nose to tail in my little VW Polo, anxious not to lose her in the power and bureaucracy of a hospital. By the time I parked and got to the ward, she was already in bed, her beautiful features framed by the starched white linen pillow case. The doctor interviewing her looked up at me, asking, 'And who are you?' To my amusement, in her illness, her head rose from the pillow, looked him directly in the eye, daring him to challenge her, and said, 'She is my *sister!*' I knew in that moment that she was acknowledging my authenticity as a sister in resistance."

The long friendship and working relationship I had the privilege to share with Paula was immensely problematic but continues to educate me in the ways of White privilege, how tenacious and elusive it is as an assumed power to those who have it, even those of us who claim to be anti-racist practitioners, and how it needs to be much more systematically analysed and understood.

Racism becomes reproduced in the everyday discriminatory practices acted out at a micro level (Bhavani et al, 2005). White people are implicated in the reproduction of inequality and need to be accountable for the role that we play in legitimising the structures that privilege Whiteness. But saying it is not enough: we need to understand the subtleties which reveal Whiteness as both invisible and hegemonic at one and the same time. Only in these ways will we be able to construct counternarratives of liberation that truly embrace the concept 'lift as we climb' (Davis, 1989, p 9) across difference and diversity.

Problematising capitalism

Capitalism has been conflated with democracy. This is problematic for social justice, as is obscures the way that capitalism is predicated on exploitation of those that it subordinates, including the natural world. For example, under capitalism 'race' is exacerbated by the relations between 'race' and property ownership, perpetuating privilege and creating unequal relations. A critical paradigm disconnects democracy from capitalism, and identifies alternative economic systems that are based on justice and sustainability. If we fail to problematise capitalism and only focus on deepening democracy, we leave the structural inequalities of capitalism intact (Ladson–Billings and Tate, 2006, p 573). The tenacity of inequality remains a conundrum simply because we miss the dialectical relationship between capitalism and democracy.

As an example, Apple raises the issue of cultural capital's exploitation of the market. For example, education is increasingly marketed as a commodity. Universities have been transformed into business enterprises which charge for the benefits of a degree at the same time as marketing their products according to demand: 'markets are marketed, are made legitimate, by a depoliticizing strategy. They are said to be natural and neutral, and governed by effort and merit' (Apple, 2006, p 471). By unquestioningly accepting these assumptions as common sense, we miss the way that the most privileged get the biggest slice, that it is a system designed for those with all the confidence, ease, wealth and natural assumptions of power so much less accessible to those who are Other. As Diane Warner raises, if we leave the system unquestioned, it produces the same inequalities, increasing dominance of the already powerful and reinforcing marginality of difference based on 'race', ethnicity, class and gender.

Linked to this analysis are the critical connections that ensure that education fails children who are from subordinated groups while maintaining its neutral stance as awarding merit. Overcrowded homes, those without books, those in which languages other than English are spoken, unemployment, cared for children, children from families that are minority ethnic or have an unemployed parent or a single parent or a 'dis'abled parent and so on are failed by the education system. Yet, *false generosity* or tokenism creates the illusion that the system is fair and just, so every so often a child from one of these backgrounds proves to be the exception.

Problematising gender

Racism, sexism and heterosexism work in overlapping but different ways. As Audre Lorde expressed as long ago as 1980: 'As a forty-nine-year-old Black lesbian feminist socialist mother of two, including one boy, and a member of an inter-racial couple, I usually find myself a part of some group defined as other, deviant, inferior, or just plain wrong' (Lorde, 1980).

Much as Whiteness is assumed, so is patriarchy. The everyday encounters between men and women reinforce gendered differences. A patriarchal hierarchy of privilege remains resilient among the myriad of hegemonies that reach from street to structures. Patrick Welsh (2010) highlights this resilience with a story from Nicaragua that tells how the impact of conscientisation on the wider social context led women to understand that their own empowerment called for changed consciousness in men. All the work done on addressing women's practical needs in health, housing, education, land, paid employment and economic independence failed to 'transform the unjust, oppressive and violent power structures, dynamics and relations that characterize patriarchal institutions' (Welsh, 2010, p 300). This is directly related to the way that 'individual men integrate hegemonic masculinity into their personal identity … as a tool to exercise and maintain power, rights and privileges that are simultaneously denied to women' (Welsh, 2010, p 301). This has led to Nicaragua being 'one of the few countries in the world with a network of male activists seeking to transform male identity from the bottom up' (Welsh, 2010, p 300).

This sort of radical questioning is central to exploring the ways that patriarchy and racism are overt oppressions, but the key to unlocking that power lies in understanding the way that they become embodied in male and White identities and played out in subtly powerful ways. Patricia Williams (1991, p 216) says that 'blacks in a white society are conditioned from infancy to see in themselves only what others, who despise them, see'. The freedom struggles that we place on Black women are powerfully expressed in this story told by Diane Watt, of Manchester Metropolitan University, about her friend Paula.

My 'sister' in struggle: a search for rebel consciousness

"My friend Paula who was also my 'sister' in struggle was born in Jamaica, the third largest of the Caribbean islands after Cuba. It is an island where the sounds of Bob Marley's 'No Woman Nuh Cry' and the rhythms of Africa are ever present, a place of oral tradition, where stories such as Nanny of the Maroons abound. In her fight against the British, and drawing upon the powers of her Ashanti heritage, Nanny is said to have bounced bullets off her bottom.

"At the age of seven, Paula left Jamaica to join her mother and stepfather in England. Although Paula was not among the thousands of children left behind with the promise that within five years their parents would return 'home' financially secure, she nevertheless found separation from her mother extremely traumatic, an effect of migration which is rarely spoken about. Paula had enjoyed sharing her mother with other members of her extended family, and these family members, in turn, mothered her after her mother left. She was surrounded, in her own words, by a battalion of little 'mothers' who all played a role in passing on the oral tradition with their parables and storytelling.

"Paula arrived in England at a time when language was seen as one of the key factors influencing the decision by many local education authorities to send an unprecedented number of Black children from the Caribbean to special educational needs schools. This was an issue of growing concern among Black parents throughout the country, and in preparing her for her first day at school, she recalled her mother telling her that, 'They'll say things to you and you won't understand, but all you have to do is to say "pardon" and they'll say it again.' Looking back, Paula felt that her mother's advice was quite radical in the sense that it was not intended to silence her. Initially, she found speaking and understanding English within the British context challenging. Paula's transition from the primary school girl who arrived at Manchester Airport in the middle of winter, wearing a little yellow and brown crinoline dress, to that of community activist was very much influenced by her mother's experience. This involvement gave her a greater understanding of the position of Black women of her mother's generation within the labour market, most of whom, irrespective of their skills, found themselves doing unskilled work. Prior to coming to England, her own mother was a successful, self-employed seamstress who found packing crisps soul destroying. This was not unlike the experience of the Jamaican feminist writer Una Marson who, despite her educational achievements and professional credentials, was unable to find employment as an office worker in England during the 1930s. Marson has since been described as the first Black British woman to speak out against racism and sexism as she did at the 12th Annual Congress of the International Alliance of Women for Suffrage and Equal Citizenship which was held in Turkey in 1935. In Manchester there were also the 'coloured' passengers on the number 53 bus, which local whites renamed the 'African Queen' in reference to the large number of black immigrants who travelled daily to what was then one of Europe's largest industrial estates.

"These are some of the experiences of the Black community that inspired Paula's involvement with community-based activism aimed particularly at championing the rights of Black women. This at times meant her active participation in deportation campaigns, as in the case of the West African woman whose marriage had broken down and along with her six children she faced deportation. Campaigns of this nature also provided her with the opportunity to engage in conscious struggles against race- and gender-related forms of social and political injustice. It was through her involvement with the Manchester Black Women's Co-op, in particular its Saturday Supplementary School activities, that Paula met the late Olive Morris, one of the founder members of the Organisation for Women of Africa and African Descent (OWAAD). In terms of political activism, she described Olive as a trooper and a young woman of wisdom who both mothered and sistered her. Throughout their friendship, Olive taught her that she didn't have to conform to all the shit to be a fighter and survive. Olive was both inspirational and fundamental to Paula's development as a young Black woman in search of that state of rebel consciousness."

Kathleen Weiler calls for counter-hegemonic opposition: 'the creation of a self-conscious analysis of a situation and the development of collective practices and organization that can oppose the hegemony of the existing order and begin to build the base for a new understanding and transformation of society' (2009, p 235). In order to resist the sexism of Black British culture and the racism of White British culture we need to understand that:

> … resistance and … 'reading' of the ideological messages of schools will differ in specific school settings. And of course girls of different class and race subjectivities will be met with varying expectations on the part of white and black, male and female teachers, depending on these teachers' own views of what is gender appropriate. By adding the categories of race and class to that of gender, we can begin to reveal the diversity and complexity of girls' and women's experiences in schools. (Weiler, 2009, p 226)

According to Gramsci, any theory of change must be grounded in the struggles of everyday life. 'The task of counter-hegemonic groups is the development of counter-institutions, ideologies, and cultures that provide an ethical alternative to the dominant hegemony, a lived experience of how the world can be different' (Patti Lather, 1984, p 55, cited by Weiler, 2009, p 226). In these ways, we can build democratic counter-hegemonies based on a critical understanding of existing society as the basis for an alternative value system based on justice and sustainability.

Feminism's emphasis on *difference* has given profound insight into the complexity of lived experience, which places us all within a matrix of oppressions, variously positioned as both victims and perpetrators. Similarly, feminism's emphasis on non-hierarchical structures of peace and non-violence has developed altered views on both human rights and environmental justice. The challenge is now to develop an integrated praxis that informs a pedagogy for our times.

bell hooks challenges feminists who separate feminist pedagogy from Freirean pedagogy:

> Unlike feminist thinkers who make a clear separation between the work of feminist pedagogy and Freire's work and thought, for me these two experiences converge. Deeply committed to feminist pedagogy, I find that, much like weaving a tapestry, I have taken threads of Paulo's work and woven it into that version of feminist pedagogy I believe my work as writer and teacher embodies. (hooks, 1993, p 150)

Male-centred models of reality, however much they offer conceptual tools that radicalise feminist consciousness, continue to validate a male way of knowing the world. Feminist approaches attempt to place women's ways of knowing at the centre of knowledge generation, not to exclude men, but because 'by looking at human experience from the point of view of women, we can understand male experience and the whole of cultural history with greater depth' (Callaway, 1981, p 460). This constitutes a critical repositioning that embraces a multiplicity of ways of knowing the world, challenging gender and cultural dominance. Within this frame, 'the act of looking back, of seeing with fresh eyes, of entering an old text from a new critical direction' (Adrienne Rich, cited in Callaway, 1981, p 457) allows us to 're-vision' Freire and Gramsci, using the analytic tools they offered us to expand our feminist consciousness in the first place. Looking back with our new awarenesses offers new ways of exposing the contradictions embedded in the taken-for-grantedness of daily life, and, in turn, 'the imaginative power of sighting possibilities and thus helping to bring about what is not (or not *yet*) visible, a new ordering of human relations' (Callaway, 1981, p 457).

Freirean pedagogy and feminist pedagogy

> How can we build upon the rich and complex analysis of feminist theory and pedagogy to work toward a Freirean vision of social justice and liberation? (Weiler, 1995, p 35)

Weiler (1994, p 18) asks a central question for activists seeking an integrated praxis: 'Where are we to look for liberation when our collective reading of the world reveals contradictory and conflicting experiences and struggles?'. Transformative change is rooted in collective action, yet the consumerist individualism that characterises neoliberalism has shifted us away from a sense of the collective.

Freire vehemently believed that empowerment is a collective experience, that true freedom is to work to transform all society (Freire, in Shor and Freire, 1987).

Pedagogy of the oppressed continues to offer critical pedagogues around the world hope, passion and theoretical justification for their work. How, then, is it possible to address the problems it presents to feminist, anti-racist pedagogy? The major problem lies not so much in its sexist language, which was addressed in Freire's later work, but in its failure to fully engage with difference and diversity, overlooking the 'possibility of simultaneous contradictory positions of oppression and dominance' (Weiler, 1995, p 27). However, Freire was emphatic that his work should always be open to critique and re-vision based on his experience, the experience of others and changing contexts:

> Many things that today still appear to me as valid (not only in actual or future practice but also in any theoretical interpretation that I might derive from it) could be outgrown tomorrow, not just by me, but by others as well. The crux here, I believe, is that I must be constantly open to criticism and sustain my curiosity, always ready for revision based on the results of my future experience and that of others. And in turn, those who put my experience into practice must strive to recreate it and also rethink my thinking. In doing so, they should bear in mind that no educational practice takes place in a vacuum, only in a real context – historical, economic, political, and not necessarily identical to any other context. (Freire, 1985, p 11)

My proposal is that Freirean pedagogy and feminist, anti-racist pedagogy are powerful and complementary in their potential for critical practice in global times. In support of this claim, I will explore the development of feminist pedagogy and consider the similarity of process and goals. The political activism of the women's movement of the 1960s and 1970s developed out of a challenge to a dominant way of seeing the world based on patriarchy and pragmatism, which denies the validity of *experience* and *feeling*. Women rose to claim the *personal as political*. There was a groundswell of grassroots activism in which women came together in leaderless groups to explore consciousness from our own experience, making feminist theory in action. We translated this into collective action for change based on a vision of peace and justice. An outstanding example of the collective potential of this movement is the way in which, in August 1981, a group of women who had never been involved in political action before marched from Cardiff to Greenham Common to protest against the siting of cruise missiles in Britain. This marked the beginning of the Greenham Women's Peace Movement, which 'highlighted the development of a new strand of community action' (Dominelli, 1990, p 119). A praxis began to evolve with emphasis on lived experience as the basis of theoretical understanding.

Many poststructuralists and postmodern feminists criticise *patriarchal* analyses of gender as *essentialist* – that by constructing *woman* as 'Other' than *man*, there is a risk of seeing this as the only way of defining women's experience. On the other hand, Sylvia Walby (1992, 1994) suggests that one of the limitations of poststructuralism and postmodernism is 'a neglect of the social context of power relations' (1992, p 16). Her argument is that postmodernism has fragmented concepts of 'race', class and gender by focusing on complexity, and that while social relations have changed, postmodernists have gone too far by denying racism and patriarchy as 'virulent social divisions'. Whereas Marxism subsumed all forms of discrimination under class, postmodernists have swung with the pendulum to disintegrate the concepts altogether. She illustrates the dangers of this in relation to Black women who raise three important aspects of analysis: (i) racist structures within the labour market; (ii) ethnic experience and racism; and (iii) locating the intersection of ethnicity and gender, both culturally and historically. Disintegration overlooks these patterns of 'race', class and gender oppressions and their local/global dimensions. For instance, the British economy not only depends on women's paid and unpaid labour at home, but also depends on the exploitation of developing world women, thus 'there is a strong case for the interconnectedness of the exploitation of First and Third World women by patriarchal capitalism' (Walby, 1994, p 232). Walby cites Swasti Mitter's call for a 'common bond on women in the newly globalised economy' (1994, p 234) within a recognition of difference, as unfolding insights enable us to work with *conscientisation* from a wider perspective as analyses of power move the dynamic of praxis further towards achieving a shared vision of freedom.

In these ways, Freire and anti-racist feminism enrich each other in the struggle for transformative social change. Together, they provide a pedagogy with which to denounce social injustices in all their complexity, 'for to be utopian is not to be merely idealistic or impractical but rather to engage in denunciation and annunciation', the 'act of analyzing a dehumanizing reality, denounce it while announcing its transformation' (Freire, 1985, p 57). For Freire, *utopia* is a fundamental necessity in the process of becoming fully human, 'in favor of dreaming, of utopia, of democracy is the discourse of those who refuse to settle and do not allow the taste for being human, which fatalism deteriorates, to die within themselves' (Freire, 2007, p 26).

The most compelling analysis of Freire from a feminist perspective continues, for me, to come from Kathleen Weiler. She profoundly influenced my thinking with her challenge to engage with 'Freire and a feminist pedagogy of difference' (Weiler, 1995, p 23). Her point is that collective action will not emerge naturally from contradictory histories and experiences. We need to engage with the contradictions of privilege, oppression and power by acknowledging our own histories and selves in process from an 'acute consciousness of difference' in order to move more critically towards our 'goals of social justice and empowerment' (Weiler, 1995, p 35). She calls for a feminist pedagogy that enriches and re-visions Freirean goals, but is framed more specifically in the context of feminist struggle. In this sense, the concept of *denunciation* suggests that we need to develop better strategies to help us name and analyse our insight into a multiplicity of oppressions, and *annunciation* suggests the need for new forms of action across difference that unite us in mutual struggle.

Weiler offers three key areas of analysis with which to extend Freirean pedagogy into feminist pedagogy: the role and authority of the teacher; experience and feelings as sources of knowledge; and the question of difference.

The role and authority of the teacher

While Freire emphasises the horizontal, reciprocal role of the educator as a co-teacher/co-learner, he fails to address issues of power according to ethnicity, gender and status. Weiler suggests that *authority* can be problematic. The vision of a mutual, reciprocal, non-hierarchical way of working can be driven by hope rather than reality if issues of power, hierarchy and culture are overlooked. Women in community are not a homogeneous group; they are diverse. They are also situated within a competitive and individualistic culture. As feminist community workers, we are vested with the role, authority and status that render us different.

If we are working towards consciousness and collective action for change with groups within which issues of power are ignored, we are not likely to be successful. However, it is possible for the anti-racist, feminist educator, through the process of *conscientisation*, to name difference and reach a shared critical understanding of the forces that have shaped that difference and, in doing so, reach a collective unity for change. For example, anti-racist, feminist thought, by engaging with male privilege as a corollary of White privilege, is able to extend beyond linear rationality to gain insight into the nature of contradictory oppressions. Let me illustrate this with a reflection from Peggy McIntosh (cited in Weeks, 2009, p 7): 'As a white person, I realized I had been taught about racism as something that puts others at a disadvantage, but had been taught not to see one of its corollary aspects, white privilege, which puts me at an advantage. I think whites are taught not to recognise white privilege, as males are taught not to recognise male privilege.' In becoming open to understanding our privileged identities as well as our oppressed identities we develop the confidence and autonomy to work collectively for the common good.

Experience and feeling as sources of knowledge

We need to identify a feminist knowledge of the world as the basis for social change. Freire placed great emphasis on the questioning of experience to come to an understanding of power in order to transform the world: in knowing it, we can recreate it. In the same way, feminist knowledge of the world is the foundation for action. Belenky et al (1997) have made an immense contribution through their research into *Women's ways of knowing*. They emphasise the quest for self and voice, which plays a key role in the process of transformation for women. The self, in an inner and outer process, is transformed: 'weaving together the strands of rational and emotive thought and of integrating objective and subjective knowing [lead to a] new way of thinking' (Belenky et al, 1997, pp 134-5). Traditionally, *feeling* has been seen as the domain of women, as of the private domain and not a reliable basis for rational action. Women are denied the value of their being in the world by a positivist, patriarchal system that places emphasis on science, on rationality, on pragmatism rather than emotion, experience or feeling. In feminist analysis, universal truths about human behaviour are challenged and increasingly *feeling* has contributed to feminist pedagogy as a balance between the inner self and the outer world, between the public and private, the personal and political. Audre Lorde captures the essence of feelings as a guide to analysis and action, keeping us in touch with our humanity:

> As we begin to recognise our deepest feelings, we begin to give up, of necessity, being satisfied with suffering and self-negation, and with the numbness which so often seems like their only alternative in society. Our acts against oppression become integral with self, motivated and empowered from within. (Lorde, 1984, p 58)

There are strong links here with Freirean emphasis on humanisation as a way of being in the world. In identifying the ways in which our experience of power relationships is structured, the act of knowing, of critical insight, generates energy and motivation for action. Out of a state of dehumanisation, we are freed to humanise ourselves, creating alternative worldviews based on justice.

The question of difference

The assumption made by White feminists of a universal sisterhood rendered Black women invisible. The racism inherent in White feminism not only failed to recognise the anti-racist struggle as central to feminism, but also overlooked the way Black people are pathologised in relation to sexuality and family relations. Black feminists and postmodern feminists challenged the unitary and universal category *woman* as fundamentally racist on the one hand, and socially constructed and shaped on the other. Feminist pedagogy has focused on narratives of lived experience as a participatory strategy with groups of women to identify the social and historical forces that have shaped these narratives. For instance, Weiler (1994, p 31) cites Sistren, a 'collaborative theatre group made up of working-class Jamaican women who create and write plays based upon a collaborative exploration of their own experiences'. The collective sharing of experience is the key to the knowledge of our socially and politically given identities. It is the process by which we discover our power as subjects in active, creative process in our world, rather than as objects that are fixed, defined and static. The Combahee River Collective argue that 'the most radical politics come directly out of our own identity, as opposed to working to end someone else's oppression' (Weiler, 1994, p 32).

In 2001, Weiler offered a further critical re-reading of Freire, emphasising that we need to pay attention to: (i) the nature of women as learners, (ii) the gendered nature of accepted knowledge, (iii) the role and authority of the teacher, and (iv) the epistemological source of knowledge and truth claims of men and women. She flags up the dangers of discourse that rests on social and cultural definitions of men's and women's natures as some *given truth*. Difference between men and women is useful in thinking about feminist knowing, but must not be seen as innate. Failing to acknowledge the social and historical construction of the idea of women's natures would be to subscribe to western patriarchy's *male rationality* versus *female nurturance* dichotomy. Weiler advocates the need to write from a discourse of *feminist rationality*. By this, she means that women have the capacity to think in rational and abstract ways: women's knowledge is not solely defined by emotion.

Gloria Anzaldúa's conception of the *new mestiza* as a postcolonial feminist emphasises that set patterns of women's behaviour are invasions of the self, and that any critique of patriarchy must include western conceptions of: (i) linear rationality, (ii) White privilege and (iii) assumptions of universal truths (1987). Anti-racist feminist educators have 'stressed that critical and feminist pedagogies, whilst claiming an opposition to oppression, are in danger of taking a kind of imperial and totalizing stance of knowing and "speaking for" those who are to be educated into truth' (Weiler, 2001, p 72). Weiler raises *social identity* and *authority* in speaking for silenced others. Are we acting out privilege by taking on an unquestioned authority in speaking? Reflecting, she asks, 'How then do I, a white woman from the US, approach the work of a Brazilian man who spoke for the subjugated and oppressed?' (Weiler, 2001, p 73).

Sylvia Walby: patriarchal sites of oppression

At this point, I want to return to the ideas of Sylvia Walby (1992, 1994) and examine their specific use in relation to a Freirean-feminist-anti-racist pedagogy.

Clearly Walby feels that postmodernism has gone too far in fragmenting concepts of class, 'race' and gender, denying the overarching theories of capitalism, racism and sexism as significant power structures in society. Her emphasis is on the centrality of patriarchy as a prime oppressive force. She agrees that postmodernists are right to identify the weaknesses of metanarratives. This has helped us gain insights into the way that unitary concepts can hide more than they reveal. Walby's argument is that patriarchy, as a blanket theory, denies the complex ways in which women's experience varies across difference. Her solution is to identify six structures of analysis within which to analyse patriarchy: (i) paid work, (ii) housework, (iii) sexuality, (iv) culture, (v) violence, and (vi) the state. She suggests that the interrelationships between these elements create different forms of patriarchy.

Walby contests that the shift from a Marxist class analysis to postmodernism has failed to reveal any pattern other than disintegration. If we fail to theorise new patterns of gender, ethnicity and class oppressions, our practice will be uncritical. For example, while the feminisation of poverty continues to be a concern within the UK, on a global level consumer-driven profit under capitalism is dependent on the exploitation of women and children in the developing (and industrialising) world who are becoming the prime producers and suppliers of some of the cheapest goods for western markets. Walby concludes that the concept of 'patriarchy' is a vital component of gender inequality, and we ignore it at our peril. Postmodernist arguments that it is founded on naive essentialism, that it defines women's experience as universal and unified in relation to men, are 'insensitive to the range of experiences of women of different cultures, classes and ethnicities' (Walby, 1992, p 2). Patriarchy as a concept and theory is essential to 'capture the depth, pervasiveness and interconnectedness of different aspects of women's subordination, and can be developed in this way to take account of the different forms of gender inequality over time, class and ethnic group' (Walby, 1992, p 2).

These are some of the ideas that have influenced feminist pedagogy. I will now move into an argument in support of a Freirean-feminist-anti-racist pedagogy that engages with the multiplicity of oppressions that diminish life on earth.

Towards a Freirean-feminist-anti-racist pedagogy: loci of oppressions

Radical community development, and by this I mean a critical approach to practice that locates it at the heart of a movement for social and environmental justice, calls for a pedagogy of difference for our times. I see Freirean pedagogy and anti-racist, feminist pedagogy as a powerful combination, informed by analyses of class, patriarchy and racism as overarching structures of oppression that intertwine with each other. These forces are woven into the fabric of life through different contexts at different levels in a complex system of domination and subordination. This is absorbed in the public psyche as *common sense*, and thus legitimate. A Freirean-feminist-anti-racist pedagogy is also profoundly concerned with other aspects of difference and diversity, seeking a worldview that is equal, harmonious and respectful of all life on earth. Exploring the ideas of Allman, McLaren and Hill from a class perspective and Spretnak and Shiva from an ecofeminist perspective, this worldview is not possible within a system of capitalism that is built on domination and exploitation for profit. In other words, capitalism is inherently incapable of reform because its success depends on exploitation and profit, and, within this, class, 'race' and gender are prime forces of exploitation that serve its interests. Douthwaite (1996), commenting on the supremacy of the market, reminds us that the elevation of the economy over the common good justifies a drive for profit that holds no accountability for human or environmental well-being, giving rise to the illusion that the problems we face in relation to justice and sustainability are inevitable rather than a consequence of capitalism.

In these ways, a Freirean–feminist–anti-racist pedagogy for radical community development practice calls for analyses of power that take thinking and action from a local to a wider collective potential for change.

A three-dimensional model might be useful here, one that moves through (i) **difference** ('race', class, gender and so on) on one axis, through (ii) **context** (family, workplace, streets, schools and so on) on another, and between (iii) **levels** (local, national, global and so on) on a third to form a complex set of interrelationships that interweave between axes, but also intertwine on any one axis. The elements are not fixed; they are interchangeable on each face: the model is designed to probe critical thinking, stimulating questions rather than offering definitive answers. It calls for three-dimensional thought, as opposed to the simplistic linear rationality of western consciousness. Students have said it helps to imagine this as a Rubik's cube, each section capable of changing and being re-examined in relation to the whole. It is only by struggling to locate these complex intersections that we begin to understand the root causes of oppression, and in doing so locate potential sites of resistance. So, for example, the model not only helps us to explore the interrelatedness of 'race' and gender on one face, but to locate this within an environmental context, and on a community level. Then, if the level is shifted from local to, say, global, different but related issues emerge.

Figure 8.1: Loci of oppressions matrix

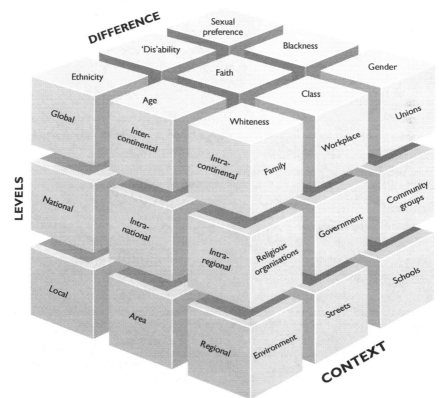

The purpose of the model is to stretch our thinking in a multidimensional way by locating the interface of different dimensions of oppressions, and, in doing so, pose questions that deepen our analysis and make our practice more critical. The critical potential of this model is that it teaches us to question in the most complex of ways. Beginning in an aspect of everyday reality, using problem–posing as part of this multidimensional model, could open us to new understandings and new forms of action. The dialogue is kept critical by using Hope and Timmel's (1994, Book 1, p 58) six stages of questioning:

(i)   description (what?)
(ii) first analysis (why?)
(iii) real life (where?)
(iv) related problems (what else?)
(v)   root causes
(vi) action planning.

Working with people in a community group, we could *problematise* a local issue by using a photograph as a *codification*, capturing the essence of this issue from the reality of their lives. The 'description' stage is merely asking what the photograph depicts. What is in the photo? What do you see? What do you think they are doing? What are they feeling? This moves into 'first analysis', which questions why this thing is happening, thus moving from observing the photograph to thinking about it. As confidence grows, and the group gets more involved, ask 'Does this happen in "real life"?' If you have chosen a generative theme, one that is relevant to the everyday lives of the people, and captured it well, it will generate a passionate response: 'It happens to me!' 'It happens every day in our community!' 'This is the way it is here!' In this way, the outward focus on the codification, in this case a photograph, shifts inward to the group and critical dialogue is generated by the relevance the issue has to the reality of its members. Curiosity and mutual inquiry will often stimulate the group to identify 'related problems'. In this way the group moves beyond the concrete situation, making connections across difference, time and space. Your role is to probe in a *problematising* way. If you challenge the group to take its analysis to a deeper level, the inquiry will go beyond the symptoms to the root causes of the problem, which truly pushes towards *critical consciousness*. New ways of knowing are explored. Social relations are transformed as people experience each other differently. There is a move towards critical thought for transformative action.

Try experimenting with some of your own experiences to see if this model extends your analysis. Consider how, on one axis, difference is compounded by, say, Whiteness, gender and age to give us profoundly different experiences of being a 'woman'. If we then consider how this is further compounded by context, say, the public world of work as opposed to the private world of family, further patterns of difference emerge. Finally, if we follow this through to make global links with local experiences, we can begin to see realities that are constructed by the interaction of these forces. By struggling to analyse these complex intersections, we get nearer to understanding the root causes of oppression, and in doing so locate potential sites of resistance. Because the elements are not fixed, the model becomes adaptable to multiple possibilities.

If you begin to see more complex connections through the matrix, consider using it as a structure for teaching to question with your community groups. Reflect on the nature of your own power, status and authority as an educator in relation to the difference represented in your groups. This may operate in half-hidden, subtle ways. How do you see the interaction of power and difference within the group? What evidence is there of different ways of knowing within the group, for example emotionality and rationality? Is your way of knowing different from that of the group? How do you see your own status, power and difference in relation to the group? In a mutual relationship as co-teachers/co-learners in process, explore the gendered, racialised nature of accepted knowledge, and discover ways in which dominant views of the world and the nature of truth may not be the same for men and women, or for different cultures. This takes us nearer to the cutting edge of a pedagogy of difference.

The matrix offers a focus for investigation of the many possible interlinked sites of oppression and deepens an awareness of the ways in which these are structurally reinforced at different levels. As the group grows in confidence and awareness, they own the process in a mutual and reciprocal way. *Critical consciousness* is an outward-flowing energy. Personal empowerment involves a sense of self in the world that gives rise to personal autonomy. This process becomes collective as critical consciousness leads to critical autonomy. Links are made with other groups in the community and alliances are formed with groups outside the community, generating a collective energy for change that has the potential to connect through levels from local to global. A coherent and strategic Freirean-feminist-anti-racist pedagogy offers community development a radical possibility. But the beginning of the process starts with critical reflection on experience: McIntosh (2004) has demonstrated that everyday experiences hold the key to power and powerlessness. In dialogue, in a process of connected knowing (Belenky et al, 1986), we pay full attention to others by suspending our own truth, and develop new insights that are the basis of counternarratives of liberation, new stories about new possibilities.

Freirean pedagogy and feminist, anti-racist pedagogy are both rooted in a vision of transformative social change and take as their starting point lived experience. They both operate from a non-hierarchical, reciprocal model. They are both committed to social justice through critical consciousness and collective action. A re-visioning of these two powerful perspectives offers the potential to contribute to critical analysis and action for change for a peaceful, just and sustainable future.

Organising for social transformation

Community development is predicated on principles of social justice and environmental justice, a sustainable world in balance, an ecosystem in which everyone and everything flourishes, a democracy based on participation and collective well-being. Its vision is that of a peaceful, just and sustainable world. Its practice is critical pedagogy, which is based on a 'profound love for the world and for people' (Freire, 1996, p 70). And 'because love is an act of courage, not of fear, love is commitment to others' (Freire, 1996, p 70). The process of liberation begins in dialogue, a critical encounter which enables people to speak their word and name their world. And Freire was clear that 'to speak a true word is to transform the world' (Freire, 1996, p 68).

Reclaiming the radical agenda

Radical community development emerged at a historic juncture: social and political change in the late 1960s and early 1970s came together with the revolutionary ideas of Freire and Gramsci available in English for the first time. This combination was the basis of a unity of praxis. The CDP challenged the pathology-based assumptions of the government's 'cycle of deprivation' theory for a structural analysis of poverty by developing a critical approach to practice. As Lena Dominelli says, 'This was not a message that the state wanted to hear, especially when coupled with the view that *poor people were necessary components in the cycle of capital accumulation*' (Dominelli, 2006, pp 55-6; original emphasis). The same analysis forms the basis of a critical approach to neoliberal globalisation, that is, that the gap between rich and poor is not due to personal pathologies, but is a direct consequence of profit generation under capitalism.

After the emergence of radical, transformative community development in the early 1970s, there was a period of sustained action against injustice, challenging class, patriarchal, racist and heterosexist traditions which erode human rights and undermine democracy. This involved campaigns to end violence against women and children, to end poverty, to end the corporate degradation of the environment, against homophobia, racism and sexism, against deportation of asylum seekers, and much more. At the same time as acting on bigger issues, practice focused on the development of cooperative local economies and healthy convivial communities. New social movements gathered momentum from grassroots practice to change the face of society. Class-based grand narratives were critiqued as inadequate analyses of discrimination and a process of deconstructing binary opposites began. Discrimination prior to this was subsumed under a class analysis in a polarity of oppressor/oppressed, and much of the critiques of Freire and Gramsci were levelled from this perspective, that is, a simplistic analysis which concealed more than it revealed. However, postmodernism became increasingly contradictory for community development: it led the way forward to dismantling binary opposites at the same time as it fragmented a sense of the collective.

During this period, community development lost its way from the radical agenda of the 1970s and 1980s, as through the 1990s neoliberalism became more embedded and we became depoliticised. Shifting boundaries between the state, the market and civil society blurred the way for us to be drawn into performing policy delivery, unwittingly playing a part in dismantling the welfare state (Craig et al, 2011). We became drawn into a culture of bureaucracy and managerialism, chasing our own funding and jumping to the tune of performance indicators. As the hijacking and dilution of our radical concepts were imported into policy, we failed to see that there were contradictions between what we said we do and what we were doing in practice. This opened the way for community development to be misappropriated in the interests of top-down agendas.

Pitchford with Henderson (2008) argues that the plethora of competing policy agendas that rename community development as community *involvement* or *engagement* or *participation* have muddied understanding of community development as a distinctive process for progressive social change. The consequence is that we have become distracted, lost our way and have little sense of direction or overarching purpose. 'The case can and should be made for how community development can deepen democracy' (Pitchford with Henderson, 2008, pp 94–5).

Without effective and relevant theoretical analyses we are vulnerable to this sort of manipulation. It is vital that we develop theoretical analyses of power that are sufficiently adequate to inform action against poverty, racism and patriarchy. For many years I have been arguing for praxis, for theory generated in action, and action informed by theory in order to bridge the persistent theory/practice divide that reduces our potential.

Critique and dissent in the process of deepening democracy

Failure to critique the political context provided a smokescreen for the ideology of the market to permeate everything about life on earth, creating a western worldview that measures success according to a strange human profit and loss account, valuing our market worth according to our relevance as consumers and producers. As Giroux (2006) so powerfully puts it, we have created a *politics of disposability*: those who are not central to the processes of production or consumption are dispensable. It is a world in which the poor, the Black, the female, the young, the old, the sick and the disabled are not key players in the game, and we saw this acted out on the world stage as Hurricane Katrina hit the largely Black communities of New Orleans in 2005. The images that remain with us are of dead and abandoned, mostly Black, mostly female, mostly poor and often young or elderly people in the floodwaters, as the ill-maintained levees gave way, while the rest of the USA, the most powerful country in the world, carried on with business as usual.

Encouragingly, Zibechi (2010a, p 11) identifies that 'societies in movement expose social fault lines, which are uncovered as society shifts away from its previous location'. This creates democratic spaces within which to create critical dissent dialogue and to build counternarratives for justice, bringing the margins of life alive as 'epistemological moments' reveal new possibilities.

Participatory democracy and global social movements

A politics of protest is not a natural component of British culture, but it is central to Latin American communities where the courage to speak one's truth is evident in public places. As Baird says, elections are a part of democracy, but do not define it: 'A deeper definition of democracy – literally "people's rule" – must also include freedom of speech, an independent judiciary, freedom from discrimination, and the rights to assembly, protest and to a fair trial. It should also include broader human rights to health, education, and the means of survival' (Baird, 2010, p 16).

There is evidence of rising dissent against a world predicated on profit at the expense of well-being. Craig et al (2011) point out that the collapse of communism played a key role in justifying capitalism, and as neoliberalism accelerated we witnessed the repositioning of traditional political parties of Right and Left to centre ground. These trends have left us with no healthy dialectical choices from which to make other worlds possible. And, as the nation state shrinks, our viable alliances are likely to be found on the local/global continuum in anti-capitalist movements for justice and democracy. Ferguson and Woodward (2009) direct our attention to the World Social Forums and the European Social Forums as contexts for challenging the commodification of the world, suggesting that 'we need to be involved in these forums and debates, both to draw on the energy that they produce and also to help us construct a positive alternative vision of an engaged work' (2009, p 144).

For an alternative political project, we need to look for inspiration to the places where participatory democracy is happening. Nicaragua was clearly a revolutionary possibility that only became unsustainable due to its undermining by the USA. Freire's role in locating educational and cultural change within political change made Nicaragua a remarkable success story in the way that it demonstrated participatory democracy in action, and this legacy is still evident (Welsh, 2010). While Latin America continues to face some of the most extreme inequalities in the world, it also has a long history of revolutionary struggles for democracy. This tradition of radical action has led to insight into critical approaches to social change (Zibechi, 2010b).

In Bolivia, social policy is based on the concept of 'living well', a concept that is rooted in local indigenous culture which contains notions of solidarity with others, lives in harmony with nature, rather than competing for more than one's fair share. It embraces the whole of life as mutual, cooperative co-existence based on personal empowerment.'In the current global context where capitalist values and excessive consumption are being questioned, this idea rings true beyond Bolivia's borders, and it provides the basis for Bolivian involvement in international meetings on climate change' (Chaplin, 2010, p 253).

Praxis is the essence of social change:

> Liberation is a praxis; the action and reflection of men and women upon their world in order to transform it. (Paulo Freire, quoted in Freire and Macedo, 1998, p 73)

In a process of reflection and action, change is based on insight and understanding. Conscientisation is driven by the desire to create a fundamentally fair and just world, but within its process it generates in subordinated groups the confidence, the autonomy, self-esteem and energy to transform 'their internalized sense of inferiority and paralysing feelings of subordination' (Pearce et al, 2010, p 268). Popular education is the 'process by which the poor come to understand that poverty and oppression is not their fault nor is it inevitable' (Pearce et al, 2010, p 268). The influence of Paulo Freire continues to generate democracy from below throughout Latin America, making an impact on state politics.

Collective action for sustainable change involves harnessing this collective power beyond neighbourhoods to national and global levels. This is why it is essential to move beyond local issues to engage with wider movements for change. Here I repeat the words of Sivanandan, which I introduced earlier, simply because they capture the essence of radical practice, expressing that global action begins in critical compassion, by being sensitive to:

> ... the oppression of others, the exploitation of others, the injustices and inequalities meted out to others – and to act on them, making an individual/local case into an issue, turning issues into causes and causes into movements and building in the process a new political culture, new communities of resistance that will take on power and capital and class. (Sivanandan, quoted in Cooke, 1996, p 22)

Theoretical analysis

Critical praxis would benefit from a re-visioning of Freire and Gramsci from a feminist, anti-racist perspective. Seeing these ideas with fresh eyes is not to ignore the interests of men but to offer a critical repositioning which embraces a multiplicity of ways of knowing the world, challenging all forms of domination. Dislocating White male supremacy aims for the heart of capitalism and the ruthlessness of a competitive, exploitative worldview which survives on domination and subordination, creating contradictions that 'are shaped within the social relations of capitalism' (Allman, 2009, p 419). Feminism seeks to create the possibility of a worldview where cooperation and participation respect diversity.

This offers not only new ways of seeing the world, but the key to what is 'not yet visible, a new ordering of human relations' (Callaway, 1981, p 457). And this is precisely why praxis is at the heart of a critical approach to community development, building new epistemologies, new ways of seeing the world, which in turn lead to new ontologies, new ways of being in the world.

Insight into the assumed superiority of Whiteness and patriarchy is a useful basis from which to re-vision Freire and Gramsci in our current global times. From a Black feminist perspective, bell hooks illustrates the contradictory nature of ideas in process which lead to new possibilities:

> It is feminist thinking that empowers me to engage in a constructive critique of Freire's work (which I needed so that as a young reader of his work I did not passively absorb the worldview presented) and yet there are many other standpoints from which I approach his work that enable me to experience its value, that make it possible for that work to touch me at the very core of my being. (hooks, 1994, p 49)

Feminism has transformed the world with its emphasis on peace, harmony and non-violence, a vision of humanity in symbiotic respectful relation with the natural world. Set against the backdrop of globalisation, which seeks out the most vulnerable people and resources in the world to meet the demands of western markets, crises of justice and sustainability escalate as new and complex forms of discrimination emerge.

These are challenging times, but they are also times of opportunity. New understandings of difference, in this context of globalisation, call for a coherently articulated *critical pedagogy*, 'that particular type of pedagogy which is concerned with issues concerning *social difference*, *social justice* and *social transformation*' (Mayo, 1999, p 58; original emphasis). The loci of oppressions matrix (see Figure 8.1 on p 193 above) is a tool of analysis which locates intersections between interlinking oppressions, the contexts in which they touch people's lives, and the levels at which they get embedded structurally. These levels of analysis are needed for community development to restate its radical purpose, and for it to become central to an emerging world movement where alliances are forming at grassroots and intellectual thought is calling for a new worldview:

> One can discern two trajectories in current history: one aiming toward hegemony, acting rationally within a lunatic doctrinal framework as it threatens survival; the other dedicated to the belief that 'another world is possible', ... challenging the reigning ideological system and seeking to create constructive alternatives of thought, action, and institutions. (Chomsky, 2003, p 236)

It is this latter perspective to which critical community development is dedicated, a worldview based on social and environmental justice through sustainability and participation. This is a time of hope for community development. We have no choice: 'unhopeful educators contradict their practice. They are men and women without *address,* and without a destination. They are lost in history' (Freire, 1998a, p 107). Yet, hope can only transform reality when it is based on criticality, a constant questioning. One potentially transformative insight into the irony of our market-dominated lives is that in rich countries, which are creating crises for the rest of the world, 'further improvements in the quality of life no longer depend on further economic growth: the issue is now community and how we relate to each other' (Wilkinson and Pickett, 2009, p 45). As Cathy McCormack, community activist, says, 'We need to try and find ways of what it means to be human. Learn to love and get along with each other and get along with the rest of the planet, species and habitats. Otherwise we really will be the generation that breaks the bank' (McCormack with Pallister, 2009, p 264).

References

Albrecht, L. and Brewer, R. (eds) (1990) *Bridges of power: Women's multicultural alliances*, Philadelphia, PA: New Society.

Alinsky, S. (1969) *Reveille for radicals*, New York: Vintage Press.

Alinsky, S. (1972) *Rules for radicals*, New York: Vintage Press.

Allman, P. (1988) 'Gramsci, Freire and Illich: their contributions to education for socialism', in T. Lovett (ed) *Radical approaches to adult education*, London: Routledge, pp 85-113.

Allman, P. (1999) *Revolutionary social transformation: Democratic hopes, political possibilities, and critical education*, Westport, CT: Bergin & Garvey.

Allman, P. (2001) *Critical education against global capitalism: Karl Marx and revolutionary critical education*, Westport, CT: Bergin & Garvey.

Allman, P. (2009) 'Paulo Freire's contributions to radical adult education', in A. Darder, M.P. Baltodano and R.D. Torres (eds) *The critical pedagogy reader* (2nd edn), New York: Routledge, pp 417-30.

Allman, P. (2010) *Critical education against global capitalism: Karl Marx and revolutionary critical education*, Rotterdam: Sense.

Allman, P. and Wallis, J. (1997) 'Commentary: Paulo Freire and the future of the radical tradition', *Studies in the Education of Adults*, vol 29, pp 113-20.

Amos, V. and Parmar, P. (1984) 'Challenging imperial feminism', *Feminist Review*, vol 17, pp 3-19.

Anthias, F. and Yuval-Davis, N. with Cain, H. (1992) *Racialized boundaries: Race, nation, gender, colour and class and the anti-racist struggle*, London: Routledge.

Anzaldúa, G. (1987) *Borderlands/La Frontera*, San Francisco, CA: Aunt Lute Books.

Anzaldúa, G. (1990) 'Bridge, drawbridge, sandbar or island: lesbians-of-color hacienda alianzas', in L. Albrecht and R. Brewer (eds) *Bridges of power: Women's multicultural alliances*, Philadelphia, PA: New Society, pp 216-31.

Apple, M. (2006) 'Producing inequalities: neo-liberalism, neo-conservatism, and the politics of educational reform', in H. Lauder, P. Brown, J. Dillabough and A.H. Halsey (eds) *Education, globalization and social change*, Oxford: Oxford University Press, pp 469-89.

Araújo Freire, A.M. (2007) 'Introduction', in P. Freire *Daring to dream: Toward a pedagogy of the unfinished* (edited by Donaldo Macedo), Boulder, CO and London: Paradigm Publishers.

Bailey, R. (1974) *Radicals in urban politics: The Alinsky approach*, Chicago, IL and London: University of Chicago Press.

Baird, V. (2010) 'The beauty of big democracy', *New Internationalist*, no 436, October, pp 15-19.

Barr, A. (1991) *Practising community development: Experience in Strathclyde*, London: Community Development Foundation.

Barr, A. (1995) 'Empowering communities – beyond fashionable rhetoric? Some reflections on the Scottish experience', *Community Development Journal*, vol 30, no 2, April, pp 121-32.

Barr, A. and Hashagen, S. (2000) *ABCD handbook: A framework for evaluating community development*, London: Community Development Foundation.

Belenky, M.F., Clinchy, B.M., Goldberger, N.R. and Tarule, J.M. (eds) (1986) *Women's way of knowing*, New York: Basic Books.

Belenky, M., Clinchy, B., Goldberger, N. and Tarule, J. (1997) *Women's ways of knowing: The development of self, voice and mind* (2nd edn), New York: Basic Books.

Benn, T. (2010) 'Every generation has to fight the same battles', *New Internationalist*, no 436, October (www.newint.org/features/2010/10/01/tony-benn-caroline-lucas-mp-agent-bristly-pioneer).

Berger, P. (1966) *Invitation to sociology*, Harmondsworth: Penguin.

Berger, R. and Quinney, R. (eds) (2005) *Storytelling sociology: Narrative as social inquiry*, Boulder, CO: Lynne Reinner Publishers.

Berner, E. and Phillips, B. (2005) 'Left to their own devices? Community self-help between alternative development and neo-liberalism', *Community Development Journal*, vol 40, no 1, January, pp 17-29.

Beveridge Report (1942) *Social insurance and allied services*, London: HMSO.

Bhavani, R., Mirza, H.S. and Meetoo, V. (2005) *Tackling the roots of racism*, Bristol: The Policy Press.

Blackburn, J. (2000) 'Understanding Paulo Freire: reflections on the origins, concepts and possible pitfalls of his educational approach', *Community Development Journal*, vol 35, no 1, pp 3-15.

Blagg, H. and Derricourt, N. (1982) 'Why we need to reconstruct a theory of the state for community work', in G. Craig, N. Derricourt and M. Loney (eds) *Community work and the state*, London: Routledge and Kegan Paul, pp 11-23.

Blair, T. (1998) *The third way: New politics for the new century*, London: The Fabian Society.

Blewitt, J. (ed) (2008) *Community, empowerment and sustainable development*, Totnes: Green Books.

Boal, A. (1994) (translated by A. Jackson) *The rainbow of desire: The Boal method of theatre and therapy*, London: Routledge.

Boal, A. (2008) *Theatre of the oppressed* (new edn), London: Pluto.

Boggs, C. (1980) *Gramsci's Marxism*, London: Pluto.

Botton, G. (2005) *Reflective practice: Writing and professional development* (2nd edn), London: Sage Publications.

Bourne, J. (1999) 'Racism, postmodernism and the flight from class', in D. Hill, P. McLaren, M. Cole and G. Rikowski (eds) *Postmodernism in educational theory: Education and the politics of human resistance*, London: The Tuffnell Press, pp 131-46.

Bowers, C.A. and Apffel-Marglin, F. (eds) (2004) *Re-thinking Freire: Globalization and the environmental crisis*, Mahwah, NJ: Lawrence Erlbaum Associates.

Bradshaw, J. (1999) 'Comparing child poverty', *Poverty*, Journal of the Child Poverty Action Group, no 104, Autumn.

Brewer, M., Browne, J., Joyce, R. and Sutherland, H. (2009) *Micro-simulating child poverty in 2010 and 2020*, London: Institute of Fiscal Studies.

Burningham, L. and Thrush, D. (2001) *Rainforests are a long way from here: The environmental concerns of disadvantaged groups*, York: Joseph Rowntree Foundation.

Burns, D. (2007) *Systemic action research: A strategy for whole systems change*, Bristol: The Policy Press.

Burton, P. (2003) 'Community involvement in neighbourhood regeneration: stairway to heaven or road to nowhere?' (www.neighbourhoodcentre.org).

Buscaglia, L. (2010) www.buscaglia.com/default.htm

Butcher, H., Banks, S., Henderson, P. with Robertson, J. (2007) *Critical community practice*, Bristol: The Policy Press.

Calder, G. (2003) 'Communitarianism and New Labour' (www.whb.co.uk/socialissues).

Callaway, H. (1981) 'Women's perspectives: research as re-vision', in P. Reason and J. Rowan (eds) *Human inquiry: A sourcebook of new paradigm research*, Chichester: Wiley, pp 457-72.

Caloustc Gulbcnkian Foundation (1968) *Community work and social change: A report on training*, London: Longman.

Campbell, B. (1993) *Goliath: Britain's dangerous places*, London: Methuen.

Cannan, C. (2000) 'The environmental crisis, Greens and community development', *Community Development Journal*, vol 35, no 4, October, pp 365-76.

Cavanagh, C. (2007) 'Popular education, social movements and storytelling: Interview with Chris Cavanagh', in C. Borg and P. Mayo, *Public intellectuals, radical democracy and social movements: A book of interviews*, New York: Peter Lang Publishing, pp 41-8.

Cavanagh, C. (2004) *Comeuppance: Storytelling and social justice*, Toronto, Canada: Catalyst Centre.

Chaplin, A. (2010) 'Social movements in Bolivia: from strength to power', *Community Development Journal*, vol 45, no 3, July, pp 346-55.

Charles, E. (2007) 'How can I bring ubuntu as a living standard of judgement into the academy? Moving beyond decolonisation through societal reidentification and guiltless recognition', Unpublished, PhD, University of Bath.

Chomsky, N. (2003) *Hegemony or survival: America's quest for global dominance*, New York: Metropolitan.

Cockburn, C. (1977) *The local state*, London: Pluto.

Cohen, R., Ferres, G., Hollins, C., Long, G., Smith, R. and Bennett, F. (eds) (1996) *Out of pocket: Failure of the Social Fund*, London: The Children's Society.

Coleman, A. (2003) 'Life in the sacrificial zone' in E. Scandrett (ed) *Agents for environmental justice: Voices from the grassroots*, Edinburgh: Friends of the Earth, Scotland.

Commission for Social Justice (1994) *Social justice: Strategies for national renewal*, London: Verso.

Community Workers' Cooperative (2004) *Tools for change: A community work resource*, Galway: Community Workers' Cooperative.

Cooke, B. and Kothari, U. (eds) (2001) *Participation: The new tyranny*, London: Zed Books.

Cooke, I. (1996) 'Whatever happened to the class of '68? – the changing context of radical community work practice', in I. Cooke and M. Shaw (eds) *Radical community work: Perspectives from practice in Scotland*, Edinburgh: Moray House, pp 6–25.

Cooke, I. and Shaw, M. (eds) (1996) *Radical community work: Perspectives from practice in Scotland*, Edinburgh: Moray House.

Coote, A. (2010) 'Cameron's Big Society will leave the poor and powerless behind' (www.neweconomics.org).

Cornwall, A. and Coelho, V.S. (eds) (2007) *Spaces for change: The politics of citizen participation in new democratic arenas*, London: Zed Books.

CPAG (Child Poverty Action Group) (2008) *Child poverty: the stats: Analysis of the latest poverty statistics*, London: CPAG.

Craig, G. (undated) 'Social justice' (available from g.craig@hull.ac.uk).

Craig, G. (1998) 'Community development in a global context', *Community Development Journal*, vol 33, no 1, pp 2–17.

Craig, G. (2008) 'The limits of compromise? Social justice, "race" and multiculturalism' in G. Craig, T. Burchardt and D. Gordon (eds) *Social justice and public policy: Seeking fairness in diverse societies*, Bristol: The Policy Press, pp 231–50.

Craig, G. and Mayo, M. (eds) (1995) *Community empowerment: A reader in participation and development*, London: Zed Books.

Craig, G., Burchardt, T. and Gordon, D. (eds) (2008) *Social justice and public policy: Seeking fairness in diverse societies*, Bristol: The Policy Press.

Craig, G., Derricourt, N. and Loney, M. (eds) (1982) *Community work and the state: Towards a radical approach*, London: Routledge and Kegan Paul.

Craig, G., Gorman, M. and Vercseg, I. (2004) 'The Budapest Declaration: building European civil society through community development' (www.cdx.org.uk).

Craig, G., Mayo, M., Popple, K., Shaw, M. and Taylor, M. (eds) (2011) *The community development reader,* Bristol: The Policy Press.

Danaher, G., Schirato, T. and Webb, J. (2000) *Understanding Foucault*, London: Sage Publications.

Darder, A. (2002) *Reinventing Paulo Freire: A pedagogy of love*, Boulder, CO: Westview.

Darder, A., Baltodano, M.P. and Torres, R.D. (eds) (2009) *The critical pedagogy reader* (2nd edn), London: Routledge.

Davidson, A. (1977) *Antonio Gramsci: Towards an intellectual biography*, London: Merlin Press.

Davis, A. (1989) *Women, culture and politics*, New York: Random House.

Deakin, N. (2001) *In search of civil society*, Basingstoke: Palgrave.

Dixon, J., Dogan, R. and Sanderson, A. (2005) 'Community and communitarianism: a philosophical investigation', *Community Development Journal*, vol 40, no 1, January, pp 4–16.

Doering, B. (1994) *The philosopher and the provocateur*, London: University of Notre Dame Press.

Dominelli, L. (1990) *Women and community action*, Birmingham:Venture Press.

Dominelli, L. (1997) *Sociology for social work*, London: Macmillan.

Dominelli, L. (2006) *Women and community action*, Bristol:The Policy Press.

Dorling, D. (2010) *Injustice:Why social inequality persists*, Bristol:The Policy Press.

Dornan, P. (ed) (2004) *Ending child poverty by 2020:The first five years*, London: Child Poverty Action Group.

Dornan, P. (2008) 'The welfare state at 60', *Poverty*, no 130, Summer, p 130.

Douthwaite, R. (1996) *Short circuit: Strengthening local economics for security in an unstable world*, Totnes: Green Books.

Doyal, L. and Gough, I. (1991) *A theory of human need*, London: Macmillan.

Dunion, K. (2003) *Troublemakers: The struggle for environmental justice in Scotland*, Edinburgh: Edinburgh University Press.

Dyer, R. (1997) *White*, London and New York: Routledge.

Emejulu, A. and Shaw, M. (eds) (2010) *Community empowerment: Critical perspectives from Scotland* (The Glasgow Papers), Edinburgh: Community Development Journal.

Entwistle, H. (1979) *Antonio Gramsci: Conservative schooling for radical politics*, London: Routledge.

Etzioni, A. (1995) *The spirit of community: Rights, responsibilities and the communitarian agenda*, London: Fontana.

Etzioni, A. (1997) *The new golden rule: Community and morality in a democratic society*, London: Profile.

Fanon, F. (2008) *Black skin, white masks* (new edn), London: Pluto.

Ferguson, I. and Woodward, R. (2009) *Radical social work in practice: Making a difference*, Bristol:The Policy Press.

Fine, M.,Weiss, L., Powell, L. and Mun Wong, L. (1997) *Off white: Readings on race, power and society*, New York: Routledge.

Fiori, G. (1990) (translated by T. Nairn) *Antonio Gramsci: Life of a revolutionary*, London:Verso (first published as *Vita di Antonio Gramsci*, Bari: Laterza, 1965).

Fisher, W.F. and Ponniah, T. (2003) *Another world is possible: Popular alternatives to globalization at the World Social Forum*, London: Zed Books.

Flaherty, J.,Veit-Wilson, J. and Dornan, P. (2004) *Poverty:The facts* (5th edn), London: Child Poverty Action Group.

Forgacs, D. (ed) (1988) *A Gramsci reader*, London: Lawrence & Wishart.

Foucault, M. (1980) Power/Knowledge: Selected interviews and other writings, Brighton: Harvester Wheatsheaf.

Frankenberg, R. (1993) *White women: Race matters:The social construction of whiteness*, London: Routledge.

Freire, A.M.A. (2007) 'Introduction' in P. Freire (ed) *Daring to dream: Toward a pedagogy of the unfinished*, Boulder, CO and London: Paradigm Publishers, pp vii–xix.

Freire, P. (1972) *Pedagogy of the oppressed*, Harmondsworth: Penguin.

Freire, P. (1985) *The politics of education: Culture, power and liberation*, London: Macmillan.

Freire, P. (1993) (translated by D. Macedo) *Pedagogy of the city*, New York: Continuum.

Freire, P. (1995) (translated by R. Barr) *Pedagogy of hope: Reliving pedagogy of the oppressed*, New York: Continuum.

Freire, P. (1996) *Pedagogy of the oppressed* (revised edition), Harmondsworth: Penguin.

Freire, P. (1998a) *Pedagogy of the heart*, New York: Continuum.

Freire, P. (1998b) *Pedagogy of freedom: Ethics, democracy and civic courage*, Oxford: Rowman & Littlefield.

Freire, P. (2005) *Pedagogy of indignation*, Boulder, CO: Paradigm Publishers.

Freire, P. (2007) *Daring to dream: Toward a pedagogy of the unfinished* (edited by Donaldo Macedo), Boulder, CO and London: Paradigm Publishers.

Freire, P. and Faundez, A. (1992) *Learning to question: A pedagogy of liberation*, New York: Continuum.

Freire, P. and Macedo, D. (1993) 'A dialogue with Paulo Freire', in P. McLaren and P. Leonard (eds) *Paulo Freire: A critical encounter*, London: Routledge, pp 169-76.

Freire, A. and Macedo, D. (eds) (1998) *The Paulo Freire reader*, New York: Continuum.

Fromm, E. (1962) *Beyond the chains of illusion*, London: Abacus.

Gamble, D.N. and Weil, M.O. (1997) 'Sustainable development: the challenge for community development', *Community Development Journal*, vol 32, no 3, July, pp 210-22.

Giddens, A. (1998) *The Third Way: The renewal of social democracy*, Cambridge: Polity Press.

Gilchrist, A. (2009) *The well-connected community: A networking approach to community development*, (2nd edn), Bristol: The Policy Press/Community Development Foundation.

Giroux, H.A. (1993) 'Paulo Freire and the politics of postcolonialism', in P. McLaren and P. Leonard (eds) *Paulo Freire: A critical encounter*, London: Routledge, pp 177-78.

Giroux, H.A. (2006) *Stormy weather: Katrina and the politics of disposability*, Boulder, CO: Paradigm Publishers.

Giroux, H.A. (2009) *Youth in a suspect society: Democracy or disposability?*, New York: Palgrave Macmillan.

Giroux, H.A. and McLaren, P. (1994) *Between borders: Pedagogy and the politics of cultural studies*, London: Routledge.

Giroux, H.A., Lankshear, C., McLaren, P. and Peters, M. (1996) *Counternarratives: Cultural studies and critical pedagogies in postmodern spaces*, New York and London: Routledge.

Goodman, A., Johnson, P. and Webb, S. (1997) *Inequality in the UK*, Oxford: Oxford University Press.

Gordon, D. and Pantazis, C. (1997) 'Breadline Britain in the 1990s: the full report of a major national survey on poverty', *Poverty*, Journal of the Child Poverty Action Group, no 98, Autumn, pp 21-2.

Graham, M. (2007) *Black issues in social work and social care*, Bristol: The Policy Press.

Graham, H. and Jones, J. (1992) 'Community development and research', *Community Development Journal*, vol 27, no 3, July.

Gramsci, A. (1971) (edited and translated by Q. Hoare and G.N. Smith) *Selections from prison notebooks*, London: Lawrence & Wishart.

Gramsci, A. (1985) (edited by D. Forgacs and G. Nowell-Smith, translated by W. Boelhower) *Selections from cultural writings*, London: Lawrence & Wishart.

Gramsci, A. (1988) (translated and introduced by H. Henderson) *Gramsci's prison letters*, London: Zwan.

Gregg, P., Harkness, S. and Machin, S. (1999) 'Poor kids: trends in child poverty in Britain, 1968-96', *Fiscal Studies*, vol 20, no 2, June.

Griffiths, M. (2003) *Action for social justice in education: Fairly different*, Maidenhead: Open University Press.

Habermas, J. (1989) *The structural transformation of the public sphere: An inquiry into a category of bourgeois society*, Cambridge: Polity Press.

Hall, S. (1996a) 'The meaning of new times', in D. Morley and K.-H. Chen (eds) *Stuart Hall: Critical dialogues in cultural studies*, London: Routledge, pp 222-36.

Hall, S. (1996b) 'What is this "black" in black popular culture?', in D. Morley and K.-H. Chen (eds) *Stuart Hall: Critical dialogues in cultural studies*, London: Routledge, pp 468-78.

Hall, S. (1996c) 'Gramsci's relevance for the study of race and ethnicity', in D. Morley and K.-H. Chen (eds) *Stuart Hall: Critical dialogues in cultural studies*, London: Routledge, pp 411-41.

Hawtin, M., Hughes, G. and Percy-Smith, J. (1994) *Community profiling: Auditing social needs*, Buckingham: Open University Press.

Henderson, P. and Thomas, D. (1980) *Skills in neighbourhood work*, London: Unwin Hyman.

Heron, J. (1981) 'Experiential research methodology', in P. Reason and J. Rowan (eds) *Human inquiry: A sourcebook of new paradigm research*, Chichester: Wiley, pp 153-66.

Higgins, P. (2010a) *Eradicating ecocide: Exposing the corporate and political practices destroying the planet and proposing the laws needed to eradicate ecocide*, London: Shepheard-Walwyn.

Higgins, P. (2010b) 'Stopping the juggernaut', *New Internationalist*, no 437, November, pp 23-4.

Hill, D. (ed) (2000) *Education, education, education: Capitalism, socialism and 'The Third Way'*, London: Cassell.

Hill, D., McLaren, P., Cole, M. and Rikowski, G. (eds) (1999) *Postmodernism in educational theory: Education and the politics of human resistance*, London: The Tuffnell Press.

Hill Collins, P. (1990) *Black feminist thought: Knowledge, consciousness and the politics of empowerment*, London: Unwin Hyman.

Hillman, M. (2002) 'Environmental justice: a crucial link between environmentalism and community development?', *Community Development Journal*, vol 37, no 4, October, pp 349-60.

Hills, J. and Stewart, K. (2005) *A more equal society: New Labour, poverty, inequality and exclusion*, Bristol: The Policy Press.

Hirshon, S. with Butler, J. (1983) *And also teach them to read*, Westport, CT: Lawrence Hill and Co.

Hoffman, J. (1984) *The Gramscian challenge: Coercion and consent in Marxist political theory*, Oxford: Blackwell.

Holland, J., Blair, M. and Sheldon, S. (eds) (1995) *Debates and issues in feminist research and pedagogy*, Clevedon: Multilingual Matters/Open University.

Holub, R. (1992) *Antonio Gramsci: Beyond Marxism and postmodernism*, London: Routledge.

hooks, b. (1984) *Feminist theory: From margin to center*, Boston, MA: South End Press.

hooks, b (1989) *Talking back: Thinking feminist, thinking black*, Boston, MA: South End Press.

hooks, b. (1991) *Yearning: Race, gender and cultural politics*, London: Turnaround.

hooks, b. (1993) 'bell hooks speaking about Paulo Freire – the man, his work', in P. McLaren and P. Leonard (eds) *Paulo Freire: A critical encounter*, London: Routledge, pp 146-54.

hooks, b. (1994) *Teaching to transgress: Education as the practice of freedom*, London: Routledge.

Hope, A. and Timmel, S. (1999) *Training for transformation: A handbook for community workers* (Book 4), London: ITDG Publishing.

Hope, A. and Timmel, S. with Hodzi, C. (1984) *Training for transformation: A handbook for community workers* (Books 1-3), Zimbabwe, Gweru: Mambo Press.

Horton, M. and Freire, P. (1990) (edited by B. Bell, J. Gaventa and J. Peters) *We make the road by walking: Conversations on education and social change*, Philadelphia, PA: Temple University Press.

Horwitt, S.D. (1997) 'Alinsky: more important now than ever', *LA Times* (www.tresser.com/alinsky.htm).

Howarth, C., Kenway, P., Palmer, G. and Miorelli, R. (1999) *Monitoring poverty and social exclusion 1999*, York: Joseph Rowntree Foundation/New Policy Institute.

Hustedde, R. and King, B. (2002) 'Rituals: emotions, community faith in soul and the messiness of life', *Community Development Journal*, vol 37, pp 338-48.

Jacobs, S. (1994) 'Community work in a changing world', in S. Jacobs and K. Popple (eds) *Community work in the 1990s*, Nottingham: Spokesman, pp 156-74.

Jacobs, S. and Popple, K. (eds) (1994) *Community work in the 1990s*, Nottingham: Spokesman.

Kabat-Zinn, J. (2005) *Coming to our senses: Healing ourselves and the world through mindfulness*, New York: Hyperion.

Kane, L. (2008) 'The world bank, community development and education for social justice', *Community Development Journal*, vol 43, no 2, April, pp 194-209.

Kemmis, S. (2006) 'Participatory action research and the public sphere', *Educational Action Research*, vol 14, no 4, December, pp 459-76.

Kemmis, S. (2009) 'What is to be done? The place of action research?', Keynote address presented to the Collaborative Action Research Network (CARN) Annual Conference, Athens, Greece, 29 October-1 November.

Kenway, J. (2001) 'Remembering and regenerating Gramsci', in K. Weiler (ed) *Feminist engagements: Reading, resisting, and revisioning male theorists in education and cultural studies*, London: Routledge, pp 47-65.

Khan, U.A. (1989a) 'Is the red flag flying here?', *Going local*, Bristol: School for Advanced Studies, University of Bristol.

Khan, U.A. (1989b) 'Neighbourhood forums and the "New Left": representation beyond tokenism?', Paper presented to the Annual Conference of the Political Studies Association, April.

Killeen, D. (2008) *'Is poverty in the UK a denial of people's human rights?'*, York: Joseph Rowntree Foundation.

Kirkwood, G. (1991) 'Freire methodology in practice', in *Roots and branches* (series of occasional papers), vol 1: *Community development and health education*, Milton Keynes: Open University Health Education Unit.

Kirkwood, G. and Kirkwood, C. (1989) *Living adult education: Freire in Scotland*, Milton Keynes: Open University Press.

Kothari, U. (2001) 'Power, knowledge and social control in participatory development', in B, Cooke and U. Kothari (eds) *Participation: the new tyranny*, London: Zed books, pp 139-52.

Kuenstler, P. (ed) (1961) *Community organization in Great Britain*, London: Faber & Faber.

Ladson-Billings, G. and Tate, W.F. (2006) 'Toward a critical race theory of education', in H. Lauder, P. Brown, J. Dillabough and A.H. Halsey (eds) *Education, globalization and social change*, Oxford: Oxford University Press, pp 570-85.

Lather, P. (1984) 'Critical theory, curricular transformation and feminist mainstreaming', *Journal of Education* vol 166, no 1, pp 49-62.

Lawner, L. (1979) (introduced, selected and translated) *Letters from prison by Antonio Gramsci*, London: Quartet Books.

Layard, R. (2005) *Happiness: Lessons from a new science*, London: Penguin.

Layard, R. and Dunn, J. (2009) *A good childhood: Searching for values in a competitive age*, London: Penguin.

Leach, T. (1983) 'Paulo Freire: dialogue, politics and relevance', *International Journal of Lifelong Education*, vol 1, no 3, pp 185-201.

Learning for Democracy Group (2008) *Learning for democracy: Ten propositions and ten proposals* (www.scutrea.ac.uk/library/Wallchart%20pdf.pdf).

Ledwith, M. (2005) *Community development: A critical approach*, Bristol: The Policy Press.

Ledwith, M. (2010) 'Antonio Gramsci and feminism: the elusive nature of power', in P. Mayo (ed) *Gramsci and educational thought*, Chichester: Wiley-Blackwell, pp 100-13.

Ledwith, M. and Asgill, P. (1998) 'Black and White women working together: Transgressing the boundaries of sisterhood' in M. Lavalette, L. Penketh and C. Jones (eds) *Anti-racism and social welfare*, Aldershot: Ashgate, pp 211–34.

Ledwith, M. and Asgill, P. (2000) 'Critical alliance: Black and White women working together for social justice', *Community Development Journal*, vol 35, no 3, July, pp 290–9.

Ledwith, M. and Asgill, P. (2007) 'Feminist, anti-racist community development: critical alliance – local to global', in L. Dominelli (ed) *Revitalising communities in a globalising world*, Aldershot: Ashgate, pp 107–22.

Ledwith, M. and Springett, J. (2010) *Partcipatory practice: Community-based action for transformative change*, Bristol: The Policy Press.

Lees, R. and Mayo, M. (1984) *Community action for change*, London: Routledge and Kegan Paul.

Lewis, M. (2000) 'Interrupting patriarchy: politics, resistance, and transformation in the feminist classroom', in I. Shor and C. Pari (eds) *Education is politics: Critical teaching across differences, postsecondary*, Portsmouth, NH: Heinemann, pp 82–106.

Lister, R. (2005) 'The links between women's and children's poverty', in V. Sharma (ed) *Women's and children's poverty: Making the links*, London: Women's Budget Group/Fawcett Society.

Lister, R (2008) 'Recognition and voice: the challenge for social justice', in G. Craig, T. Burchardt and D. Gordon (eds) *Social justice and public policy: Seeking fairness in diverse societies*, Bristol: The Policy Press, pp 105–22.

Little, R.M. and Froggett, L. (2010) 'Making meaning in muddy waters: representing complexity through community based storytelling', *Community Development Journal*, vol 45, no 4, October, pp 458–73.

Lockhart, J. (1999) 'Re-examining Paulo Freire and his relevance for community intervention: the source of my "surprise"', in D. Scott and T. Ireland (eds) *'Vidas secas: Lutas fecudas': Community and development in the Brazilian Northeast*, London: Whiting & Birch.

Lorde, A. (1980) 'Age, race, class and sex: women redefining difference', in M. Evans (ed) (1994) *The woman question*, London: Sage Publications, pp 36–41.

Lorde, A. (1984) *Sister outsider*, New York: The Crossing Press.

Lovett, T. (ed) (1982) *Radical approaches to adult education: A reader*, London: Routledge.

Lovett, T., Clarke, C. and Kilmurray, A. (eds) (1983) *Adult education and community action*, London: Croom Helm.

Lupton, R. and Power, A. (2005) 'Diasdvantaged by where you live? New Labour and neighbourhood renewal', in J. Hills and K. Stewart (eds) *A more equal society? New Labour, poverty, inequality and exclusion*, Bristol: The Policy Press, pp 119–42.

Macmurray, J. (1996) (selected and introduced by P. Conford) *The personal world: John Macmurray on self and society*, Edinburgh: Floris Books.

McCormack, C. with Pallister, M. (2009) *The wee yellow butterfly*, Glendaruel: Argyll Publishing.

McIntosh, A. (2001) *Soil and soul: People versus corporate power*, London: Aurum.

McIntosh, P. (2004) 'White privilege: unpacking the invisible knapsack', in M. Anderson and P. Hill–Collins (eds) *Race, class and gender: An anthology*, Belmont, CA: Wadsworth Publishing.

McLaren, P. (1995) *Critical pedagogy and predatory culture: Oppositional politics in a postmodern era*, London: Routledge.

McLaren, P. (2000) *Che Guevara, Paulo Freire and the pedagogy of revolution*, Oxford: Rowman & Littlefield.

McLaren, P. (2002) 'Afterword: a legacy of hope and struggle', in A. Darder, *Reinventing Paulo Freire: A pedagogy of love*, Boulder, CO: Westview, pp 245-54.

McLaren, P. (2009) 'Critical pedagogy: A look at the major concepts' in A. Darder, M.P. Baltodano and R.D. Torres (eds) *The critical pedagogy reader* (2nd edn), London: Routledge, pp 61-83.

McLaren, P. and Leonard, P. (eds) (1993) *Paulo Freire: A critical encounter*, London: Routledge.

McLaren, P., Hill, D. and Cole, M. (1999) 'Postmodernism adieu: towards a politics of human resistance', in D. Hill, P. McLaren, M. Cole and G. Rikowski (eds) *Postmodernism in educational theory: Education and the politics of human resistance*, London: The Tuffnell Press, pp 203-13.

McLaren, P., Finschman, G., Serra, S. and Antelo, E. (1998) 'The specter of Gramsci: revolutionary praxis and the committed intellectual', *Journal of Thought*, Winter, pp 1-33.

Mack, J. and Lansley, S. (1985) *Poor Britain*, London: George Allen & Unwin.

Mackie, R. (1980a) 'Contributions to the thought of Paulo Freire', in R. Mackie (ed) *Literacy and revolution: The pedagogy of Paulo Freire*, London: Pluto, pp 93-119.

Mackie, R. (ed) (1980b) *Literacy and revolution: The pedagogy of Paulo Freire*, London: Pluto.

Marcuse, H. (1991) *One-dimensional man* (2nd edn), London: Routledge.

Maruyama, M. (1981) 'Endogenous research: rationale', in P. Reason and J. Rowan (eds) *Human inquiry: A sourcebook of new paradigm research*, Chichester: Wiley, pp 227-38.

Mason, J. (2002) *Researching your own practice: The discipline of noticing*, London: Routledge.

Mayo, M. (ed) (1977) *Women in the community*, London: Routledge and Kegan Paul.

Mayo, P. (1999) *Gramsci, Freire and adult education: Possibilities for transformative action*, London: Zed Books.

Mayo, P. (2004) *Liberating praxis: Paulo Freire's legacy for radical education and politics*, London: Praeger.

Mayo, P. (2010) 'Antonio Gramsci and his relevance to the education of adults', in *Gramsci and educational thought*, Chichester: Wiley-Blackwell, pp 21-37.

Milne, S. (undated) 'Fifty years on, Labour discovers a guru', *Guardian*.

Milne, S. (1994) *The enemy within: MI5, Maxwell and the Scargill affair*, London: Verso.

Morley, D. and Chen, K.-H. (eds) (1996) *Stuart Hall: Critical dialogues in cultural studies*, London: Routledge.

Moustakas, C. (1990) *Heuristic research: Design, methodology and applications*, London: Sage Publications.

Nairn, T. (1982) 'Antonu su gobbu', in A. Showstack Sassoon (ed) *Approaches to Gramsci*, London: Writers and Readers, pp 159-79.

New Economics Foundation (2010) *Ten big questions about the Big Society: And ten ways to make the best of it* (www.neweconomics.org).

Novak, T. (1988) *Poverty and the state*, Milton Keynes: Open University Press.

O'Donohue, J. (2004) *Beauty, the invisible embrace: Rediscovering the true sources of compassion, serenity and hope*, New York: HarperCollins.

Ohri, A., Manning, B. and Curno, P. (eds) (1982) *Community work and racism: Community work seven*, London: Routledge and Kegan Paul/Association of Community Workers.

Opie, A. (1992) 'Qualitative research, appropriation of the "other" and empowerment', *Feminist Review*, no 40, Spring, pp 52-69.

Oppenheim, C. (2007) 'Child poverty in London', *Poverty*, no 126, Winter, pp 15-17.

Oppenheim, C. and Harker, L. (1996) *Poverty: The facts*, London: Child Poverty Action Group.

Page, M. (1997) *Women in Beijing one year on: Networks, alliances, coalitions*, London: Community Development Foundation.

Pearce, J., Howard, J. and Bronstein, A. (2010) 'Editorial: Learning from Latin America', *Community Development Journal*, vol 45, no 3, July, pp 265-75.

Pheterson, G. (1990) 'Alliances between women: overcoming internalized oppression and internalized domination', in L. Albrecht and R. Brewer (eds) *Bridges of power: Women's multicultural alliances*, Philadelphia, PA: New Society Publishers, pp 34-48.

Pitchford, M. with Henderson, P. (2008) *Making spaces for community development*, Bristol: The Policy Press.

Popple, K. (1995) *Analysing community work: Its theory and practice*, Buckingham: Open University Press.

Poverty (2010a) Journal of the Child Poverty Action Group, Issue 137, Autumn.

Poverty (2010b) Journal of the Child Poverty Action Group, Issue 136, Summer.

Power, A. and Tunstall, R. (1995) *Swimming against the tide: Polarisation or progress on 20 unpopular council estates, 1980-1995*, York: Joseph Rowntree Foundation.

Randall, R. and Southgate, J. (1981) 'Doing dialogical research', in P. Reason and J. Rowan (eds) *Human inquiry: A sourcebook of new paradigm research*, Chichester: Wiley.

Ransome, P. (1992) *Antonio Gramsci: A new introduction*, London: Harvester Wheatsheaf.

Reagon, B. (1983) 'Coalition politics: turning the century', in B. Smith (ed) *Home girls*, New York: Kitchen Table – Women of Color Press, pp 343-58.

Reason, P. (ed) (1988) *Human inquiry in action: Developments in new paradigm research*, London: Sage Publications.

Reason, P. (1994d) 'Human inquiry as discipline and practice' in P. Reason (ed) *Participation in human inquiry*, London: Sage, pp 40–56.

Reason, P. (1994a) 'Future participation', in P. Reason (ed) *Participation in human inquiry: Research with people*, London: Sage Publications, pp 30–39.

Reason, P. (1994b) 'Inquiry and alienation', in P. Reason (ed) *Participation in human inquiry: Research with people*, London: Sage Publications, pp 9–15.

Reason, P. (ed) (1994c) *Participation in human inquiry: Research with people*, London: Sage Publications.

Reason, P. (2002) 'Justice, sustainability and participation: inaugural lecture' (p.w.reason@bath.ac.uk).

Reason, P. and Bradbury, H. (eds) (2001) *Handbook of action research: Participative inquiry and practice*, London: Sage Publications.

Reason, P. and Rowan, J. (eds) (1981) *Human inquiry: A sourcebook of new paradigm research*, Chichester: Wiley.

Ridge, T. (2004) 'Putting children first: addressing the needs and concerns of children who are poor', in P. Dornan (ed) *Ending child poverty by 2020: The first five years*, London: Child Poverty Action Group, pp 4–11.

Rikowski, G. and McLaren, P. (1999) 'Postmodernism in educational theory', in D. Hill, P. McLaren, M. Cole and G. Rikowski (eds) *Postmodernism in educational theory: Education and the politics of human resistance*, London: The Tuffnell Press, pp 1–9.

Riordan, S. (2008) 'NGOs: the *sine qua non* of adapting to climate change in Africa', in J. Blewitt (ed) *Community, empowerment and sustainable development*, Totnes: Green Books, pp 33–58.

Robson, T. (2000) *The state and community action*, London: Pluto.

Roderick, I. with Jones, N. (2008) 'The converging world', in J. Blewitt (ed) *Community, empowerment and sustainable development*, Totnes: Green Books, pp 17–32.

Rowan, J. (1981) 'Dialectical paradigm for research', in J. Reason and J. Rowan (eds) *Human inquiry: A sourcebook for new paradigm research*, Chichester: Wiley, pp 93–112.

Rowan, J. and Reason, P. (1981) 'On making sense', in P. Reason and J. Rowan (eds) *Human inquiry: A sourcebook of new paradigm research*, Chichester: Wiley, pp 113–40.

Rude, G. (1980) *Ideology and popular protest*, London: Lawrence & Wishart.

Rutter, M. and Madge, N. (1976) *Cycles of disadvantage*, London: Heinemann.

Schuler, D. (1996) *New community networks: Wired for change*, New York: ACM Press.

Schutzman, M. and Cohen-Cruz, J. (eds) (1995) *Playing Boal: Theatre, therapy, activism*, London: Routledge.

Scottish Education Department (1975) *Adult education: The challenge of change* (Alexander Report), Edinburgh: HMSO.

Seebohm Report (1968) *Local authority and allied personal social services*, London: HMSO.

Shaw, M. (2004) *Community work: Policy, politics and practice*, Hull and Edinburgh: Universities of Hull and Edinburgh.

Shor, I. (1992) *Empowering education: Critical teaching for social change*, London and Chicago, IL: University of Chicago Press.

Shor, I. (1993) 'Education is politics: Paulo Freire's critical pedagogy', in P. McLaren and P. Leonard (eds) *Paulo Freire: A critical encounter*, London: Routledge, pp 24-35.

Shor, I. (2000) '(Why) education is politics', in I. Shor and C. Pari (eds) *Education is politics: Critical teaching across differences, postsecondary*, Portsmouth, NH: Heinemann, pp 1-14.

Shor, I. and Freire, P. (1987) *A pedagogy for liberation: Dialogues on transforming education*, London: Bergin & Garvey.

Shor, I. and Pari, C. (eds) (2000) *Education is politics: Critical teaching across differences, postsecondary*, Portsmouth, NH: Heinemann.

Showstack Sassoon, A. (1987) *Gramsci's politics* (2nd edn), London: Hutchinson.

Sinfield, A. (2009) 'Recession: a major threat in tackling poverty', *Poverty*, no 132, Winter, pp 81-93.

Skeffington Report (1969) *People and planning*, London: HMSO.

Smith, B. (ed) (1983) *Home girls*, New York: Kitchen Table – Women of Color Press.

Social Exclusion Unit (SEU) (1998) Bringing *Britain together: A national strategy for neighbourhood renewal*, London: HMSO.

Social Exclusion Unit (SEU) (2001) *A new commitment to neighbourhood renewal: National strategy action plan*, London: HMSO.

Southgate, J. and Randall, R. (1981) 'The troubled fish: barriers to dialogue', in P. Reason and J. Rowan (eds) *Human inquiry: A sourcebook of new paradigm research*, Chichester: Wiley, pp 53-62.

Spretnak, C. (1993) 'Critical and constructive contributions of ecofeminism' in P. Tucker and E. Grim (eds) *Worldview and ecology*, Philadelphia, PA: Bucknell Press, pp 181-9.

Spretnak, C. (1997) *The resurgence of the real: Body, nature and place in a hypermodern world*, Harlow: Addison-Wesley.

Steedman, C. (2000) *Landscape for a good woman: A story of two lives* (2nd edn), London: Virago.

Tandon, R. (2008) 'Participation, citizenship and democracy: Reflections on 25 years of PRIA', *Community Development Journal*, vol 43, no 3, pp 284-96.

Taylor, M. (1995) 'Community work and the state: the changing context of UK practice', in G. Craig and M. Mayo (eds) *Community empowerment: A reader in participation and development*, London: Zed Books, pp 99-111.

Taylor, P. (1993) *The texts of Paulo Freire*, Buckingham: Open University Press.

Thomas, D. (1983) *The making of community work*, London: George Allen & Unwin.

Thompson, N. (2000) *Theory and practice in human services* (2nd edn), Buckingham: Open University Press.

Thompson, N. (2003) *Promoting equality: Challenging discrimination and oppression in the human services* (2nd edn), London: Macmillan.

Thompson, N. (2006) *Anti-discriminatory practice* (4th edn), Basingstoke: Palgrave Macmillan.

Thompson, N. (2007) *Power and empowerment*, Lyme Regis: Russell House.

Tomlinson, M., Walker, R. and Williams, G. (2008) 'Child poverty and well-being in the here and now', *Poverty*, Issue 129, Winter, pp 11-17.

Torres, C.A. (1993) 'From the *Pedagogy of the oppressed* to a *luta continua*', in P. McLaren and P. Leonard (eds) *Paulo Freire: A critical encounter*, London: Routledge, pp 119-45.

Townsend, P. (1979) *Poverty in the UK*, Harmondsworth: Penguin.

Townsend, P. (1988) *Inner city deprivation and premature death in Greater Manchester*, Ashton-under-Lyne: Tameside Policy Research Unit.

Townsend, P. (1995) 'Poverty: home and away', *Poverty*, Journal of the Child Poverty Action Group, no 91, Summer.

Townsend, P., Phillimore, P., Beattie, A. and Helm, C. (1988) *Health and deprivation: Inequality and the North*, London: Croom Helm.

Treleaven, L. (2001) 'The turn to action and the linguistic turn: Towards an integrated methodology', in P. Reason and H. Bradbury (eds) *Handbook of action research: Participative inquiry and practice*, London: Sage Publications.

Twelvetrees, A. (1991) *Community work* (2nd edn), London: Macmillan.

Twelvetrees, A. (ed) (1998) *Community economic development: Rhetoric or reality*, London: Community Development Foundation.

UNICEF (2005) *State of the world's children 2005: Childhood under threat*, Wetherby: UNICEF Publications.

UNICEF (2007) *Child poverty in perspective: An overview of child well-being in rich countries*, Innocenti Report Card 7 (www.unicef.org.uk).

Waddington, P. (1979) 'Looking ahead – community work into the 1980s', *Community Development Journal*, vol 14, no 3, October, pp 225-36.

Waddington, P. (1994) 'The values base of community work', in S. Jacobs and K. Popple (eds) *Community work in the 1990s*, Nottingham: Spokesman, pp 3-12.

Walby, S. (1992) *Theorizing patriarchy*, Oxford: Blackwell.

Walby, S. (1994) 'Post-postmodernism? Theorizing gender', in *The Polity reader in social theory*, Cambridge: Polity Press.

Weekes, K. (ed) (Foreword by Peggy McIntosh) (2009) *Privilege and prejudice: Twenty years with the invisible knapsack*, Cambridge: Cambridge Scholars Publishing.

Weiler, K. (1994) 'Freire and a feminist pedagogy of difference', in P. McLaren and C. Lankshear (eds) *Politics of liberation: Paths from Freire*, London: Routledge, pp 12-40.

Weiler, K. (1995) 'Freire and a feminist pedagogy of difference', in J. Holland, M. Blair and S. Sheldon (eds) *Debates and issues in feminist research and pedagogy*, Clevedon: Multilingual Matters/Open University, pp 23-44.

Weiler, K. (ed) (2001) *Feminist engagements: Reading, resisting, and revisioning male theorists in education and cultural studies*, London: Routledge.

Weiler, K. (2009) 'Feminist analysis of gender and schooling', in A. Darder, M.P. Baltodano and R.D. Torres (2nd edn) *The critical pedagogy reader*, New York: Routledge, pp 217-39.

Welsh, P. (2010) 'Community development: a gendered activism? The masculinities questions', *Community Development Journal*, vol 45, no 3, July, pp 297-306.

Wilkinson, R. and Pickett, K.E. (2009) *The spirit level: Why more equal societies almost always do better*, Harmondsworth: Allen Lane.

Williams, F. (1989) *Social policy: A critical introduction*, Cambridge: Polity Press.

Williams, P. (1991) *The alchemy of race and rights*, Cambridge, MA: Harvard University Press.

Winter, R., Sobiechowska, P. and Buck, A. (eds) (1999) *Professional experience and the investigative imagination: The art of reflective writing*, London: Routledge.

Witte Garland, A. (1988) *Women activists: Challenging the abuse of power*, New York: The Feminist Press.

Young, A. (1990) *Femininity in dissent*, London: Routledge.

Young, I.M. (1990) *Justice and the politics of difference*, Chichester: Princeton University Press.

Younghusband, E. (1959) *Report of the working party on social workers in the local authority health and welfare services*, London: HMSO.

Zibechi, R. (2010a) (translated by Ramor Ryan) *Dispersing power: Social movements as anti-state forces*, Oakland, CA and Edinburgh: AK Press.

Zibechi, R. (2010b) 'The rising power of slum democracy', *New Internationalist*, no 436, October, pp 26-8.

Index